DAUGHTER OF GOOD FORTUNE

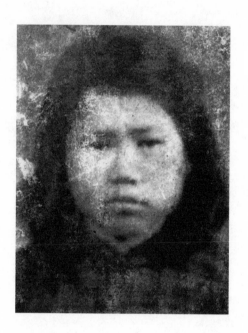

Chen Huiqin

DAUGHTER OF GOOD FORTUNE

A TWENTIETH-CENTURY CHINESE PEASANT MEMOIR

With Shehong Chen
Introduction by Delia Davin

UNIVERSITY OF WASHINGTON PRESS
Seattle and London

© 2015 by the University of Washington Press
Printed and bound in the United States of America
Design by Thomas Eykemans
Composed in Fanwood, typeface designed by Barry Schwartz
19 18 17 16 15   5 4 3 2 1

UNIVERSITY OF WASHINGTON PRESS
www.washington.edu/uwpress

LIBRARY OF CONGRESS CATALOGING-IN-PUBLICATION DATA
ISBN 978-0-295-99471-0 (hardcover)
ISBN 978-0-295-99492-5 (paperback)
Complete cataloging information for this title is available
from the Library of Congress.

The paper used in this publication is acid-free and meets
the minimum requirements of American National Standard
for Information Sciences—Permanence of Paper for Printed
Library Materials, ANSI z39.48–1984.∞

FRONTISPIECE: Chen Huiqin, 1940s

Dedicated to Yang Xi (Beibei) and Chen Li

CONTENTS

PREFACE AND ACKNOWLEDGMENTS

THE narrator of *Daughter of Good Fortune*, Chen Huiqin, is my mother. As is the custom in China, her family name, Chen, precedes her given name, Huiqin. Because it is not respectful in Chinese culture for children to address their parents directly by their names, I avoid doing so here.

Mother was born in 1931 in Wangjialong, Wang Family Village, in Jiading County near the city of Shanghai. Mother helped her family farm and maintain a subsistence life, took refuge with her family when the Japanese attacked Shanghai, lived through the Japanese occupation of her hometown between 1937 and 1945, witnessed the march of Communist troops through her village in May of 1949, took part in the Land Reform Movement, endured shortages of material goods in the 1950s, participated in the Great Leap Forward, experienced ordeals during the Cultural Revolution, moved to become a factory worker and an urban dweller in the 1980s, visited the United States, welcomed the relocation of her village with mixed feelings in 2003, and finally returned to live on her ancestral land in 2012. Since the 1990s, she has been lighting incense and chanting Amitabha every day at home.

About ten years ago, I started a research project to understand the process of transformation rural peasants experienced in China during the radical Communist revolution as well as in the following waves of industrialization, urbanization, and globalization. My native place, Jiading County, where I still knew many people, was the focus of my research.

I utilized my summers and a sabbatical semester to do research in Jiading District Archives and to interview local men and women.[1] While in Jiading, I lived with my parents. Many times, when I shared a piece of information from the archives or an interview, my mother would add her own recollection of the particular event. My pursuit of information about life in the past thus led to many conversations with Mother about her past.

It is a great regret in my mother's life that she had no formal schooling. When I realized she had wonderful memories and that her life paralleled the challenges and changes of the modern Chinese nation, I decided to be the pen through which Mother's personal experiences would be written down. I put aside my initial project on the transformation of a collective peasant experience and listened to my mother as she narrated her own personal experiences.

I returned to Jiading during my non-teaching summer months, sat down with Mother at her house, and listened to her stories and experiences, taking notes. I expanded on the notes as much as I could and entered them into my laptop every day. I asked Mother for more details whenever I needed them. I did this for two summers. When I returned to work in the United States, I wrote chapters based on my expanded notes. I called Mother on the phone many times to ask for more information or clarification when I found problems in my notes. Mother commented several times in a loving tone that I was "silly" to pay for an international phone call just to get "useless" information. In the spring of 2012, I spent a sabbatical semester in my native home, where I continued to listen to Mother's stories and finished writing the book.

I recorded Mother's narrative in her own words, with the exception of adjusting occasional second-person speech ("Do you remember the time when . . .") to first-person for consistency. In the process of writing, I asked Mother for more detailed descriptions of items and practices that would otherwise be unclear to readers.

Although Mother narrated in Chinese, I wrote the book manuscript in English. Every time I completed a chapter, I translated it into Chinese and emailed the Chinese version home. Either my brother or my father would read the chapter to my mother. During the summer months, I read the chapters to her myself. For every chapter, she listened carefully, corrected inaccuracies, and often praised my ability to write down her story in her own words. Everything in the final version is thus an accurate recording of Mother's narrative.

Daughter of Good Fortune is my mother's story, and I want the reader to hear her voice without much distraction. I have done archival research and read scholarly works concerning the eighty-one years covered in this book; however, I have included explanations or references in endnotes only when absolutely necessary.

The writing of this book has been a journey of learning for me. As the first surviving child in the family, I developed a very close bond with Mother. The process of listening to Mother's stories and writing them down in English enabled me to appreciate the bond in a much deeper sense. Mother's stories are now constant sources of inspiration and courage in my life.

As this book goes into print, I would like to express my deepest gratitude to Mother for all the love and support she has given me and for her willingness to tell me her life stories. I also want to thank my father for his confidence in me and his support for my pursuit; my brother and sister and their spouses for taking care of our parents while I live and work half a globe away and for their enthusiasm and assistance in the writing of this book; and my husband for his comments and suggestions, which helped to improve the narrative flow.

My wonderful colleagues Jeannie Judge and Mary Kramer, both professors of English, read the entire manuscript and gave me detailed editorial and stylistic suggestions and comments, which helped to make the writing read more smoothly. I thank both of them wholeheartedly. In the same breath, I thank my best friend and colleague Dean Bergeron, professor of history and political science, for his unwavering support for this book, his insightful and encouraging comments after reading the manuscript, and his sustained enthusiasm.

This book project was supported by Joseph Lipchitz, chair of the History Department, Charles Carroll, Nina Coppens, and Louis Falcón, deans of Fine Arts, Humanities, and Social Sciences, provost Ahmed Abdelal, and chancellor Martin Meehan with reduced teaching loads and a sabbatical semester. My colleagues Christoph Strobel and Michael Pierson helped lessen my worries during the process of writing the book and getting it published. My other colleagues Christopher Carlsmith, Chad Montrie, Patrick Young, and Lisa Edwards also supported me along the way. I thank all of them sincerely.

My gratitude is also due to Mitchell Shuldman, Richard Harvey, John Callahan, and Paul Coppens of the Media Center and Deborah Friedman and Rose Paton of O'Leary Library for their patient help in scanning and cleaning photos, burning CDs, and getting books from off-campus libraries.

I owe my deep gratitude to Lorri Hagman, executive editor of the University of Washington Press, for recognizing the value of my mother's stories, for arranging an introduction by Delia Davin, and for providing help and guidance in the publishing process. My sincere appreciation goes to Delia Davin, an eminent scholar of modern Chinese history, politics, and gender issues, for putting my mother's stories into a broad historical framework. I also thank the two anonymous readers for their helpful comments and constructive criticism, as well as Mary Ribesky of the Editorial Department and other staff members at the University of Washington Press for their prompt and kind help. My heartfelt thanks also go to Amanda Gibson for her meticulous copyediting and insightful queries. Her edits and queries definitely helped to make the narrative read more idiomatically and smoothly.

Shehong Chen

NOTES

1   Jiading became a district in Shanghai Municipality in 1992.

DAUGHTER OF GOOD FORTUNE

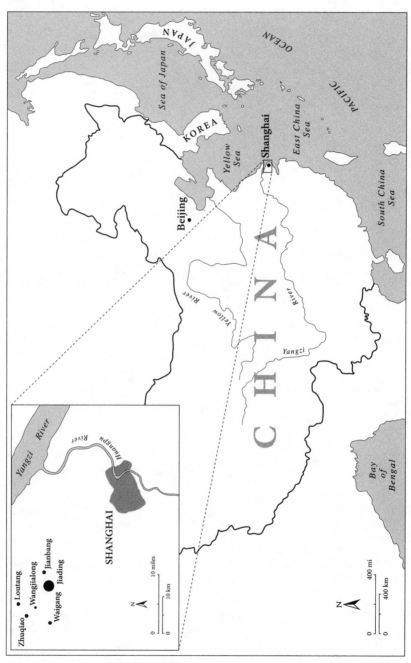

Wangjialong's location in China. Inset: Wangjialong and vicinity.

INTRODUCTION

Delia Davin

F IRSTHAND memoirs of ordinary people's lives in modern China are extremely rare: those that recount the lives of peasant women still more so. *Daughter of Good Fortune*, the autobiography of Chen Huiqin, born in 1931, the only child in a peasant family in Wang Family Village, in Jiading County near Shanghai, is therefore a precious addition to the literature on rural China. It should become a standard text for students of Chinese society. Chen's daughter, Chen Shehong, a professor of history and gender studies at the University of Massachusetts Lowell, interviewed her mother about her life over a number of years. She transcribed her mother's narrative and then condensed and translated the material to produce an autobiography that offers a peasant woman's own perspective on the way her community was affected by land reform, agricultural collectivization, the Cultural Revolution, economic reforms, industrialization, and the rapid growth of prosperity. Accessibly written and rich in political and cultural detail, it will be a most useful text for all those interested in the transformation of Chinese rural society, first through revolution, and subsequently through industrialization and globalization.

Much of what we know of rural Chinese society in the decades before the establishment of the People's Republic in 1949 comes from anthropological studies. Some of the best of these were Fei Xiaotong's study of village life in the lower Yangzi valley (a region not so far from Chen Huiqin's Jiading County),[1] Martin Yang's description of society and life in Taitou, his home village in Shandong Province,[2] and Francis Hsu's investigation of West Town, a remote semi-rural community in Yunnan Province where he took refuge during the Japanese occupation of coastal China.[3] These studies focused on the Chinese peasant family, and its treatment of birth, marriage, death, and inheritance. They showed that despite local variations, filial piety, the preference for sons over daughters, and the lesser value of girls to the natal families that they would leave on marriage were part of a system intended to assure the continuation of families that were both patriarchal and patrilineal.

A rural survey conducted by Mao Zedong in 1930 in Jiangxi Province, where the Communist movement was then based, offered a more political approach.[4] It contained much detail on the agricultural and commercial economy, as well as on social and family relations, educational levels, and religious practice. It also emphasized land ownership, class relationships between landlords and peasants, gender inequality, and the impact of the Communist land redistribution. Later, land reform and rural society were also described in William Hinton's *Fanshen*,[5] a book based on his observations in a village in Shanxi Province from 1946 to 1948, and in *Revolution in a Chinese Village* by Isabel and David Crook, who were teachers in this region in the same period.[6]

After 1949, as access to the rural areas by scholars and foreign observers was severely restricted and carefully supervised, studies of rural China had largely to depend on official documents and refugee interviews.[7] Isabel and David Crook wrote a study of the commune movement based on a short visit in 1959 to the area in which they had earlier studied land reform.[8] However, as they later learned, much of the truth about the difficulties there was withheld from them at the time.[9] In 1962, Jan Myrdal, a Swedish visitor, was allowed to conduct interviews with peasants in a Shaanxi village for a month. His report gives interesting glimpses of collectively organized work, the struggle to raise production, the rather mixed effects of the efforts to liberate women through the new marriage law, and the campaign to limit the size of families.[10] Although he does show how dreary and unvaried the diet of the northern countryside was at this time, there is no hint of the terrible three-year famine from which most of China was just beginning to emerge. Presumably the area he visited had been carefully chosen for having escaped the worst of the hunger.

From the 1980s, after the economic reforms, access to the countryside gradually became easier for social scientists and publications based on fieldwork began to appear.[11] Among these, Gail Hershatter's *The Gender of Memory*, based on one hundred interviews in Shaanxi villages over a ten-year period, gives the strongest voice to rural women, reflecting their roles as political activists, farmers, workers, and members of their families in the revolutionary period.[12] Increasingly, young Chinese social scientists trained in the West have also produced valuable insider studies of their home villages.[13]

Memoirs and oral history have also given us access to the stories of a few ordinary Chinese people. Perhaps the most remarkable is that of Ning Lao Tai-tai, an illiterate Shandong woman born in 1867 to a small-town family with a business in market gardening.[14] Ida Pruitt, an American brought up in China by missionary parents, befriended this woman in the 1930s and wrote her "autobiography" on the basis of two years of conversations with her. In addition to a brief spell in market gardening, Ning's father had worked in shops and as a peddler selling bread, but he was a failure in all these occupations. His opium habit had contributed to the family's gradual impoverishment. He strictly enforced the traditional restrictions on the females in his family. Although as a small child Ning Lao Tai-tai had enjoyed considerable freedom to play, as she grew older she suffered from the traditional restrictions visited on females. She was not allowed to attend school, her feet were bound when she was nine, and by the time she was thirteen she was no longer allowed to go out of the house alone. That same year her parents betrothed her to an older man. Her

marriage, two years later, turned out to be a disaster. Her husband
spent his money on opium and did not bring home enough to feed his
family. Unable to bear the sight of her children starving, Ning eventually broke with convention and went out to do odd jobs or to beg.
Finally, when her husband sold one of their daughters to raise money
for drugs, she decided she could no longer stay with him. She found a
job as a maid in a well-to-do household and supported herself for the
rest of her life. As an old woman, she was content that her children
had obtained schooling and that her granddaughter had even studied in America. Although she worried that this granddaughter was
still unmarried at thirty-five, she recognized that the young woman's
achievements—a good salary and economic independence—were
positive and would have been impossible for earlier generations. Ida
Pruitt lost touch with Ning Lao Tai-tai when Beijing was occupied by
the Japanese in 1938, so we do not know how her life ended.

Daughter of Good Fortune is also the story of an individual
woman. Chen Huiqin was born in 1931 and her story therefore carries
on chronologically from that of Ning Lao Tai-tai. Relationships in
Chen's peasant family seem to have been closer and happier than
those in Ning's. Chen was a child at the time of the Japanese occupation and the civil war that followed. She lived through the revolutionary enthusiasm and the extreme frugality of the 1950s and 1960s
as a young wife and mother. The Cultural Revolution brought fear
and difficulty to her family at a stage when her life might otherwise
have been becoming easier. Finally, from the time of the post-Mao
economic reforms of the 1980s, the family began to prosper. Deprived
of the schooling her father wanted for her by the civil chaos of her
childhood, Chen Huiqin never really learned to read. However, her
perceptive narration is proof that illiteracy does not preclude understanding of the intricacies of economic and social change.

Her account of the Land Reform is nuanced. During the Land
Reform, land confiscated from landlords was given to households who
had no or very little land. Its egalitarian ideals were supported by the
majority of peasants, as they stood to gain from the redistribution.
However, as Henrietta Harrison points out, the outcomes of the Land

Reform sometimes involved luck rather than justice.[15] In her story of
three Shanxi brothers, two older men had sold their inherited land
to support their addictions. Penniless at the time of land reform, they
were classified as poor peasants and received redistributed land. Their
younger brother, a hard worker who had retained his inheritance,
received nothing. Moreover, he was classified as a rich peasant, a polit-
ically disadvantageous label that would not be lifted until the 1980s.
The outcome of land reform in Chen Huiqin's family also reflects
the role of luck. Her great-uncle's sons had both died. As his family
had no adult men of working age, he had to hire laborers to work his
fifty *mu* of land. He was thus defined as a landlord—someone who
owned land but did not work it, depending instead on hired labor. As
a landlord not only was his land subject to confiscation, but he also
lost part of his house and some of his furniture. For the next three
decades his descendants would suffer discrimination as members of
a landlord family. Yet if he had had sons to work the land, he would
have been labeled a rich peasant, not a landlord, and thus protected
from confiscation. Chen's own family was classified as middle peasant. Her father had saved hard in the 1940s to buy land, but fortunately his holding was modest at the time of the Land Reform. His
family had once been wealthy and he joked that he should be grateful
to his father, who had gambled away the family fortune.

Chen's father was a Daoist priest before 1949. After 1949, he
supported the new regime and became a cadre. He had an enlightened attitude toward women and was clearly deeply fond of his only
daughter. He was determined that they should find her a husband
who would come to live with her family. Although in Chinese society
women normally married into their husbands' families, parents who
had no sons would sometimes arrange a matrilocal marriage for a
daughter. Their family line would thus continue and they would
have young people to care for them in their old age. Interestingly,
although Chen's father later prevailed, Chen's mother at first opposed
a matrilocal marriage for her daughter on the grounds that she would
have problems with his relatives, who would usually have expected to
inherit after his death.

Usually, only poor families would allow their sons to make a matrilocal marriage, as it was considered a demeaning arrangement for a man. The husband found for Chen was indeed of poor peasant origin. However, in the new society, the label of poor peasant had advantages. Chen's husband, a land reform activist, was later admitted to the Communist Party and rose to be quite an important local cadre. He treated Chen well and proved to be an enlightened parent in matters such as their daughters' education and their children's right to select their own marriage partners. It seems probable that Chen's matrilocal marriage allowed her to develop the strength of character and the clear views demonstrated in her life story. She lived in her parents' household and her mother's help in bringing up the children left her free to work outside. Her husband's work took him away from the village for much of the time and after her parents' deaths she effectively ran the household.

Chen is positive about collectivization but records the economic dislocation that accompanied the Great Leap Forward and the hardships and food shortages that followed. She does not mention deaths from the starvation, perhaps because her comparatively prosperous region had more food security than less fortunate ones. Of all the political movements that marked the Maoist period, the Cultural Revolution hurt Chen's family most. As cadres, both Chen's father and her husband were perceived by the Red Guards as members of the pre–Cultural Revolution establishment. Both were accused of being counterrevolutionaries and her husband spent a long time in detention, while her father attempted suicide under the strain.

The Cultural Revolution period saw much stricter prohibitions on traditional practices that had been merely discouraged in earlier years. Chen's mother, father, and father-in-law all died in this period and Chen always regretted that they had to be cremated without any of the rituals she considered proper. Even incense was unobtainable. The extravagant banquets that normally accompanied weddings and house building also had to be foregone in those years. Later, after Mao's death and the introduction of economic reforms, such restrictions were lifted and old customs were revived. Chen records in loving detail the arrangements made for each family celebration from then on, such as food preparation, clothes, and decorations. She began to chant and burn incense to Buddhist deities daily and used shamans to contact her deceased parents. Having discovered through the shamans what her parents needed, she paid professionals to make a modern paper house with a car and bought household goods that could be burned, along with paper money, for her parents' use in the afterworld.

Until the economic reforms, Chen's life was characterized by poverty, frugality, and hard work. She recalled, for example, that her three children had only ever had one store-bought toy among them—a clockwork frog that her husband purchased for the eldest. But her family was well placed to take advantage of the great economic opportunities that accompanied China's growing prosperity after the economic reforms. Her husband, as a cadre of long-serving, had a pension. He was also allowed to purchase apartments in the county town at a discount. The family later benefited from a number of advantageous property deals. The value that Chen's father had taught his family to attach to education also paid off. Her eldest daughter was admitted to university in Shanghai, thanks partly to a Cultural Revolution admissions policy that favored peasants. She later became a university professor in the United States. Her second daughter trained to be an accountant and married a man who later set up a successful business. The youngest child studied engineering and was a university professor in Shanghai before he also set up a flourishing business. Growing prosperity transformed lives and expectations. Chen's mother had never traveled even as far as the county town. Yet in 2001, Chen and her husband flew to the United States to visit their daughter. They also made other trips for pleasure within China. When their grandson was leaving Shanghai to do graduate work in Japan, the couple who had once treated their children with a clock-work frog gave him an Apple laptop.

Chen worked in subsistence agriculture for much of her life and lived in a house without electricity, running water, or drainage. She now enjoys such amenities as a flush lavatory, a washing machine, a telephone, and air conditioning. Her children drive cars. She enjoys video-chats with her grandchild living abroad when her children living nearby bring laptops to her house. Modern technology makes it possible to maintain the traditional closeness of intergenerational relationships in a Chinese family despite the distances brought about by modern geographical mobility. Despite all this change, some things that are important to Chen—family relationships, the celebration of traditional festivals, the observance of ritual, and the belief in communication with dead relatives—would be familiar to those who studied the Chinese family in the early twentieth century. For the moment, also, her children help to organize and participate in the traditional rituals. Will this continue or will it disappear with the passing of her generation?

NOTES

1   Fei Hsiao-tung (later written Xiaotong), *Peasant Life in China: A Field Study of Country Life in the Yangtze Valley* (London: Routledge and Kegan Paul, 1939).

2   Martin Yang, *A Chinese Village: Taitou, Shantung Province* (New York: Columbia University Press, 1945).

3   Francis L. K. Hsu, *Under the Ancestors' Shadow: Chinese Culture and Personality* (London: Routledge and Kegan Paul, 1949).

4   Mao Zedong, *Report from Xunwu*, translated with an introduction and notes by Roger R. Thompson (Stanford, CA: Stanford University Press, 1990).

5   William Hinton, *Fanshen: A Documentary of Revolution in a Chinese Village* (New York: Monthly Review Press, 1966).

6   Isabel and David Crook, *Revolution in a Chinese Village: Ten Mile Inn* (London: Routledge and Kegan Paul, 1959).

7   One of the best of these is William L. Parish and Martin K. Whyte, *Village and Family in Contemporary China* (Chicago: University of Chicago Press, 1978). Among the document-based studies that focus on rural women in the 1950s are Phyllis Andors, *The Unfinished Liberation of Chinese Women, 1949–1980* (Bloomington: Indiana University Press, 1983), and Delia Davin, *Woman-Work: Women and the Family in Revolutionary China* (Oxford: Clarendon Press, 1976).

8   Isabel and David Crook, *The First Years of Yangyi Commune* (London: Routledge and Kegan Paul, 1966).

9   David Crook, *Hampstead Heath to Tian An Men: The Autobiography of David*

Crook, ch. 11, accessed July 12, 2014, http://www.davidcrook.net/pdf/DC14_Chapter11.pdf.

10 Jan Myrdal, *Report from a Chinese Village* (London: Heinemann, 1965).

11 See, for example, Edward Friedman, Paul G. Pickowicz, and Mark Selden, *Chinese Village, Socialist State* (New Haven, CT: Yale University Press, 1991), and *Revolution, Resistance, and Reform in Village China* (New Haven, CT: Yale University Press, 2005).

12 Gail Hershatter, *The Gender of Memory: Rural Women and China's Collective Past* (Berkeley: University of California Press, 2011).

13 See, for example, Yan Yunxiang, *Love, Intimacy and Family Change in a Chinese Village, 1949–1999* (Stanford, CA: Stanford University, 2000), and Mobo Gao, *Gao Village: Rural Life in Modern China* (Honolulu: University of Hawaii Press, 1999).

14 Ida Pruitt, *A Daughter of Han: The Autobiography of a Chinese Working Woman* (Stanford, CA: Stanford University Press, 1967).

15 Henrietta Harrison, *The Man Awakened from Dreams: One Man's Life in a North China Village, 1857–1942* (Stanford, CA: Stanford University Press, 2005).

1

Ancestral Home

I was born in 1931 in Wangjialong, Wang Family Village. Mother said that after giving birth to me, she could not stop bleeding. A cushion filled with kitchen stove ash was placed under her to absorb the blood. The cushion had to be replaced every several hours. A traditional Chinese doctor was called in. The doctor said that he could prescribe a traditional Chinese medicine to stop the bleeding, but the medicine would prevent Mother from having any more babies.

My father was nineteen and Mother was twenty-one years old at the time.[1] Despite the fact that I was a girl, Father decided to save Mother's life and my grandmother agreed. Mother took the medicine. Her life was saved, but she never got pregnant again. According to traditions at the time, only a son could inherit family property and carry on a family's surname. A daughter was destined to leave her parents' home and become a child bearer for another family. Families in the village tried various ways, including "borrowing the belly" of a house maid, to produce a son. The worst curse that anybody at the time could utter was *juezisun*, which means "not having sons or grandsons." Parents ending up with only daughters had to give all their property to the man's nearest male kin. There were plenty of examples of such parents being maltreated in their old age by those who were to inherit their property, because these heirs were not the parents' own flesh and blood.

Thus, the decision to give my mother the medicine was quite extraordinary. It showed that both my father and grandmother had enlightened minds. They valued life, my mother's life and my life. They knew that if my mother died, I would not have the milk I needed to survive and would also die. They believed in their own principles and were not swayed by traditional beliefs or other people's opinions.

Father was the eldest brother in a family of four children. He had an elder sister, a younger brother, and a younger sister. Father said that Grandfather was a nice and loving man, but he gambled a lot. He had inherited a lot of land from our ancestors. When he signed away the last piece of land, he did not realize that it was the last piece. He continued to bet, and when he lost again, he signed again, believing that he still owned that piece of land. Discovering that piece of land belonged to someone else, the winning party sued Grandfather and he was thrown into jail. He became depressed and sick and died in jail. Father was nine years old at the time and his little sister was born after Grandfather's death.

Grandmother was a wise woman. She apprenticed my father to the locally well-known Zhang Family Daoist priests (Zhangjia Daoshi), and her second son to a rice store as soon as they were old enough. Since feeding an apprentice was the responsibility of the master family, she saved them from starvation. A Daoist priest was a respected man, and people used the title *xiansheng*, "mister," when they addressed a Daoist priest. To be trained as a Daoist priest, a person had to spend six years learning reading and writing as well as all the rituals and formalities of ceremonies. Rice was an important staple food, but people in Jiading County could not grow enough of it locally. So importing rice from rice-producing areas and selling it locally were profitable businesses. By apprenticing the boys to such respectable and profitable trades, Grandmother was astutely assuring the future for her sons.

Grandmother was also a brave woman. She ignored local gossip and openly courted a bachelor man. The man moved into her house and helped her sustain the family. I grew up calling this man Grandpa Bai, Bai being his surname, although Grandmother and Grandpa Bai were never married. Grandpa Bai was too poor to marry a wife when he was young. In midlife, he developed a small business of buying and selling salt. When he moved in with Grandmother, he piled salt in the corner of our guest hall (*ketang*). I grew up with a pile of salt inside our house all the time.

Father grew up fast and gained a strong sense of responsibility, for after Grandfather's death, he was considered head of the household. In the 1930s, Father's little sister, or my Little Aunt (Niangniang), was employed at Jiafeng Textile Mill (Jiafeng Fangzhi Chang). Little Aunt was a pretty young woman. She lived in the dorms because she had to work the three shifts in the mill. A famous local hoodlum saw my young aunt and began a sexual relationship with her. Father quickly decided to ask his sister to quit the job and return home. My aunt was already hurt. She resorted to folk ways of keeping herself from pregnancy and thus ruined her body. Later, she was married properly to a nice man, but she never gave birth to any children.

Father's elder sister is my Big Aunt (Momo), who was married to a man whose last name was Lu. After giving birth to a daughter and a son, Big Aunt had another baby boy. Since I was the only child, one who was destined to be another family's child bearer, Big Aunt tried to persuade my father to adopt her new baby boy. She said that an adopted son would not be allowed to inherit family property and carry down the family name; but, she added, if an adopted son had family blood, he would be accepted as the inheritor and carrier of the family lineage.

Father did not quite like the idea. At that time, I was eight years old. He was already thinking of keeping me at home and having me take in a husband when I grew up. But Mother was afraid that having me marry matrilocally would lead to family controversy and ultimately hurt me. She said that when I grew up, I would be able to find a good man and establish a happy family.

In the end, Father agreed to adopt Big Aunt's baby boy. I thus had a little brother. When Mother and Father went to work, I cared for him. At the same time, I was braiding yellow straw to increase the family income. We got yellow straw, a locally grown crop, from a station in West Gate of Jiading Town. My mother and I braided the straw, returned it to the station, and received payment. The braided yellow straw would be sewed together to make mats. Such mats were for export. I had never seen any local family using such mats.

I had to soak the yellow straw in water to make it soft so that I could braid it. One day when I went to soak the yellow straw in the river behind our house, I took my brother, about three years old at the time, with me and seated him on a stone step near the water. When I bent over to soak the straw, he kicked me in the rear and I fell into the river. I yelled for help and my yellow-straw-braiding friends pulled me out of the water.

Later that same year, my brother ran a high fever. A doctor was called in and we were told that it was too late and nothing could be done to save his life. The fever had already damaged his lungs, and he died. A little coffin was made for him and he was buried beside my grandpa's grave.

As head of the family, Father had to move Big Aunt's family back to our village in the 1940s to protect her. Big Aunt's husband was working as a commercial painter, painting paper fans, in the city of Shanghai. She and her children, three of them at the time, lived in her husband's village. A bachelor neighbor became interested in her. When she gave birth to another child, the bachelor neighbor said that it was his. She denied ever having had a sexual relationship with the man and refused to give him the child. The bachelor threatened to destroy her family.

With Big Aunt's husband away working in urban Shanghai, Father believed that his sister was no longer safe in her husband's village and decided to move her and her children back to our village. The house in her husband's village was dismantled, and bricks, tiles, and beams were shipped to our village. Local masons and carpenters were hired and a three-room house was built right outside our residential compound. The bachelor neighbor soon got into other trouble and was arrested and died in jail. The child in dispute did not survive its infancy.

Big Aunt had one more child, a girl, after she moved to our village. Having to deal with poverty and already with three children, she gave her baby girl to her sister, Little Aunt. Little Aunt and her husband had been married for a few years and did not have any children, so they accepted the girl and raised her as their daughter.

While my father's family became poor only after Grandpa gambled away the wealth, my mother came from a destitute family. In fact, my mother's native village, Tang Family Village (Tangjiazhai), was known for its poverty. There was a saying that it had only two and a half rice strainers. Rice had to be washed in a bamboo strainer before cooking. Although rice was the preferred staple food, many families did not own the more expensive irrigable land and so grew rye, beans, and potatoes in poor and marginal lands for sustenance. In the entire Tang Family Village, only two families owned rice land and could afford to eat rice. A third family owned a little rice land, thus qualifying them as "owning half a rice strainer."

Mother's mother, my grandmother (Waipo), was a capable woman. She gave birth to four children. Her family was so poor that they could not even afford to use a midwife. Grandmother delivered all her babies without midwifery help. Her babies were all born into a wooden basin. After the baby came out, she sat on the bed and asked her husband to lift the baby from the basin and give it to her. She would cut the umbilical cord, and clean and wrap the baby herself. Because she had been successful four times, she became a midwife herself and helped other poor women in the surrounding area.

Mother's father, my grandfather (Waigong), worked as a year-long hired hand (changgong) for a rich family with the surname of Zhou in Zhou Family Village (Zhoujiazhai). One night a baby girl was born in the Zhou family but died within a couple of days. On the same day, Grandmother gave birth to her fourth child, a girl. Grandfather offered the Zhou family his newborn girl for adoption. The family accepted the offer. The baby was adopted when it was three days old and grew up drinking the adopted mother's milk. Zhou Family Village was on the west side of the Xijing River (Xijing He), a river that flowed in the north-south direction on the west side of our village. Therefore, I refer to her as West River Aunt (Hexi Niangyi).

The Zhou couple who adopted my West River Aunt did not produce any children of their own. After having adopted my aunt, they adopted a boy and raised him. When the boy and my aunt were old enough, the parents had the young people married and made them legitimate inheritors of the family property. They were able to do so because my aunt's adopted father was the only biological son in the family. He had an adopted brother, who had been given only one-eighth of the family property. Further, this adopted brother did not have any children either, and had also adopted a girl. The extended Zhou family was rich in property but was poorly blessed with posterity. West River Aunt and her husband, however, would have four sons and one daughter.

West River Aunt and her husband, my uncle (Yifu), were hard-working farmers and good managers. They worked in the fields together with hired laborers. Nobody could idle time away because they were there working by them.

West River Aunt and Uncle loved children and their first child was not born until I was ten years old. When I was little, quite often, Aunt or Uncle would come and get me to spend a few days at their house. They would send me with a bamboo basket to gather chicken eggs in the grain barn. They opened the grain barn during the day and laid a lot of dry rice stalks there for chickens to lay eggs. Aunt and her family ate well, with every meal containing rice and meat. Laborers working for them also ate meat and rice with them. Poor people in nearby villages competed for an opportunity to work for them. Theirs was a landowning family known for good food as well as hard work.

Mother had another younger sister, and this one was given to a family in Song Family Village (Songjiacun) as a child bride. Poor families did not see why they should spend limited resources on a daughter who was destined to be a child bearer for another family. Poor families with sons were worried that they would be too poor to get a wife for their son and so were willing to raise an adopted girl as their son's future wife. Song Family Village was on the east side of our village, so I refer to this sister of my mother's as East River Aunt.

The Song family had East River Aunt and their son married. But the son never agreed to the marriage. He was a professional cook and worked for families far and near. After the marriage with my aunt, he stayed away from home and eventually married another woman. His father vowed to kill him if he ever returned home, so he rented a house away from his village and had a son with the wife of his choice. East River Aunt was a capable woman and her in-laws liked her and regarded her as the lawful daughter-in-law. With her in-laws' support, she adopted a daughter and raised her. She never married again.

Mother's elder brother worked as a year-long hired hand for a well-to-do family in his own village. My uncle (Niangjiu) and his family were so poor that nobody wished to send their daughter to suffer such poverty. Grandfather died young. Grandmother did manage to buy a wife for Uncle, but the woman did not stay long. She sneaked out one day, taking with her my uncle's clothes, the only valuable items in the house.

After the brief marriage, Uncle was again a bachelor working as a hired hand for the well-to-do family. The man of this family was sick with tuberculosis. His wife became sexually attracted to my uncle, a tall young man with a strong body. Unfortunately, Uncle got a venereal disease from the woman. The disease exposed the affair, and Uncle was kicked out by the family. Since he did not have the money to get any treatment, Uncle almost died from the disease. It was his strong body that helped save him from death. After that, he worked as a hired hand for my West River Aunt's family until Liberation.

When I became aware of things, I saw with my own eyes how poor a family my mother came from. Grandmother's house had a leaky roof. Two of the bedroom walls were collapsing and I could see the outside while staying inside. In winter, snow came through the collapsed places into the bedroom. Grandmother's bed was placed in the corner away from the collapsing walls and under the part of the roof that leaked the least. Uncle's bed was easily movable, allowing him to move it around to avoid dripping water from the roof.

In the kitchen, Grandmother had a run-down brick stove. Brick stoves had to be rebuilt from time to time, for bricks and mortar cracked from daily cooking. But Grandmother and Uncle could not afford to buy new bricks and mortar. They kept the stove, for its wall was where a portrait of the Kitchen God was pasted. For cooking, she used a movable stove (*xingzao*), a big earthen vat with a side opening for fuel. A wok would sit on the wide opening of the vat to get the heat from below. That was where Grandmother cooked her meals.

Grandmother owned three-tenths of a *mu* of land.[2] She grew vegetables, beans, rye, and a bit of cotton on it. She used the cotton to clothe herself and her son. The land also served as the family burial ground. When you did not have enough land, not only did you not have enough to eat, but you also had a shortage of fuel for cooking. The main source for cooking fuel in our area in the old days was crop stalks. That was another reason Grandmother used the movable stove to cook, for the movable stove was more efficient in fuel consumption.

When I was little, I liked the food Grandmother cooked on the movable stove. I thought it tasted more delicious. As I got older, I realized how hard life was for Grandmother and Uncle. Today, when I think of poverty, I think of the life they lived before Liberation.

ANCESTRAL COMPOUNDS

My paternal ancestors were rich people. They moved from North Hamlet (Beicun) to South Hamlet (Nancun), where they built two compounds, the West Compound and the East Compound. They were side by side, facing the south. A house needed to be near a river for washing purposes, so the compounds were built on the south bank of the Zhangjing River (Zhangjing He). On the western side of the West Compound, my ancestors had a branch river dug up. This branch river ran from the Zhangjing River southward and turned eastward on the southern side, covering about one-third of the width of the West Compound.

In the old days, the location of a house and the way a house was built were determined through consultation with geomancy (*fengshui*) masters. I do not know what the geomancy masters said, but I see two practical reasons for digging the branch river. First, it provided earth to raise the site on which the houses were to be built. In fact, the West Compound I grew up in never had water come in, not even when other houses in our village were flooded in severe storms. Second, the branch river provided occupants of the compounds secure access to river water for washing purposes. In the old days, thieves and robbers usually used boats for transportation, so access to water behind the house in the Zhangjing River was dangerous.

The West Compound had four main quarters connected by two guest halls and two side rooms with a sky well (*tianjing*) in the middle. The sky well was an open space with a drain for rain water. Adults also used it to dump laundry water. The sky well was also space for the occupants to dry washed clothes on bamboo poles. When it rained, adults got the washed laundry into the guest halls.

My nuclear family occupied the northeast quarter of the West Compound. Father's brother, my uncle (Bobo), and his nuclear family lived in the southwest quarter. The northwest and southeast quarters as well as the rooms on both sides belonged to my father's cousins. The guest halls were shared spaces for large furniture such as a loom and for ceremonies such as weddings and funerals. Ancestral tablets, which were wood blocks recording the names of our ancestors, were also placed in the guest halls. Father's family owned another two rooms in the East Compound, which was where my paternal grand-mother slept.

Inside the rear guest hall, the one connecting my nuclear family's quarter with the northwest quarter, there was an inscribed wooden board two and a half feet high by six feet long. On the board were three Chinese characters: *Dun Hou Tang*, Hall of Honesty and Sincerity. The board was an official present to our ancestors. It must have been presented at the time when the compound was built, for it was an integral part of the second beam on the north side of the guest hall. The inscribed board was shown most prominently when an important ceremony took place inside the hall. The inscribed board showed a kind of recognition of our family by the officials in the earlier days. The East Compound had a different layout. There were two main quarters connected by a guest hall, which was bigger than either the front guest hall or the rear guest hall inside the West Compound. Stretching southward were two side rooms and a sky well. All were bigger than the ones in the West Compound. Closing in the compound on the south side were five more rooms, with the middle being the Fortune Gate Room (*xiangmenjian*).

Our ancestors must have entertained official guests with grand ceremonies. Adults said that the Fortune Gate Room was where the family ushered in important guests when they held a grand ceremony. After guests were formally welcomed, they would be entertained with tea and snacks in the rooms on each side.

When I grew up, the extended family no longer expected any official guests. The Fortune Gate Room was turned into a space where a pestle and mortar was installed for all of us to pound sweet rice into flour for glutinous rice balls with sweet or meat fillings (*yuantuan*). My grandmother lived in the two small rooms on the west side of the Fortune Gate Room.

There was a narrow, dark, and often damp alley between the East and West Compounds. The East Compound was parallel to the West Compound's front half. There was no roof that covered the meeting place of the two compounds. Rainwater dropped down from the two roofs into a drain ditch in the alley. When it rained heavily, dripping rainwater splashed, wetting the narrow alley. Since the eaves of the two roofs literally touched each other, the alley was never exposed to any sunshine.

Since the East Compound was parallel to the front half of the West Compound, there was an open space behind the East Compound. This open space was right outside my nuclear family's quarter.

Inside my family's quarter, we divided the space into two rooms. One was our bedroom with two beds and the other our kitchen-dining room. In the kitchen-dining room, there was a brick stove, a square table with benches around it, and two big earthen vats, one for storing well water and the other for river water. Well water was for cooking food, while stored river water was for washing. My father had a particular way of purifying river water in our earthen vat—he would put alum in the water, stir it, and wait for silt to settle down to the bottom of the vat. He would then use a bamboo stick that had been hollowed inside to suck up the silt. Thus we always used clean water even for washing purposes.

Right behind our quarter was a thatched house where we stored crop stalks for cooking fuel and raised pigs, sheep, and rabbits. Outside the thatched house was an earthen vat that stored night soil to use as fertilizer.

We had to go through the sky well and the front guest hall in order to get to the stone steps to the water (*shuiqiao*) in the branch river, to fetch water and to wash things. This was the only set of stone steps for all of us in the two compounds. The only well, which was located on the southeast corner outside the East Compound, was also shared by all of us.

By the mid-1940s, my father said that the one set of stone steps to the water and one well were no longer enough for all the families occupying the East and West Compounds. He decided to build another set of stone steps to the water in the Zhangjing River behind our living quarter.

But Father ran into a problem. The open space right outside our quarter was owned by Father's uncle. This granduncle inherited from the same father as did my grandfather. When Grandfather gambled away his inherited wealth and property, his brother kept his share and worked it. By my time, this uncle of my father's had become a rich landowner and had to hire hands to work on the family land. He had turned the space right outside our quarter into an ox pen. He scolded Father and said that a set of stone steps behind the compound would make all the families unsafe, for thieves and robbers could get up from the river and rob the homes.

My father gave his reasons, but his uncle would not listen. Father went ahead and had the stone steps built anyway. As time went by, the steps Father built were used by more and more people in the two compounds. The old ones were gradually abandoned, as silt built up there while silt from the river behind our house was regularly collected as fertilizer. The original set of stone steps was at the end of the branch river. Silt-collecting boats could not easily turn around there so they neglected the area.

LIVELIHOOD

Father finished his six-year apprenticeship as a Daoist priest at the age of nineteen. Although he helped during planting and harvesting seasons, he worked mainly as a Daoist priest. In his profession, he sometimes worked alone; many times, he worked with the Zhangjia Daoist priests. When someone in a well-to-do family died, eight priests would be hired to chant for a day, called *daochang*, to send the dead off to the other world with blessings. Well-to-do families also held a chanting ritual, called *dajiao*, around the Mid-Autumn Festival. This ritual was to remove various evil spirits from the house and ask for blessings from Heaven and Earth. In order to show sincerity, the performing priests and the hosting family ate only vegetarian food on the day.

Around winter solstice, Father would again be very busy chanting on behalf of families, thanking Heaven and Earth for a good year and asking for blessings for a better year. Families moving into new houses also called a Daoist priest to preside over a ceremony called *zhenzhai*, calming the homesite. Daoist priests were also hired by families with sicknesses that were believed to be caused by having disturbed various gods and goddesses. A priest would go to the family and perform a ritual to calm the disturbed god or goddess.

Father's profession was a respectable one. He wore a long gown (*changshan*) year-round. In summer, the long gown was made of palace textile, a thin and wrinkle-free material. In winter, the long gown was made of homespun cotton cloth. He had to wear a long cotton-padded gown inside to keep him warm. When he went to work, he carried a candle lamp made of oiled paper. The one-day chanting rituals always lasted into the evening and the host family provided the candle. The lamp was necessary because in those days, there was no electrical lighting and roads were unpaved and narrow.

Father's profession required sitting on hard wooden benches for twelve or fourteen hours. One year in early autumn, a heat rash on Father's buttocks turned into a huge abscess. He was bedridden. A doctor who was famous for his expertise in treating abscesses came every day to change the dressing for Father. He would take off the wrapping and pull up a solid piece of medicine he had put in the previous day. As he did this, pus gushed out into a container he brought. He would clean the wound and put in another solid piece of medicine and then wrap it again.

Father was bedridden for more than ten days. Mother went into the fields during the day. I was about ten years old at the time. I sat next to the bed my father slept in, brought him the urinal when he needed it, and emptied and cleaned it afterwards. I brought him drinking water when he asked for it. In early autumn, taro was in season. Mother cooked some before she went into the fields. By mid-afternoon, I got a bowlful of the cooked taro, peeled them one by one, and feed them to Father.

In the late 1940s, Father earned ten *jin* of rice each day for his service.[3] At that time, professionals like Father preferred rice as payment for their services, for money was very unstable.

Like many women from poor families, Mother worked for other families as a day laborer and grew crops on a piece of land my family rented. Later, she worked on our own land. But women usually did not participate in transplanting rice seedlings. Female bodies had to be protected for child-bearing and child-nursing functions, for families depended on them for their continuation. In the old days, there were no contraceptive methods. Women were menstruating, pregnant, or breastfeeding babies most of their adult lives. Traditional Chinese medicine said that during any of those times, the female body was weak and should be protected from exposure to cold temperatures. Rice transplanting usually took place in early summer and the water in rice paddies could still be cold then. In fact, if the transplanting season was rainy and cold, transplanters had to wear cotton-padded vests. When they got up from rice paddies for lunch and supper, they would drink high-proof Chinese liquor to drive away the cold from their bodies.

After we bought irrigable land, we planted rice every three years. For the other two years, we planted cotton one year and soy beans the other. We contracted out the work of transplanting rice seedlings and of irrigating our rice paddies to rich families, paying for the service. Rich families used draft animals to turn a waterwheel to bring water to the rice paddies. Many families like ours contracted out transplanting and irrigating work.

There was another way for not-very-rich families to grow rice. They would transplant rice seedlings and use human power to bring water to rice paddies themselves. After rice seedlings were transplanted, both male and female adults in the family would pedal a waterwheel day and night to bring water from a river or a pond into the rice paddies to keep the paddies irrigated throughout the growing season. That was a lot of work.

I started to help from very early on. We raised sheep to provide manure for our crops and for their meat and I collected weeds for them. I started to braid yellow straw when I was about seven years old. Mother and I would walk about nine *li* to the West Gate of Jiading to get yellow straw.[4] Mother would carry six bundles on a shoulder pole and I would carry two bundles on my shoulders. We took the braided straw to West Gate, where it was checked for quality and measured by length for payment.

In 1946, when I was sixteen, I worked in a factory in Zhuqiao Town, about three *li* north of home, making yellow-straw mats. I walked to work every day and brought my own lunch. We sewed yellow-straw braids together into one-square-foot pieces. At the end of the day, the foreman would come, examine the quality, and count the pieces. If the quality was not good, you would be fined. I was a good worker and earned about three *jin* of rice per day.

After I worked there for about a year, the business closed. I then worked at a factory that spun a kind of hair. I do not know what hair it was, but it felt like human hair that had been processed. This factory

1.1   Chen Huiqin's bamboo
lunch basket

was at Eight Letter Bridge (*baziqiao*), which was about three *li* south of
home. I again walked to work every day and brought lunch with me.

Several of us young girls in the village went to work together. We
would leave home at sunrise and come home before it got dark. I still
have the bamboo basket that I used to carry my lunch (fig.1.1), which
usually consisted of a bowl of rice and a little something salty. The
factories heated lunches for us workers.

In the late 1940s, I learned the warping skill from Big Aunt, who
acquired the skill when she lived in her husband's village. Warping
was the necessary step between spinning the yarn and weaving the
cloth (figs. 1.2 and 1.3). Although individual families spun and wove
at home, warping was more complicated and required tools that most
families did not own. People took starched yarn, which had been
wound onto bamboo bobbins, to the warping shop. There, bobbins
were put on thin bamboo sticks and warp threads were drawn from
them and then reeled onto a weaving beam. The process established
the lengthwise threads for weaving with the shed for the heddle. People paid a small fee for the warping service. After Big Aunt moved to
our village, she set up her own warping shop in a thatched house and
had her elder daughter working with her. When her daughter went to

1.2   Spinning wheel   1.3   Loom

work in Jiafeng Textile Mill, I became the helper in the shop.

Our family lived a frugal life, but we always had enough to eat. Around Chinese New Year, Father would buy malt sugar and we would make sweets with peanuts and sesame seeds we grew. We roasted peanuts and sesame seeds in a wok and mixed in melted malt sugar. When the mixture was cool enough to handle, Mother would knead it and press it into flat pieces. When it was completely cold, Father would cut the pieces into small squares. We would have this candy for most of the spring.

I got along very well with my parents. I remember when I was little, Father bought me a silver hair pin with about twenty-five inlaid pearls in the shape of a flying butterfly. It was beautiful and I treasured it. I put it on my left-side parted hair, but the butterfly was upside down. I tried to part my hair on the right side, and the butterfly hair pin was perfect. I got used to parting my hair on the right side and wore my hair that way for many decades. After I moved to the apartment we bought in Xincheng in urban Jiading, I got to know a hairdresser very well and went to her every time I needed a haircut. Every time she finished cutting my hair, she would blow-dry it and part it on

the left side, for most people part their hair that way. She would realize it was a mistake and do it again. She jokingly complained about it,
and I decided to part my hair on the left side and have been combing
my hair that way since then.

My mother was the most loving and caring person on this earth.
She never scolded me or beat me. Whether we worked in fields or at
home, we talked to each other softly. Other mothers and daughters
in our village quarreled or argued or cursed each other. We never did
any of that.

Mother suffered from severe headaches, which affected her
eyesight. When Father took Mother to see an eye doctor at West Gate
about the headaches, I went with them. The doctor was a big and tall
Indian. He spoke Chinese and had a local woman as his assistant. He
was very expensive, but my mother's headaches were not cured. The
headaches ultimately led to the total loss of vision in her right eye.

Mother was good at weaving and spinning but was not very good
at sewing. When her right eye lost vision, sewing became an impossible task. As a teenager, I took over the responsibility of sewing clothes
and making shoes for the family. I sewed all the family clothes, including my father's long gown and his cotton-padded long gown.

Most tradesmen in Wangjialong were from poor families. Chen
Qixiang was a carpenter from North Hamlet. His family owned less
than one *mu* of land. Chen's wife worked as a day laborer for a rich
family. The couple had two sons. When the boys were little, they
followed their mother to work during the day and got food from the
rich family. When the boys became teenagers, their father took them
along and trained them as carpenters. Tradesmen such as carpenters,
brick masons, tailors, and bamboo craftsmen all worked in customers'
houses and were given lunch and dinner.

There were several kinds of jobs that few local people wanted and
so people from poorer places came to do them. One of these jobs was
to redo cotton quilts. After some use, quilts became so pressed that
they were no longer soft and warm. They needed to be dismantled
and napped into quilts again. In Wangjialong, there was one man who
napped new cotton into quilts, but he would not redo old ones. The

dismantling of the old quilts that had been pressed flat produced dust. It was very unhealthy work that caused choking. He would charge a lot if he accepted the job.

Every year, after the fall harvesting and planting season was over, a tall, thin man would come to our village from Huizhou in Anhui. He was willing to redo cotton quilts without charging too much. He brought with him his own tools, including a brush-like implement that he used to dismantle old cotton quilts, a bow-like tool he used to make cotton fluffy, and a plate-shaped wooden piece he used to press the fluffed cotton into shape. He brought with him his own bedding. Every day, he was provided with food by the family for whom he worked. At night, he usually unrolled his bedding and slept in a corner of that family's guest hall. Not all families allowed him to sleep in the guest hall. In some cases, families did not have a guest hall. So sometimes, he ended up sleeping outside, under the eaves of a house.

My father invited him to sleep inside our guest hall. Father said that it was wintertime, sleeping in the open must be cold, and there was some open space in our guest hall. So this Huizhou man came and slept in our house. In the morning, he would roll up his bedding, leave it in a corner, and go to work. In the evening, he would come back to our guest hall and sleep.

One evening, my mother cooked taros and asked me to take one to the Huizhou man. Each taro plant produced one huge taro and many small ones. The one Mother asked me to bring to the Huizhou man was a huge taro. The Huizhou man peeled it with a smile on his face. He opened his mouth so wide in order to bite into the taro that he dislocated his jaw.

The Huizhou man came year after year and slept in our guest hall. He became a friend. When I gave birth to my first child in 1952, he presented me with a maternity gift (she'm'geng).

Another job that was done by people from poorer areas was scraping river silt. Young men or men in their prime rowed their own boats to our area and were willing to work for low pay. They were hired by land-owning rich families to gather river silt as fertilizer. They slept on their own boats at night and got food from the family for whom they worked. Our rich, land-owning neighbor hired such men. I remember seeing each of them eat three big bowls of staple food, which consisted of rice and flattened rye.

Poor people from Jiangsu and Anhui also worked as peddlers. In the old days, women seldom went to town to buy things such as needles and thread, so peddlers brought such things to them. The peddlers used a cluster of shells and metal pieces to make a sound, announcing their visits. As a child, I would go out to see the little things the peddlers carried. There were also candy peddlers, who played a flute to announce their visits. We children loved candy peddlers. We would take old and worn-out clothes, old shoes, and other sellable scraps to the candy peddler and exchange them for candy. I was told that such peddlers lived in improvised huts along the river that circled the town of Jiading.

LAND

Mother and Father worked hard and saved to buy two *mu* of dry land when I was little. Dry land was much cheaper than rice or irrigable land. We grew cotton on the dry land. Cotton needed a lot of care. Mother worked hard, and I started to help by weeding and picking cotton when I was very young. After cotton was dried, it was packed and stored in the attic of our bedroom.

In the 1940s, you would need four bales (250 kilograms) of cotton or 10 *shi* (780 kilograms) of rice to acquire one *mu* of rice land. I remember that when I was about eleven years old, my parents dug up an earthen jar full of silver dollars at night. The silver dollars were darkened a bit. My parents had buried the jar under the threshold between our bedroom and our kitchen-dining room. They had to dig at night and pour the silver dollars out into a bag slowly and carefully so that they did not make a lot of noise. They were worried that if somebody heard the noise, they would be robbed. We bought four *mu* of land with that money.

One *mu* of the land was located right in front of our residential compound. Father was a reasonable man and was well aware of local traditions and customs regarding family inheritance. He said that he would give the house he inherited from his father to the eldest son of his brother. Now he used the money he, Mother, and I earned through our labor to purchase land, which he said he would keep for me. Father said further that he, Mother, and I would now work hard to earn more money so that we could build a house on that piece of land right in front of our original home. He added that when I grew up, he wanted me to take in a husband and raise a family in that house.

Although Mother continued to protest Father's suggestion of having me marry matrilocally, she and I gathered broken bricks and tiles in our spare time and piled them up for a building site. We would bring a bamboo basket and go to riverbanks for broken bricks and tiles. People would dump such things on a riverside after building a house. Water washed them downriver and when the river water receded, they would be exposed and we could pick them up.

Besides broken bricks and tiles, we needed more dirt to build a raised site for our future house. Father used bamboo baskets and a shoulder pole to bring dirt from the other pieces of land we owned. He always did this in wintertime. He did not take dirt randomly. He dug up dirt only at places where a ditch was needed for drainage. That way, he prepared the land for crops while getting the dirt we needed for our potential building site.

At that time, land changed hands for various reasons. The man from whom we bought the four-*mu* land was the only son in a well-to-do family. He gambled and ate the "white powder" (heroin). He sold land to pay for his gambling and drug addictions and totally neglected his family, which included his wife, a daughter who was my age, and his mother. His wife was so starved that she walked away from home, taking the daughter with her. This man's mother, who worked for other families for food, asked my grandmother, who was a well-connected and outgoing person, to keep an eye open for her granddaughter. The mother said that she had given up all hope for her useless son and that the little girl was the only grandchild she would ever have. My grandmother asked around and finally found the

runaway woman and the little girl. The woman had begged her way
south and married a poor man about twenty-five *li* from our village.
This was about five years after she had left our village. She and her
new husband already had two children. Grandmother persuaded the
mother to allow her to take the girl back to her grandmother.

Some families sold land because of unfortunate events at home. A
Yan family owned four *mu* of rice land. In 1942, the family decided
to grow rice on three *mu* of their land and cotton on the other *mu*.
Yan's wife was a diligent woman, while Yan liked drinking and was a
slacker. People who grew rice hoped that it would be a wet year, for
rice demanded a lot of water, and those who planted cotton hoped for
a dry year, because too much rain would allow weeds to grow too fast,
overwhelming cotton plants. The year 1942 was a dry one. Yan's wife
had to pedal a waterwheel day and night to bring enough water to
their rice field. She developed a little bump under her nose. She was
too busy and poor to see a doctor. When the bump grew large quickly,
the family realized that it was a deadly illness called *ding*. *Ding* was
curable if it was treated in time. But when she went to see a doctor,
the *ding* had broken and the virus had gotten into her blood. It was
no longer curable. She died of it, leaving behind her five-month-old
daughter.

Yan's mother "borrowed milk" in the village to raise the girl. Yan
grieved over his wife's death and was depressed. He escaped from
life's reality by drinking excessively. The family's rice land dried up
and was taken over by tall weeds. People from near and far came and
gathered weeds from Yan's land that fall. When the cotton produced
fiber balls, he picked three or four *jin* every day and sold it at the
local market to get the money for his alcohol addiction. He sold the
land that winter. Father bought two *mu* from the Yan family and his
brother, my uncle, bought the other two *mu*.

Uncle and Father were not the only ones buying land in the 1940s.
Yan Shoufu was another one. He inherited a little land. When he had
some money, he bought an ox and a plow. He plowed land for other
families, and the families he worked for paid him a fee for the service. In our area, we only had two planting seasons in which plowing

service was needed. But on the outskirts of urban Shanghai, people grew vegetables for the big city. Vegetables had much shorter growing seasons and land had to be plowed for each new crop. Therefore, when it was not a busy planting season in our area, Yan Shoufu brought homemade snacks and walked about sixty *li* with his ox and plow to villages near urban Shanghai and plowed land for families who needed his help. The families provided him with room and board and paid him for his labor.

He bought not only more land with the money he earned but also a boat. He planted garlic on his land. After the garlic was planted, he rowed his boat far and near to get wild water plants, which he placed on the rows of garlic before the garlic plants sprouted through the soil. Then he rowed out to gather river silt. He spread river silt between the rows of garlic. When the silt was dry, he pounded it into small pieces. Both water plants and river silt were very good fertilizers for garlic. The garlic from Jiading was exportable, thus making it a very profitable cash product. While others would harvest 100 or 200 *jin* of garlic from one *mu*, Yan would harvest 1,000 *jin* from the same amount of land. With the money he gained from selling garlic, he bought more land.

By the late 1940s, Father was a respected man in the village. He was educated and wrote beautiful calligraphy. Villagers consulted him on matters of ritual and ceremony and asked him to write couplets for special occasions. People addressed him politely as Mr. Chen. He was made head (*jiazhang*) of South Hamlet. In that position, Father executed orders from the higher-ups, known as *baozhang*.[5] Such orders included collecting money or grain from each family to support various local projects and activities. For instance, when a young man from the area enlisted in the military service, Father would go to every house in the hamlet to collect "soldier rice," which was for the soldier's family to make up for the loss of the young man's labor. Father would hand over the rice he collected to the higher-ups for distribution.

I remember Father would take a container to families to collect grain. A lot of times, he would return home and add our own grain to what he had collected to bring it up to the quota set by the higher-ups. He had to do so because some poor families just could not afford to give grain. Father would say that so long as we could afford it, we would do the good deed.

NOTES

1 In Wangjialong, as soon as a baby is born, it is considered one year old. This method of calculating age is used throughout the narrative.
2 One *mu* is about one-sixth of an acre. Grandmother owned approximately one-twentieth of an acre.
3 One *jin* is about half of a kilogram, or one pound. Ten *jin* is the equivalent of about five kilograms, or ten pounds.
4 One *li* is about half of a kilometer, or three-tenths of a mile. Nine *li* is approximately four and a half kilometers.
5 *Jiazhang* and *baozhang* were heads of the most basic administrative units, known as *jia* and *bao*, in China before 1950. Although theoretically a *jia* contained ten families and a *bao* contained ten *jia*, in some cases, such as in Wangjialong, a natural village became a *jia* and several natural villages formed a *bao*.

2

War and Revolution

I HAVE lived a long life and experienced changes that turned the world upside down. In my youth, I witnessed Japanese invasion and then Communist revolution. When I was three months old, in early 1932, the Japanese attacked Shanghai.[1] Mother said that she took me and fled to Grandmother's village, which was west of Wangjialong. The Japanese were bombing from the east. Our own house was too close to the Big Road (Dalu), where troops were marching. Mother said that when bombing and shooting came close, she took me into the bamboo grove near Grandmother's house, put me on the ground, and covered me with her body arched above me. That way, if a bullet came, it would hit her body so that I would be saved, Mother said. When Mother told me this story, she admitted that it was a foolish action, because if she was killed by a bullet, I would not have her milk any more and would starve to death. Mother loved me and would die for me.

A couple of months later, the Japanese occupied Jiading. My family ran away and took refuge in Qingpu County, which is in the west. Mother told me that we were given three meals of porridge every day in the refugee camp. Earlier, when my mother gave birth to me, our relatives presented meat as maternity gifts. My family could not eat all the meat within a short period of time, so my parents salted some to preserve it. The adults took the salted meat with them when they fled. At the refugee camp, Mother went out to gather dry straw and leaves during the day. Mother said that I was a good baby and people in the camp played with me when she was away. The adults dug a hole in the ground and cooked the meat in a wok with fire fed by the straw and leaves Mother gathered. Mother always worked the hardest in the extended family.

When I was seven years old, in 1937, the Japanese came again.[2] We again went into refuge, this time at a place called Xiemaqiao, Resting Horse Bridge, in Qingpu County. We stayed there almost half a year this time. My family became friends with a local man named Ah Quanlin, who visited us many times afterward.

We went with Chen Jixi's family from North Hamlet. Chen Jixi owned a boat so we fled in the boat. One foggy morning, when we were rowing on the Baihe River (Baihe Jiang), two Chinese soldiers forced themselves onto our boat and demanded that we take them to a certain place. The adults on the boat were afraid of the soldiers and wanted to get rid of them. So Mother pinched my thighs to make me cry, thinking that the soldiers would be bothered by my crying. At that time, there appeared a boat rowed by a single white-bearded man. The old man offered to take the soldiers on his boat. The soldiers got onto the old man's boat and our boat turned around and went in the opposite direction. The old man's boat disappeared into the morning fog. A few minutes later, we heard the explosion of a bomb into the Baihe River. The explosion pushed a big column of water into the air, in the opposite direction not very far from us. My uncle, who was with us on the boat, said that the old man was a fairy sent by our ancestors to save our lives.

At Resting Horse Bridge, I saw women walking around with their breasts totally uncovered. In the evening, men and women took off clothes and bathed in rivers. This place was not very far from our home village, yet their customs and habits were different.

In those days, people did not buy furniture or build pretty houses. There were too many wars and we never knew when we would have to run away. When we ran away, we did not even lock our doors, for there was not much to be stolen. When we had saved money, we bought land, which could not be taken away when we fled. When we came back, we put in seeds and could start a livelihood again in a few months.

After we returned home from Resting Horse Bridge, we lived under Japanese control. The Japanese were always looking for "flower girls." When I became a teenager, I had to pretend that I was an ugly, dwarfed old lady when I worked in the fields. I smeared ashes from the back of the kitchen wok on my face, wore Mother's old clothes, which were too big for me, added a worn-out work skirt at my waist, and put on my grandmother's old headcloth. When Grandmother, Mother, and I worked in the fields, I stood between them. Wherever possible, I stood in ditches or hunched over to pretend that I was dwarfed when Japanese soldiers passed by.

Young women had to hide when the Japanese came into the village. During the Qingxiang Yundong, or Clearing the Villages Movement,[3] Japanese soldiers came into our compound several times. Little Aunt and Uncle's wife were pretty young women at the time. They had to hide on the roof behind a decorative wall above our sky well. One day, the Japanese came to our compound and stayed the whole day, cooking and eating what we had. The two young women stayed on the roof for the whole day. They did not eat or drink the entire time and had to urinate there. When their urine dripped down the eaves into the sky well, they feared that the Japanese would discover them. Fortunately, the Japanese were busy cooking and eating, which helped save them from trouble.

When the Japanese were about to be defeated, they were desperate. They snatched young men to dig trenches for them; they cut down all the trees in our village for wood to support their trenches; they came into homes and slaughtered chickens and ducks and cooked them and ate them; they were very rude people.

When the Japanese were here, the prices of many things went up. The price for matches was one of them. Poor families could not afford to buy matches and so kept foot warmers in summer for the seed of fire. When they needed to start a fire to cook food, they stuck a rolled-up piece of paper into a foot warmer and waited for it to catch fire.

I spent my school-age years under Japanese control. Public security was poor; people had to take care of themselves. Some people owned firearms; robbers, bandits, and hoodlums were everywhere. Father worried that I would be hurt if I walked to school every day. The only school at the time was in Zhuqiao Town, which was about three *li* from home. Between Zhuqiao and our home were a deserted house that had nothing but tablets for the family's ancestors, a thick bamboo grove, a temple, and a narrow road with crops growing tall and dense on both sides. These structures and the bamboo and crops provided hiding places for robbers, bandits, and hoodlums. So I never went to school.

Father taught me Chinese characters at home. He used square cards and grouped characters of the same radicals for me. For instance, with the radical of gold, there were the characters of silver, copper, iron, and tin. When I remembered these characters, he presented another group. In my teens, I knew about five hundred characters.

But I did not practice writing characters. I was busy braiding yellow straw, sewing, and embroidering when I was not working in the fields or in a factory. I always wanted to do something to help the family. Since I did not see how reading and writing would benefit the family, I did not go beyond recognizing characters. This is a big regret in my life. Today, when I see people reading newspapers and novels, I am envious. Now that I have so much free time in my retirement, I wish I could read and write.

Although the reason I did not go to a formal school was not my gender, other families treated girls and boys very differently. Girls were expected to learn needlework and spinning and weaving. They were also expected to help tend younger siblings and do other house chores. Not a single girl in Wangjialong went to school for a day in the 1940s, but all families, even those that were not well-to-do, tried to send sons to school. A few boys I grew up with went to school. None of them liked school and all of them quit after a couple of years. In one of our neighboring villages, there was a widow who risked her life to send her son to school. During the Clearing the Villages Movement, the Japanese built a fence at Penglang Town, a town on the west side of Jiading County. West of Penglang Town was a rice-producing region. Before the fence was built, people from Jiading went there to buy rice. Once people could not cross the fence to buy rice, the price of rice in Jiading went up dramatically. So the widow, a brave and shrewd woman, used a boat to avoid the Japanese-guarded fence. She put on long white mourning clothes, placed a coffin in the boat, and wailed loudly and sadly when she approached the checkpoints, indicating to the Japanese that she was taking her dead husband to a burial site. The Japanese did not want to stop and check a coffin, but the coffin was full of rice. She made a lot of money this way and sent her son to school. Her son happened to be a smart boy and went all the way to college.

The different expectations of girls and boys were based on the conventional belief that only male children were legitimate heirs in a family. So most families tried to send their sons to school. If a son was smart, then, with education, he could bring fame and fortune to the family. On the other hand, a girl was to be married out, so investing limited family resources in her was just a waste from her parents' point of view. Also, if the parents wanted their daughter to be happy and successful, then they would prepare her with womanly skills so that a good and well-to-do family would choose her as a daughter-in-law.

The Japanese employed local despots and hoodlums to run affairs for them. In Jiading, there were the Ji brothers. They were so famous as hoodlums that nobody dared to offend them. Before this time, the road between Jiading Town and Zhuqiao Town was a footpath, although it was known as Big Road. The Ji brothers demanded that the road be widened so that they could come to visit Zhuqiao in rickshaws. I remember one day a man beat a gong and marched along the road, shouting, "An eight-feet-wide official road will be built between

2.1   Chen Huiqin, 1940s

Jiading Town and Zhuqiao Town. Two ditches will be dug to flank the official road."

This was a big project and many local people participated in it. The bridge spanning the Zhangjing River (Zhangjing He) behind our house used to be made of two stone slabs. During the project, two more stone slabs were used to match the width of the new road. The widened road became known as Big Official Road (Daguanlu).

During the Japanese occupation of my hometown, people who needed to enter an urban area or travel to another town had to show a "good-citizen" identification card with a photo. Little Aunt was working at Jiafeng Textile Mill (Jiafeng Fangzhi Chang) in the town of Jiading. She wanted to take me to urban Jiading for a visit. So I had a photo taken (fig. 2.1) and then obtained a "good-citizen" identification card. That was the first photo taken of me in my entire life.

LIBERATION

In May of 1949, troops marched past Wangjialong. We later learned that these troops were the People's Liberation Army (PLA). They were marching from the north to the south on the Big Official Road right outside our village. It was around midnight when the army started to pass our village. We did not dare to sleep, nor did we dare to go out. Families living right beside the road came and spent the night with us. We were all afraid of troops. From time to time, we would go to the bamboo grove in front of our compound to watch the marching men. During the night, we could vaguely see columns of troops and sometimes horses carrying things on their backs.

As the PLA troops marched, they announced through hand-held loudspeakers that they were the common people's army and would not hurt anybody or take anything without payment. After daybreak, some young people ventured out to the road. They came back to report that the marching soldiers had shaken their hands and given them food to eat. After hearing this, those whose houses were along the road returned home. We went to Big Aunt's house, which was in the front of our compound, and watched the marching troops through its east window. It was around eight or nine o'clock in the morning when the last of the troops marched past our village.

Right after the Communists arrived, my father still worked as head of our hamlet. He helped borrow things such as dry rice straw and wooden doors from various families to support the army. The troops either slept on wooden doors or on the ground cushioned with dry straw. They were on their way to take over Shanghai. They spoke a strange dialect and so only after some time did we begin to understand some of what they said.

Very soon after the Communists arrived, we experienced big changes. A new political structure was established in our area. The three hamlets in Wangjialong were organized as three groups. The old heads of hamlets were replaced by heads of groups (*zuzhang*). Replacing my father was a tailor, a poor man with little land, from our hamlet. Above the group was the administrative village (*xingzheng-cun*).

Heading the Wangjialong Administrative Village was Chen Yuanxiang, a man from North Hamlet. Chen had a little education and ran a seasonal small business that collected harvested crops to sell for a profit. His family owned a few *mu* of land and also worked on rented land. He was among the first supporters of the new regime.

In the spring of 1950, the new head of the administrative village invited a few people from outside the village and had a feast in the house of a well-to-do family in Wangjialong. Chen and his followers cooked what was available in that house, drank the wine in the house, and ate to their hearts' content. Chen was quickly disciplined and was replaced by Lu Weixin, Big Aunt's husband, who had lost his job in Shanghai and returned to the village. Being poor and having little land, he actively supported the new system.

The Communists initiated a new organization, called the Peasant Association. The first chairman of the Peasant Association in Wangjialong was Chen Pingli, a poor man with a little education who was making a living as a tailor. My family, together with many other families, joined the Peasant Association.

The third element of the local political structure was the militia. The head of the militia in our village was a young man named Chen Xianxi. Chen was from a poor family, had a little education, worked as a carpenter, and showed enthusiasm for the changes. Young people, including me, volunteered to stand guard in a militia hut built along the Big Official Road.

Father was very cautious in accepting the changes. When the Communists first arrived, I went to a meeting for young people held at Yang Family Temple. I brought home an application form to join the Communist Youth League and showed it to Father. He tore it up right in front of me and said, "You can go to meetings, but do not join any political organization." Father made another rule for me: I could go out and participate in activities during the day, but I should not go out in the evening. Because of this rule, I volunteered to be on duty in the militia hut only during the day.

The militia was necessary because some people did not accept the Communists and were resisting the changes. In Jiading County, the Ji brothers were die-hard anti-Communists. After the Japanese were defeated, one of the Ji brothers became a local gangster chief and the other an officer in an anti-Communist organization. After the Communists arrived in Jiading, the two brothers gathered local supporters and killed Communists and activists and raided grain warehouses. In the spring of 1950, we heard that they had appeared in Penglang Town and raided a grain warehouse. Penglang was west of us. Then we heard that they had killed a Communist official in Loutang Town, which was east of us. They also broke into the town office in Xuhang, which was southeast of Wangjialong, and stole a telephone.[4]

Related to the Ji brothers' anti-Communist activities was a murder in Tang Family Village, my mother's native village. A man named Hang Genquan from the village was a member of a gang associated with the Ji brothers. After raiding grain warehouses, Hang Genquan and his people stored looted grain in the compound occupied by several poor families, all of whom were surnamed Tang. Living in the compound was a child bride, who was about ten years old. The mother of the child bride was a widow who treated the child bride badly, including not giving her enough to eat. The child bride said to the adopted mother, "There is so much grain stored in our house, but you only allow me to eat leftover porridge." After the child bride threatened to tell people about the grain stored in the house if she continued to be treated badly, the mother decided to get rid of her.

One night, as one neighbor woman stood on guard outside the compound, the adults brutally killed the girl and threw the dead body in the river behind the compound. The next morning, the dead body was discovered by a fishing boat. The mother joined the alarmed public, pretending to be in shock and asking why her child had committed suicide. But the dead body showed violent blows and cuts on the head, clearly indicating that it had not been suicide, but murder.

An investigation was carried out. Seven people were proven to be involved in the murder. The mother of the child bride was sentenced to death. One man was sentenced to jail for life. The woman who stood on guard was sentenced to three years of imprisonment. The others served jail terms between two and seven years.[5]

Hang Genquan was not involved in the murder, but he was arrested for his involvement with the Ji brothers' activities. He was released from jail in the 1950s and died of tuberculosis soon after he was released. The Ji brothers were also arrested. There was a public trial in Jiading Town and both brothers were sentenced to death.[6]

Many Communist cadres in the new structure were from outside areas and spoke with an accent. One of them, a tall Shandong man, became acquainted with my female cousin Lianzhen, Big Aunt's daughter. Lianzhen had been working in Jiafeng Textile Mill and she went to the night school run by the factory after Liberation and learned enough to read newspapers. She had been living in urban areas and learned to understand different dialects. Lianzhen married this tall Shandong man in the early 1950s, and they established their home in urban Jiading. One day, this man came to visit his in-laws. Villagers went to see the new son-in-law. It was summer and he was offered watermelon. To be polite, he said *wobuyaochi*, I do not want to eat. After that, villagers referred to him as *wobuyaochi*; many villagers never knew or remembered his real name, which is Qian Caiqing.

My father supported the new system in his own ways. After some watching, he volunteered as a teacher at the village night school. Only a few young men in the village had received some schooling before Liberation. The night school was free, and many young people, men and women, attended. Father encouraged me to take advantage of the night school to review the Chinese characters he had taught me. I went to the night school diligently and enjoyed learning. When I attended the night school, I always went and returned home with my father.

Chen Jixi, another educated man in the village, was the former head of hamlet in Beicun. His family owned good rice land, a warping shop, and a store in Zhuqiao Town. Like my father, Chen Jixi volunteered as a night school teacher and sent his school-aged daughter, Yunqing, to a formal school inside the Yan Family Temple. From there, Yunqing would go to college and finally become a medical doctor.

Communists did not believe in superstition: Daoist chanting was considered superstitious. My father stopped performing as a Daoist priest, although others still continued the practice. Father worked on our land, taught at the night school, and served as the work-hour recorder and accountant in the mutual aid team[7] formed in our hamlet in 1952.

The New Marriage Law of 1950 caused a lot of changes.[8] The new law said that marriages should be based on free love between a man and a woman. It also said that arranged marriages were no longer lawful. A young lady from Bai Family Hamlet found her own love and declared that she was going to be married. Her parents protested but she insisted. When she married the man she had found for herself, her parents refused to recognize the union. It was only after many years, when her parents were already old, that they established relations again.

Quite a few married couples obtained divorces because they said that their marriages had been arranged and were loveless. One divorced couple was in our hamlet. I grew up with both the man and the woman, and we were very good friends. This woman was among the girlfriends who pulled me up from the river when I was about ten years old and had been kicked into the river by my little brother while I was soaking yellow straw behind our house.

My girlfriend was raised by the man's parents as a child bride. By the time they were old enough to be married, the family was extremely poor and the father had passed away. So the young man and the woman were joined together as husband and wife without a formal ceremony a couple of years before Liberation.

After the marriage, the young man and woman were given their own bedroom. Although they slept in the same bed, they were not having any children. There was a local theory that if a married couple did not produce a child after marriage, then an adoption would help them conceive. It was believed that when a child called the married woman "Mom," her body would react to the calling and produce its own baby. Therefore, the family adopted a baby girl for the couple.

But the child's calling did not produce a pregnancy. There were signs of problems between the man and woman, although they remained very polite to each other. One day, when the man was visiting at our house, Father, who liked this young man very much, asked him to be good and to not let his widowed mother down. The man answered, "I am being good. But my 'little guy' is not being good." We learned later that he did not like his wife and could not get excited about her. But the couple continued to live as husband and wife, and they raised the adopted child together.

Under the New Marriage Law the couple divorced each other. The man married a woman who was the only child in her family and thus the marriage was a matrilocal one. He left our village and soon became a father. The woman also married again soon and produced five children with her new husband. After both the man and woman left the house, the little girl grew up with the grandmother who had made the decision to adopt her.

Here is another example. A man in North Hamlet was supposed to marry the child bride the family had raised for him. He told his parents that he did not like the girl, but his parents went ahead and held a wedding ceremony for them before Liberation. As the man was told to kneel down to Heaven and Earth in the matrimony ceremony, he ran out of the house and went into a nearby river. He said he would rather die than marry the chosen bride. This was shocking news and people in Wangjialong talked about it for days. But the ceremony was still considered valid. When the man and woman did not produce a child, the parents also adopted a daughter for them. When the New Marriage Law was proclaimed, this marriage also ended. The woman got married and left the house, taking the little girl with her. The man married a wife of his own choice and had three children with her.

Others, who were still traditional in thinking, remained married to the husband or wife their parents had arranged for them. One man in South Hamlet told me when he was in his seventies that he had lived a loveless life. His parents raised a child bride for him and he was married at the end of the 1940s. When the New Marriage Law came out, he and his wife already had a son. He did not love his wife, but he did not ask for a divorce because he did not want to hurt his parents or his young son. He said he was too filial as a son and too responsible as a father. One day, I heard that he was sick, so I went to visit him. He slept in a one-person bed. In the same bedroom, there was a big bed that his wife slept in.

East River Aunt was divorced by her husband after the New Marriage Law came out. My mother advised her sister to find a husband for herself. But East River Aunt did not take the advice. She said that she was the lawful daughter-in-law in the Song family and would not give up her position for the woman her husband had married. She did not win this fight, because she only raised a daughter, who was married out. The son of the Song family and his second wife had a son, who carried on the family name. My aunt lived her entire life a single woman and died at the age of eighty. In her old age, she lived with her daughter's family.

Under the protection of the new law, all the child brides in Wangjialong, about ten of them, were treated as daughters and were married out when they reached marriage age. The sons of these families found suitable spouses one way or another.

LAND REFORM

The Land Reform Movement in our area was carried out during 1950 and the first half of 1951.[9] We received our new land titles in July 1951.

The movement went through several stages. First, meetings were held to publicize the Land Reform policies. We learned a song entitled "Who Provided Livelihood for Whom?" The song proclaimed that the poor labored and the rich enjoyed the profits of the labor. This changed the old thinking, which was that poor people should be grateful for the opportunity to earn a livelihood by working on land rented from the rich or by working as laborers for the rich. Now we realized that those who worked the land provided the livelihood for the rich. It was the opposite of the old thinking and it made sense.

A Land Reform team was formed in Wangjialong. The team members included the head of the village militia, the head of the village Peasant Association, and other activists from poor families. They went through some training regarding the Land Reform policies. The team encouraged poor peasants to speak up against the rich. Pan Guanghua, one of the very poor, was the most active at these speaking-bitterness meetings. He exposed Pan Shouwen, a rich man and *baozhang*, for exploiting poor people like him and for using his position to oppress villagers. Pan Guanghua, in fact, was from the same lineage as Pan Shouwen.

Each family had to report to the Land Reform team how many *mu* of land it owned, how many *mu* were rented out or cultivated by hired labor, and how many *mu* of rented land the family worked on. The team investigated to verify the information. The investigation included physically measuring land and talking to hired hands and families who rented land from rich families. The collected information was displayed in public and all adult villagers gathered at meetings to discuss which class category each family should belong to.

There were five class categories. The first category was landlord, for people who used hired labor to work on their land and/or rented land out to other families. We learned that this class of people exploited others for a living. My father's uncle's family belonged to this category. The family owned about fifty *mu* of land. My father's uncle was in his sixties. Both of his sons had died. His grandsons were not yet experienced farmers, so the family used hired labor to work the land.

The second category was rich peasant. There was no rich peasant family in our hamlet, but several families in North Hamlet belonged to this category. One family owned thirty-some *mu* of land. The family included some strong and capable farmhands and thus did not use hired labor to work the land.

The third was middle peasant. My family owned fifteen *mu* of land and my uncle's family owned fourteen *mu*; both were categorized as middle peasants. We worked the land ourselves and were self-sufficient families. Quite a few families in Wangjialong belonged to this self-sufficient category.

The fourth was poor peasant, whose own land was too little to support the mouths in a household. Such families worked on rented land and/or worked as hired labor for others. Therefore, they suffered exploitation. Many families in Wangjialong belonged to this category.

The fifth was hired laborer, a person who had little or no land and mainly depended on selling his labor to make a living. My grandmother's family in Tang Family Village belonged to this category. The only land Grandmother and Uncle owned was a small piece where the family's ancestors were buried. Uncle worked as a year-long hired hand.

The landlord families also experienced the Land Reform team's counting of the number of rooms they owned and pieces of furniture they had. Houses and furniture were considered the result of exploiting other people's labor. My father's uncle's family experienced that.

When the Communists first arrived, my father's uncle was nervous. One day, he asked my father if it was true that Communists would kill people. Father told him not to believe in such rumors. Although nobody physically bothered him, the process of reporting and verifying the land he owned made him more nervous. At the speaking-bitterness meetings, people who had worked for his family complained about ill-treatment they had received. That added to the stress he lived under.

My father's uncle had been complaining about pains caused by his inguinal hernia. His pains became worse as he lived under pressure and fear. With both of his sons dead and his grandsons not knowing what to do, my father stepped in to help. Father borrowed a boat and, together with the old man's son-in-law, rowed him to a hospital in West Gate of Jiading Town. He quickly underwent surgery, but it was already too late. He died in the hospital. According to a local tradition, a dead body could not enter a house, so the body rested in the open air outside the compound while a simple funeral service was performed. The old man died before the Land Reform ended, so he did not see the confiscation of some of his family's property.

As a result of the Land Reform, my father's uncle's family, now with Ah Bing, the old man's elder grandson, as head of the household, retained only thirteen of their fifty *mu* of land. In addition, the family lost the ownership of the southeast quarter and the east side room of the West Compound. Those rooms were given to Big Aunt's family, which belonged to the poor peasant category. Ah Bing's family was reduced to the northwest quarter and the west side room. Some of the family's furniture was also confiscated.

Ah Bing's wife, who married into the family just before Liberation, wailed at the memorial table of her husband's grandfather, complaining that she was the victim. She said that it was not fair for her furniture to be confiscated, for it was part of the dowry her parents gave her. She further complained about the grandfather's refusal for his second son to take a concubine, which led to the son's death from lovesickness. After the son died, the son's baby boy also died. After that, the son's wife married another man and left. If the second son had been allowed to take in a concubine, he would not have died and would have established his own family. His family would have provided the labor so that no hired labor would have been necessary. The fifty *mu* of land would have been divided and shared by two families. The family would thus have avoided the fate of belonging to the landlord category and suffering the loss of land, house, and furniture.

My family and my uncle's family did not lose any land, house, or furniture; nor did we gain any. Father said that he should thank his father for having gambled away the family fortune.

In North Hamlet, there were a landlord family surnamed Chen and another one surnamed Pan. The Chen family's memorial hall (*citang*) was confiscated. After the coffins were removed by the family, the several rooms that used to be the memorial hall were used for village meetings. The new village leadership was headquartered in the rooms confiscated from the landlord named Pan.

The Land Reform turned the old society upside down. The impact on West River Aunt's family was severe. The family had inherited seven-eighths of its ancestral property while her cousin's family got the remaining one-eighth. Aunt and Uncle were good farmers and managers, so the family wealth grew under their care. By 1950, their family was rich.

During the Land Reform, my aunt's family was categorized in the landlord class while the cousin's family belonged to the poor peasant category. The poor cousin acted unjustly toward my aunt and uncle. The former accused the latter of cruel treatment of laborers before Liberation. The accusation of cruelty ultimately served as the reason to send Uncle to jail as a "tyrant landlord."[10]

Although Uncle was released from jail in a few years, he was labeled a member of the four categories of class enemies (*sileifenzi*), and he worked and lived under surveillance until 1979, when the labels were lifted.[11] His cousin was an activist in local politics. The two never spoke again. When Uncle died in the early 2000s, the cousin finally came over and kowtowed to the dead man. One of his children had persuaded him to make the gesture of reconciliation.

After the Land Reform, some confiscated pieces of furniture such as desks with drawers, moon tables, and chairs were put up for sale. This was precisely the time I was getting ready for my wedding. In the bridal bedroom, we needed a desk with drawers. I saw such a desk at the sale and talked to my father about buying it. Father flatly refused. He said that it was not good to buy things that had been confiscated from other families.

The following spring, when I was already married, my father and I went to a temple fair in Waigang Town on March 28 of the lunar calendar. This was a traditional day for local people to gather for festive activities such as the local opera performance and to sell or buy things. At the fair, we visited an exhibition of new furniture and saw desks with drawers for sale. We bought one for twelve yuan. We had to come home to get a rope and a pole. My father and I carried the desk home on our shoulders from Waigang, which was about nine *li* from our village.

NOTES

1   This is known as either the Song-Hu War or the Shanghai War of 1932. For detailed information about the war, see Donald Jordan, *China's Trial by Fire: The Shanghai War of 1932* (Ann Arbor: University of Michigan Press, 2001).

2   Japanese and Chinese armies were engaged in heavy fighting in Shanghai from August to October 1937. The fighting ended when the Chinese army was defeated and Shanghai fell under Japanese control for the duration of WWII. Jonathan Spence, *The Search for Modern China*, 2nd ed. (New York: W. W. Norton, 1999), 422–23.

3   Qingxiang Yundong, which started in mid-1941 and was part of Japan's "rural pacification" program, was an effort to work with Chinese collaborators to control

rural people and prevent them from organizing resistance activities. Yung-fa Chen, *Making Revolution: The Communist Movement in Eastern and Central China, 1937–1945* (Berkeley: University of California Press, 1986), 81–84.

4   *Jiading Xianzhi* describes the two brothers and their gangster and anti-Communist activities in detail. *Jiading Xianzhi* [Annals of Jiading County] (Shanghai: Shanghai renmin chubanshe, 1992), 713.

5   This event is briefly mentioned in "Zhujiaqiao Zhi: Dashiji" [Annals of Zhujiaqiao: chronology of events] (unpublished manuscript, no date, in Shehong Chen's possession), 15.

6   *Jiading Xianzhi*, 27.

7   See chapter 3 for more information on the mutual aid team.

8   "Zhonghua renmin gongheguo hunyinfa" [Marriage Law of the People's Republic of China], *Renmin Ribao* [People's daily], Apr. 16, 1950, accessed Mar. 5, 2014, http://www.china.com.cn/guoqing/2012–09/04/content_26746185.htm.

9   "Zhonghua renmin gongheguo tudi gaigefa" [Land Reform Law of the People's Republic of China], June 28, 1950. In Zhonggong zhongyang wenxian yanjiushi, ed., *Jianguo yilai zhongyao wenxian xuanbian* [Selected important documents since the founding of the People's Republic of China], vol. 1 (Beijing: Zhongyang wenxian chubanshe, 1992), 336–45.

10 According to the Land Reform Law, only someone who committed crimes against the implementation of the Land Reform Law would be charged as an "unlawful landlord." Someone who killed laborers, raped them, or used unlawful agents or organizations to bully and harass people who were too poor to pay rent or debt would be charged as a "tyrant landlord." Both categories had to involve criminal activities. There was no clear criminal activity involved in this case. But during the Land Reform there were excessive cases, and this is one of them.

11 The four categories are landlords, rich peasants, counterrevolutionaries, and bad elements. For details of surveillance and control, see "Guanzhi fangeming fenzi zanxing banfa" [Provisional methods to control counterrevolutionaries], June 27, 1952. In Zhonggong zhongyang wenxian yanjiushi, ed., *Jianguo yilai zhongyao wenxian xuanbian* [Selected important documents since the founding of the People's Republic of China], vol. 3 (Beijing: Zhongyang wenxian chubanshe, 1992), 244–46. For lifting of the labels, see "Zhonggong zhongyang guanyu dizhu funong fenzi zhaimao wenti he difu zinu chengfen wenti de jueding" [Chinese Communist Party Central Committee's decision on lifting of labels on landlords and rich peasants and class categories for sons and daughters of landlords and rich peasants], Jan. 11, 1979. In Zhonggong zhongyang wenxian yanjiushi, ed., *Sanzhong quanhui yilai zhongyao wenxian huibian* [Collection of important documents since the Third Plenary Session], vol. 1 (Beijing: Renmin chubanshe, 1982), 76–77.

3

Benefiting from the
New Marriage Law

W HEN I was about nine or ten years old, a fortune-teller told
my parents that I would bring good fortune wherever I went.
Father had always wanted to keep me home despite his
understanding of traditional practices regarding family inheritance.
The fortune-teller's words made him even more determined to keep
me home. Whenever Mother said that keeping me at home would
lead to controversies within the extended family, which would in turn
hurt me, Father would say, "She is too precious to be married out." He
would then turn to me and ask, "You are not to be married out; you
will stay home, right?" I would always answer, "Right, I will not marry
out. I will always be with mom and dad." Father would then say to
Mother, "See, our child wants to stay home."

My mother's worry was well-grounded. Before Liberation, no family in Wangjialong had attempted to have a daughter marry matrilocally, although quite a few families only had a daughter or daughters.
They bent to the conventional practice and gave their property to
their nephews. Some of these people lived miserable lives in their old
age because their nephews, having no flesh-and-bone connections,

took the properties but neglected the old folks' needs. A married-out daughter could come for a visit and bring gifts to the parents, but she had her own family to care for.

One man in our hamlet married his only daughter out and his nephews expected to inherit his property. After marriage, the daughter and her husband, who could mend wool clothes, emigrated to Singapore. My father used to read aloud letters the parents received from Singapore and wrote letters on behalf of the parents to the daughter and her husband. In the late 1940s, when the old man became sick and was on his deathbed, he decided to give the property to his daughter and called her home. The daughter obeyed and brought her family back to Wangjialong.

But the old man's nephews wanted his property and believed that they deserved it. According to local customs, the inheritor held the dead man's head when the corpse was put into the coffin. The daughter and two nephews scrambled to hold the dead man's head while relatives, neighbors, and curious villagers watched. After the event, everybody talked about this fight, and so I know the details. Ultimately, the daughter inherited the house and most of the land, while the two nephews each got some land from the deceased man.

The New Marriage Law of 1950 directly addressed the old conventions and customs and proclaimed that women now had the same rights as men in inheriting family property. Under the new law, my parents no longer had to worry about the inheritance problem, and I had the legitimate right to stay home as the inheritor of my family's property.

One woman in South Hamlet had married out her daughter, her only child, a couple of years earlier. After she heard about the law, she told my parents that she regretted having married out her daughter. She blamed herself for not being wise enough and admired my parents' wisdom in keeping me unmarried. In my teenage years, my grandmother had suggested various families for me to marry into. Father always told her not to bother about it. Our relatives had also tried to arrange marriages for me. My father turned them all down.

At the time of Liberation, we owned fifteen *mu* of land, which allowed us a very comfortable life. Father bought me whatever I wanted. When I became aware of a machine-made cotton fabric with a pretty blue color, known as *shilinbu*,[1] Father bought some for me and I made a traditional Chinese dress (*qipao*). Unlike our homemade cloth, this machine-made fabric would not fade from washing, and it would not wrinkle. Father also bought me wool yarn in navy blue and bright red. I knitted a pair of pants with the blue yarn and a sweater with the red yarn. When I went to a meeting in Waigang, the seat of the district our village belonged to at the time, I wore the navy blue pants and the *shilinbu* dress, over which was the red sweater. All of the materials, the colors, and the styles were in fashion in those years. I was the envy of my girlfriends.

At the night school, I learned more Chinese characters, including liberty, youth, and fortune. Father wrote beautiful calligraphy. I asked him to write these characters out and I sewed them into the work skirts (*zuoqun*) I was making.

I brought my knitting and sewing work to the militia hut when I was on duty. One spring day in 1951, when I was at the hut sewing the *shilinbu* dress, a woman came to visit me. Having watched me sewing for a while, she told me that I had dexterous fingers. I knew she was one of Chen Jiaxiang's daughters from North Hamlet and had been married out several years earlier.

Sometime after that, a woman from our hamlet came to visit my parents and said that Chen Jiaxiang from North Hamlet had asked her to be a matchmaker for his son. The matchmaker said that Jiaxiang had two sons and the elder one was already married. He was willing to marry his second son out and knew that my father was determined to keep his only daughter home. The matchmaker put a red piece of paper in the niche under our Kitchen God. On the piece of paper was Chen Jiaxiang's second son's birth information.

I did not participate in discussions about the marriage. I let my parents and my grandmother make the decision for me. Father said that he had observed Jiaxiang's second son at the night school and liked him because the young man was quick in learning and very quiet. When a fellow villager told my parents and grandmother that this young man was reserved and did not like greeting people, Grandmother replied, "It does not matter. We shall greet him first."

The second son was Chen Xianxi, head of our village militia. This Chen family was very poor at that time. Chen Xianxi's mother had died. Before Liberation, he had followed his father and big brother, both carpenters, for food and learned the carpentry trade. Liberation temporarily interrupted the carpentry business, which was the main way for his family to make a living. My father did not mind the poverty of the family. He said, "What we want is the young man." He told Chen Jiaxiang that he did not have to worry about anything regarding the wedding. Father said, "We will bring food over for the after-the-wedding visit (*huimenri*) so that you can hold a banquet to announce the marriage to your close relatives."

I had seen Chen Xianxi myself during the Land Reform. When it was decided that my rich neighbor was a landlord, the Land Reform work team came to count the pieces of furniture in that household. Chen Xianxi was in charge of recording the pieces of furniture. Unlike some other work team members who were loud and abrasive toward the people in our neighbor's family, Chen Xianxi stood to the side, had a notebook in his hand, and quietly recorded the pieces of furniture in the book. I never talked to Chen Xianxi alone before our wedding, but I saw him on some other occasions, such as at meetings.

My elders made the decision that I was to marry Chen Xianxi matrilocally on December 24, 1951. My wedding was a three-day affair—the rehearsal day, the wedding day, and the after-the-wedding home visit day.

To prepare for the wedding banquet, we raised two pigs, two sheep, and many chickens. We always raised sheep for the manure we needed as fertilizer for our land, but we seldom raised pigs. We learned that feeding pigs with roasted sesame seeds would help them grow leaf fat, which was needed to cook banquet dishes. That year, all the sesame seeds we harvested from our land were kept for the two pigs. We waited until the last month before the wedding to feed the seeds to the pigs. Indeed, when the pigs were slaughtered, they contained thick leaf fat.

The two pigs yielded more than four hundred *jin* of pork. After the wedding banquet, which was attended by thirty tables of guests, or 240 people, and after we delivered two tables of banquet food to Chen Xianxi's native home for the after-the-wedding visit, we still had two legs of pork left. We salted the remaining pork. I remember that the following spring we had salted pork as well as salted fish to eat almost every day.

We also slaughtered the sheep and the chickens we raised for the wedding banquet. That year, my mother planted more taro than usual. Taro was used as a dish at the dinner on the rehearsal day as well as at the lunch on the wedding day. These two meals were rich, but they were less formal than the banquet dinner on the wedding day.

We made our own wine for the wedding banquet, too. West River Uncle, who would be thrown into jail as a "tyrant landlord" later, helped us make the wine. In early summer, he came and made the fermentation starter from wheat. We ground fifteen *jin* of wheat into coarse grits on a stone mill. Uncle kneaded the ground wheat grits into two big cakes, which were wrapped in dry rice straw and hung from a ceiling beam in a drafty place in our guest hall.

About one month before the wedding, my uncle came to make rice wine. We steamed one hundred *jin* of sweet rice in our big steamer. Uncle mixed dry wine yeast into the cooked and rinsed sweet rice. The mixed rice was then put into big earthen vats (fig. 3.1). We wrapped the vats with mats made with dry rice straw to keep the contents at a consistent warm temperature for fermentation. During the next few days, Uncle came a few times to check on the fermentation process.

When the rice had been fermented enough, Uncle came again. He took down the two big cakes from the ceiling beam and pounded them into powder. He put the powder, seasoned orange peels, peppercorns, and water into the fermented rice. Every day after that, we used a long-handled wood tool to stir the contents several times. This second

3.1 Earthen vat, for fermenting rice or storing water

round of fermentation took another couple of weeks. We did this in our guest hall, but the whole house was permeated with a fragrant wine smell.

We then poured the completely fermented rice mix into a bamboo presser, which squeezed out wine from the pulp. We made a total of three hundred *jin* of raw sweet wine (*shengganjiu*). The wine was raw because it was not pasteurized. It was similar to yellow wine (*huangjiu*), but had a lighter color.

I was quite particular about the clothes I prepared for the wedding. In those days, the standard materials for a bridal set of clothes were red silk and satin with flowers in them. I did not like silk or flowers in clothing. I chose wool, fur, and camel-hair materials and selected solid colors. My favorite piece of the wedding clothing was the green wool traditional dress with a lining. I did not think the tailors in the village would do a good enough job, so I had it custom-made by a well-known tailor in West Gate of urban Jiading. This tailor was so careful about his product that I had to go try it on before he put the finishing touches to the dress. The other pieces of clothing I prepared for the wedding were a silk-padded coat, a sheepskin coat, and a camel-hair coat. At the time, women's formal clothes were long, about halfway below the knees.

My mother and grandmother did not like my choice of clothes. They thought that bridal clothes should be in red silk and have flowers. They said that I was too willful about my choices. But father was quite open-minded and allowed me to do what I wanted.

For the wedding, I embroidered four pairs of pillowcases in the traditional fashion. I followed a pattern, counted the stitches, and embroidered accordingly. At the time, I was learning crewel embroidering with a hoop. I bought a pattern, rendered it onto cotton cloth, and finished one pair of pillowcases with crewel embroidering for the wedding.

Members of my family had always been known for having small appetites. Some villagers said, "You people eat like cats. You'd better be prepared for the coming young man with a big stomach." We had actually experienced what a big stomach was like. Several months before the wedding day, Chen Xianxi and his father made a new bed and delivered it to our house. They brought the bed over on a boat and came up the stone steps my father had built behind our house. This was in the early morning and Mother offered them breakfast. It was only breakfast, but they ate a wok of rice and a big bowl of pork, the amount of food that would have fed my family for a couple of days.

My parents took the villagers' advice. That autumn, we salted one hundred *jin* of fish. About ten days after the wedding, my husband packed his own bedding and clothes, packed an enamel bowl, a spoon, and a pair of chopsticks, and went to a training course in Jiading Town. He was gone for one month. We gave some of the salted fish to my maternal grandmother and shared the rest with our neighbors before it went bad.

My family only had one bedroom at the time. My parents and I had shared it for the last twenty years. To prepare for my wedding, we had a wooden partition put up in the bedroom, turning it into two rooms—one for my parents and one as my bridal bedroom. Chen Xianxi and his carpenter father came and put up the partition. Afterward, the two bedrooms had their own separate doors to the kitchen-dining room.

My father also asked them to put down a wood floor in the bedrooms at the same time. Like most houses in Wangjialong at the time, our house had a dirt floor. In spring during the rainy season (*huang-mei*), dirt floors could be very damp. Wood floors helped reduce the dampness. In West Compound, only the bedroom in the southeast quarter, owned by our rich neighbor, had a wood floor.

On the rehearsal day of my wedding, the professional chefs my father hired came to prepare food. Bowls, chopsticks, plates, and spoons were rented from a local merchant. Neighbors and close relatives helped with the food preparation, and we borrowed square tables from neighbors and villagers. That evening, we offered the rehearsal dinner, a rich but not formal meal, to everyone who helped and relatives who had arrived from afar. These relatives spent the night in our compound.

On the formal wedding day, Chen Xianxi, the groom, walked to our house in the late afternoon. He and his companions were entertained with tea and snacks. For the marriage ceremony, I wore a rented red wedding gown. The gown came with a headpiece, but I refused to wear it, for I did not like the hangings on the headpiece. I said that they would prevent me from seeing the ceremony. Again, Mother and Grandmother complained about my stubbornness, but Father allowed me to go without the hanging headpiece.

Our marriage ceremony was considered a new type. We obtained a marriage certificate (fig. 3.2) and my father personally filled out the certificate with a Chinese writing brush. The marriage ceremony took place in our guest hall, the Hall of Honesty and Sincerity. Two square tables were put in the middle of the guest hall. A huge red candle on each table was lit. Chen Xianxi and I stood on a red carpet, facing the tables and the lit candles. Behind us were our guests and villagers watching the ceremony.

My father presided over the ceremony. He stood on the north side of the tables. While facing us and the watching audience, he thanked our guests for coming to the wedding and introduced us as bride and groom. He then introduced our matchmaker, the lady who brought Chen Xianxi's birth information to our house. The matchmaker said a few words about acting as a bridge between me and Chen Xianxi. My father then introduced the head of township (*xiangzhang*), who

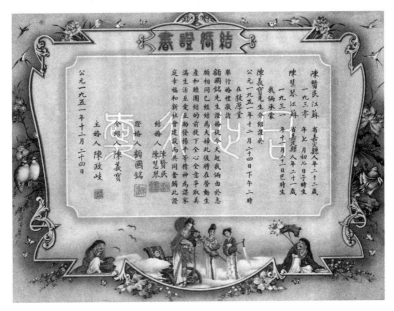

3.2   Chen Huiqin's marriage certificate

was invited to witness our marriage. Standing on the north side of the tables, the witness read aloud what was written on the marriage certificate. He then asked me and Chen Xianxi to put our seals on the certificate. After that, he put his seal on the certificate and declared Chen Xianxi and me husband and wife. As newlyweds, we bowed to our matchmaker and to our marriage witness while a ceremonial mistress my father had hired guided us.

Following the marriage ceremony was the meeting ritual. Two chairs were placed on the south side of the tables. My father and mother were the first to take the chairs. Chen Xianxi, now my husband, called them father and mother for the first time. My parents gave him meeting-ritual money (*jianlitian*) wrapped in red paper. After my parents, then my grandmothers, uncles, aunts, and all other relatives who belonged to the elder generations took the chairs and my husband was officially introduced to them. In this meeting ritual, I accompanied my husband.

Two young men, our relatives, moved the big red candles into the bridal bedroom and they were kept lit for the night. At the time, it was very difficult to buy new furniture or wood for furniture making, so we did not even have a desk with drawers, a standard piece of bridal suite furniture, in our bedroom. The red candles stood on a borrowed desk.

A ceremony to inform my ancestors about the marriage followed. A table with banquet food was set in the guest hall. My husband and I kowtowed to my ancestors. After that, we kowtowed to the Kitchen God in all the kitchens inside West Compound.

On the third day I accompanied my husband to his native home in North Hamlet for the first visit after the wedding. I wore my favorite green wool dress. That was the only time I wore that dress. I treasured it too much to wear it on any other occasion.

My parents regarded my husband as an adopted son. Father gave my husband a new name, Chen Xianmin, which is on the marriage certificate. My family, relatives, and neighbors call him Xianmin. But he kept his own name, Chen Xianxi, professionally. To his own family, his relatives, and people in North Hamlet, he is Ah Qiu, which is his nickname.

My name, Chen Huiqin, is not my original name. When I was born, Father gave me two names, a nickname and an official name. My nickname is Linshe. The Chinese character "lin" (林) is made up of two parts. Each of the two parts means "wood" and the combined word means "woods." In the old days, after a baby was born, the family would consult a fortune-teller to determine if the baby lacked any of the Five Elements, which were Metal, Wood, Water, Fire, and Earth. It was believed that a person needed all the elements to live a healthy and balanced life. If one lacked any of the Five Elements, a name that contained a character or half of a character related to the element was supposed to help. When I was growing up, I heard adults say that I was called Linshe because I lacked wood. Father, however, never explained that to me in a serious way.

My official name was Chen Tian'e, Chen the Swan. I never liked Tian'e as my name and told my father so. Nothing was done about it. When I went to night school after Liberation, I needed an official name. One of my female cousins was ten years younger and went to the formal school inside Yan Family Temple after Liberation. There, her school teacher gave her an official name, Chen Huijun. I followed her example and chose Chen Huiqin. My father accepted it, and it became my official name. While I continued to be called Linshe at home and by my relatives and neighbors, my husband's family members, relatives, and neighbors all addressed me as Chen Huiqin.

MUTUAL AID TEAM

After our marriage, my husband stopped being a carpenter and joined us in farming our family land. The Land Reform was over, but he continued to be involved in local politics and went to many evening meetings and attended training courses in Jiading Town.

In the spring of 1952, my husband introduced the idea of organizing mutual aid teams for farming in our village.[2] Father supported the idea. Before Liberation, families like ours did not own large farm implements such as plows or draft animals such as oxen and had to rent them. Many families also helped each other in planting and harvesting seasons, so mutual aid was not a totally novel idea to us. But before Liberation, many families had been too poor to own rice land. Now, all families owned dry land and rice land, and we all needed implements and draft animals in order to farm. The idea of organizing mutual aid teams was thus welcomed by many.

Yan Shoufu's family, our family, and five other families joined to form the first mutual aid team in Wangjialong. My father was the work-hour recorder and accountant for the team. The seven families shared draft animals and a waterwheel and worked together in planting, weeding, and harvesting crops. We still kept our land titles and claimed the harvests from our own land. Our work hours were recorded. At the end of the year, the families that owned more land and contributed fewer hours had to pay families that owned less land and worked more hours.

The crop yield of our mutual aid team in the first harvest was higher than that of an average family which did not belong to a team.

We became an example and other families in the village followed us and organized their own teams in the following year. My husband was invited to talk about his experience of successfully organizing the mutual aid team in Waigang, where the district headquarters were located, and even in Jiading Town, the county seat.

After the first harvest, my husband went for another training course in Jiading Town. He came home and talked to my father about joining the Communist Party. Father supported him. Father said that the Party had been working for the poor and the downtrodden. With Father's support, my husband joined the Communist Party.

My husband worked quietly and diligently. He was a fast learner. Everyone in my family supported him and never held him back. He was away from home a lot and usually did not come home until late at night. We were worried about his personal safety walking at night and told him to be careful every time he left for evening meetings.

In the latter part of that same year, my husband was promoted to head of township (*xiangzhang*). Before he accepted the position, he again asked my father's opinion. The *xiangzhang* position would make him a *bantuochan ganbu*, one who worked half of his/her time as a cadre and the other half as a peasant, earning a twelve-yuan monthly salary for the non-peasant work. Although the pay was not much and the position was not attractive, my father still gave him a positive answer. Father said, "Let him be a representative for the poor."

FIRST CHILD

Our first child was born in October 1952. It was a boy and the whole family was very happy. On the twelfth day after he was born, we made a lot of red eggs and gave them out to our relatives and neighbors. This was a customary practice. Red eggs were an appreciation of the maternity gifts relatives had presented as well as an announcement of the birth of a new baby to neighbors. Eggs were boiled first and then dyed red. When we boiled the eggs, many broke, which was considered a bad omen.

The child was growing fast and was healthy. He also seemed very smart. When he was about eight months old, he started to say *ma* and *die*.[3] One hot summer day, when I came home from the fields, the baby was hungry and my breasts were tight with milk. So I sat down and fed him immediately. The hot milk made him sick. He ran a fever. It was a busy farming season and I continued to go out and work in the fields while my mother was home taking care of the baby. When the baby's fever became worse, we sent for a doctor. The doctor came and said that it was already too late. The fever had burnt him from the inside. He died soon afterward.

The first night after I lost my child, I had to spend it away from my own home, according to a local belief. This was to secure the safe rearing of other babies I would have later on. I spent the night at my husband's native home in North Hamlet. That was the only night I spent there before or since. After I got there in the evening, a Chen family in the hamlet brought their infant daughter to me and said that they wanted me to adopt her. They had had one daughter and they were trying to have a son, so they wanted to give away the second daughter.

My husband's family and my family all thought the adoption was a good idea. They said that having a child calling me "mom" would help sow a seed for me and it would be easier to raise my own later on. They even gave me examples of local women who had adopted other people's babies and now had their own. I breastfed the baby and slept with the baby that night, but I refused to adopt her. When my family tried further to persuade me, I replied, "You go ahead and adopt it; I only want my own."

After I returned home, another family asked me to adopt their baby. This baby girl was born out of wedlock in Tang Family Village. The girl's mother was an unmarried young woman, whose family did not want her to keep the baby, because in those days nobody would want to marry somebody who already had a child. The father's family had to raise her, but they did not have any milk. In those days, there was no alternative food for infants. At the same time, the new government had a law protecting all babies, girl or boy, born out of wedlock or to a married couple. In this case, if the infant died, her father would have to be jailed for killing the baby. So the father's family brought the girl to me and begged me to adopt the baby to save her as well as the father. I said I would not adopt the baby, but I agreed to breast-feed her and take care of her. When the infant first came to me, she was thin and sickly. She was with me for many months, until she was able to eat other food and no longer dependent on mother's milk. She returned home and grew up with her paternal grandparents.

Later, when the grandparents wanted me to recognize the girl as my goddaughter, I declined. I did not grow up with godparents and did not wish to have godchildren.

NOTES

1   *Shilinbu* literally means *shilin* fabric. *Shilin* comes from the English word "indan-threne," the water-insoluble blue dye.
2   "Guanyu nongye huzhu hezuo de jueyi (caoan)" [(Draft) Resolution concerning agricultural mutual aid cooperation], Dec. 15, 1951. In Zhonggong zhongyang wenxian yanjiushi, ed., *Jianguo yilai zhongyao wenxian xuanbian* [Selected important documents since the Founding of the People's Republic of China], vol. 2 (Beijing: Zhongyang wenxian chubanshe), 510–22.
3   In the local dialect, the pronunciation of mom is *m'ma* and that of dad is *diedie*.

4

Rushing into Collective Life

T HESE days, as long as you have money, you can get practically
anything you want from a store. Right outside our residential
compound, there is a supermarket. Both my husband and I are
now retired and have a lot of free time. We go to the supermarket
quite often. Many times when I am leisurely browsing aisle after
aisle of food items, I am reminded of the life we lived in the 1950s.
Life then was hard. I worked long hours and ate rationed and coarse
food.

In 1953, my husband, now head of Zhuqiao Township (*xiangzhang*), chose South Hamlet to experiment with organizing an
initial-stage cooperative (*chujishe*),[1] whose membership was again
voluntary. Most families in the hamlet joined it because the mutual
aid teams, which had immediately preceded the experimental cooperative, had yielded good harvest in the autumn of 1952. My father
supported the experiment and acted as its accountant.

When we joined the cooperative, we still kept our land titles, but
the pieces of land each family owned were now merged together.
The merging allowed easier irrigation and eliminated the ditches,

footpaths, trees, and tree stumps that served as demarcations of each family's land holdings.

By the time of Liberation, land in our area had been chopped into very small pieces. This was due to buying and selling as well as to family divisions. For example, my family owned fifteen *mu* of land, divided into thirteen distinct pieces which were spread in all directions. The one *mu* of land at Big Stone Bridge was one of the earliest pieces of land my nuclear family bought. At that time, we were only able to afford one *mu*. Later we bought more land, including the piece located right in front of our compound. The smallest piece of land we owned at that time was one-twentieth of a *mu* and it was located on the west bank of the branch river right outside the West Compound. My nuclear family acquired this piece of land from our ancestors. Surrounding that little piece of land were strips owned by my uncle's family and by my father's uncle's family.

In the winter of 1953, we in the cooperative adopted the method of pulling the roots of harvested rice stalks from fields before we sowed other crops such as wheat. This helped to eliminate crop diseases that caused rotten roots in the next crop. The spring harvest of 1954 for us was a good one, with a per-*mu* yield that was 20 to 40 percent higher than the yield of land cultivated by individual families.

The cooperative benefited families with working adults because work hours were rewarded with pay. A good harvest, like the one we had in the spring of 1954, made each work hour worth more. I remember that one woman who had three adult sons and lived in a nearby village said to me, "Meimei,[2] we really envy you. I wonder when somebody will help us form a cooperative like the one you belong to." Before the Land Reform, such families would have hired out labor to those families with lots of land and fewer working adults. Now no families hired extra labor, so that woman welcomed the cooperative as a way to utilize her family resources and earn more income.

Our cooperative at first did not have a formal name. After it became a success and many more such cooperatives were organized in our neighboring villages, my father came up with a name, Limin, meaning "benefit the people." When the name was sent up to be reg-

istered, we were told that it had been used already by another cooperative in the same district. My father then changed the two Chinese
characters, but did not change the sound. Limin now meant "dawn."[3]
Father said it was still meaningful, for it indicated that the cooperative
was the beginning of a good day.

In 1953, a popular election for people's representatives was held
in Wangjialong.[4] My father was among the elected who represented
Wangjialong at Zhuqiao Township. From that group Father was
again elected, and he went to Jiading Town, the county seat, for
meetings.

We had a lot of rain in the early summer of 1954. Weeds grew fast
in our cotton field. We had to sit on small stools and pull up weeds
carefully to avoid hurting young cotton plants. I was big with a baby
inside me. A nice old man from our village told me that I should not
sit on such a low stool any more because my sitting and bending over
was rubbing off the baby's hair. But I wanted to help. Also, we earned
from the hours we worked in the field. I just would not give up any
opportunity to earn more income.

I am just that way. Now that I look back at it, I think I was silly.
These days, people are so particular about what you should and
should not do during a pregnancy. In those days, nobody talked about
such things. I did worry what would happen if that nice old man were
right. Furthermore, I even wondered if my sitting and bending over
might hurt the baby's development and make the baby dumb. That,
however, did not stop me from going to work in the fields every day.

In the last month before the baby was born, we were able to use
hoes to weed in the cotton fields. I developed a problem known
locally as *jisuhun*, chicken night blindness. After the sun went down,
I could not see anything. Candlelight or oil lamps meant nothing to
me. Mother had to take care of me after sunset. I learned to return
home from the fields right before sunset so that I could walk home on
my own and clean myself for bed. I would wait for everyone else in
the family to return home from the fields. My mother would get me
supper. After that I went to bed.

I cried a lot. People told me that the problem was related to pregnancy, but I was worried. If the problem did not go away after the child was born, then what would become of me?

My elder daughter, Shezhen, was born in the summer of 1954. On the day she was born, I woke up feeling heavy in my lower body. Mother said that I should not go to the fields and should rest at home. When they came back for breakfast, Mother asked me how I was feeling. I said it was the same. After breakfast, they went back to the fields again and I took up the crewel embroidery I had been working on. Very soon, I started to feel contractions. I used the chamber pot and my water broke. I immediately emptied the chamber pot and cleaned it at the stone steps behind our house. Then I thought to myself that the chamber pot was deep and might be stifling for the baby, making it mentally slow. So I prepared a wooden basin.

After that, I went out to the front of our compound to see if anybody was around. Kaiyuan, Big Aunt's second son, was playing there. He was a schoolboy and this was during his summer vacation. I told him to go to the field and call my parents back. He asked why and I told him, "Just say I want them back and they will know why."

Kaiyuan was a teenager and fast with his legs. My mother and grandmother rushed home. Father went straight to North Hamlet and brought back a midwife, Panjia Mama.[5] When the midwife arrived, the baby was just about to emerge into the world. Panjia Mama said to me, to my parents, and to my grandmother, "You people take risks. You should have called a midwife much earlier." The baby was born around nine o'clock in the morning.

By that time, midwives had received modern midwifery training. Panjia Mama came with sterilized scissors to cut the baby's umbilical cord. I delivered the baby while lying on my bed and Panjia Mama received the baby with her hands. The baby was not born into the chamber pot or the wooden basin that I had prepared.

A couple of days after the baby was born, I was able to see the light after sunset. There was a skylight right above my bed. After supper when it had turned dark outside, I saw the skylight. I called Mother and told her that I could see the skylight. A big stone was lifted off me.

My father came up with the name Shezhen for my daughter. *She* means cooperative, which Father supported and praised, and *zhen* means precious. Other families in the village consulted my father for their newborn babies' names. Names he had given around that time were Shegao, "cooperative high," Shefa, "cooperative prosperous," and Shemin, "cooperative people." Father was open-minded, sincerely supported the new system, and believed that it was good for everyone.

When Shezhen was big enough, we pierced one of her earlobes and made her wear a gold earring. Wearing a little piece of gold was supposed to protect her from harm. After I had recuperated from childbirth, I went to work in the fields and Mother stayed home to take care of Shezhen.

Long clothes such as the Chinese traditional dress were no longer in fashion. Long coats and jackets were not very convenient, either, when we had to work in the fields throughout the year. I turned my camel-hair long coat into a short jacket for daily wear. I turned the part I cut from the long coat into a little skirt to keep Shezhen warm during winter. In those days, little children wore split pants, which were open in the middle to make going to the bathroom easier. I also cut short my sheepskin coat and used the cut-off piece as a cushion for Shezhen to sleep or sit on during cold days.

My father started to teach Shezhen characters when she was still little. Kids usually learned to walk first and then to speak, but Shezhen learned to speak earlier than she was able to walk on her own. Father thought Shezhen was smart. He made Chinese character cards himself and used them to teach her. Shezhen was a good learner and Father was so encouraged. I know he felt bad that I had grown up in difficult times and lost the opportunity for formal education. Now he wanted to do everything possible to give his granddaughter the opportunity.

My husband (fig. 4.1) was often away from home. Once he went to Nanjing to study. When he left, Shezhen was about twelve months old. When he returned home after seven months, Shezhen was walking. When her father tried to hold her, she ran away to a corner in the kitchen-dining room. We told her that he was her father and asked her to call him father. But she stayed in the corner and replied, "No."

4.1 Chen Huiqin's husband,
Chen Xianxi, 1955

Then her father took out a toy he had bought for her. It was a wind-up jumping frog. He wound the frog up and put it on the kitchen floor. The frog jumped around. Shezhen got so excited that she went to catch the jumping frog. After that she called him *diedie*. That was the only toy we bought for Shezhen. In fact, it was the only store-bought toy she and her sister and brother, who arrived in this world later on, ever had.

My parents helped me take care of Shezhen. Father took down one of the wood planks that made the partition between the two bedrooms. At night, Mother would get up and come over into my bedroom to check on me and the baby.

UNIFIED PURCHASING AND MARKETING

The government policy of unified purchasing and marketing (*tonggou tongxiao*) was bad for us.[6] We had always lived a frugal life and saved for rainy days. The new policy said that in addition to the public grain (*gongliang*) we had been selling to the state, the state now wanted to buy planned grain (*jihualiang*) from us peasants. In addition to public grain and planned grain, the policy encouraged peasants to sell any surplus grain to the state rather than to privately owned stores or private collectors.

My family grew four *mu* of rice in 1953 and so had quite a bit of rice in stock. After having fulfilled the quotas for the public and planned grain, we sold the rest of the rice to the state. In those days, selling grain to the state was a glorious event, accompanied by beating drums and striking gongs. If you did not do what the higher-ups encouraged you to do, you were a "backward element." My father was always conscious of "face" and did not want to be regarded as backward. My husband was an activist and had already become a cadre. He wanted to lead by setting a good example.

After selling all the rice, my family, just like all other families in the village, relied on rationed grain for livelihood. In my maternity confinement, I was supposed to get additional rice according to a local government policy, but any additional rice allocation had to be decided by the village cadres. Among them was Yang Ji'an, chairman of the Peasant Association at the time. Yang believed that our family, which was famous for its prosperity and frugality, must still have rice in stock and therefore should not be entitled to additional allocation.

I had to eat pumpkin and coarse grains such as rye. This led to loose bowel movements that bothered me as a chronic illness for many years to come. Traditional Chinese medicine said that an illness that started in maternity confinement could be cured when one had another baby if great care was given. The only other opportunity for a cure was when one went through menopause. I had a problematic intestinal system until my menopausal years.

My problem became very bad in late 1954. I had bowel movements more than twenty times a day. What came out was no longer stool; it was blood and pus-like stuff. I went to see a renowned Western medicine doctor, Dr. Ge Chenghui, in Jiading Town. Dr. Ge had gone to school in the United States and was running a private business in her hometown, Jiading, at the time. The Western medicine she prescribed for me stopped the problem, but only temporarily. Once I stopped taking the medicine, the problem came back again.

I then consulted Wang Zhicheng, a traditional Chinese medicine doctor in Jiading Town. The same thing happened. While I was taking the herbal medicine he prescribed, I was fine. Once I stopped it, the problem returned. After several rounds, Doctor Wang said that his herbal medicine could not get to the root of the illness. He asked me to buy two *jin* of walnuts and two *jin* of dried longan and bring them to him. He would then mix walnuts and dried longan with herbal medicines. He believed that only that mixture would cure my illness. My father and husband asked everywhere for walnuts and dried longan. During those days of scarcity in everything, they failed to find them.

The scarcity of food-related materials was unbelievable. When Shezhen was five months old, I stayed in a hospital for twenty-five days to have hemorrhoids removed. The hospital was in Jiading Town. My father borrowed a boat and rowed me to the hospital. I had to take Shezhen with me, for she was still dependent on my breast milk for life. Grandmother came with us to take care of me as well as to help take care of the baby.

Next to the hospital, there was a store that sold freshly made noodles. The store was rationed to make and sell only a certain amount of noodles each day. Every night before going to sleep, Grandmother would go to the noodle store and use a brick or a piece of dry rotten wood to line up in front of the store. She would get up at dawn and go stand in the line. She had to do so because it was first come, first served until the daily amount was sold out. The store only sold one *jin* to each person who stood in line.

Grandmother brought back to the hospital one *jin* of noodles every day. She would make the fresh noodles into the shape of a traditional woman's hairdo and dry them outside the window of my hospital room. When I was discharged from the hospital and returned home, we brought back more than ten *jin* of dried noodles.

My father again rowed a borrowed boat to the hospital to get us home. When we arrived at the stone steps behind our house, Mother was waiting there. She took the baby and kissed her many times. She said, "The baby has grown quite a bit." Twenty-five days was a long time for Mother. She must have missed the baby very much.

In 1955, another policy, called "Three Fixes," came out. The three fixes were fixed production output, fixed purchase, and fixed sales.[7] The first two "fixes" affected us peasants. Fixed production output was based on the average per-*mu* yield of the 1954 harvests. Each family reported the amount of land as well as the quality of the land. Good rice land yielded more than poor, dry land. Each family's report was verified. From this information, each family's production output was determined. The second "fix" was really not "purchase" for us peasants, but "retention." Each family was to retain a fixed amount of grain for the mouth (*kouliang*) according to the number of persons in the household. In addition to this grain, each family would also retain pig-feed grain and seeds for the next crop. The total of grain for the mouth, pig-feed grain, and seeds was the fixed amount each family could keep from harvests. We sold the rest of our harvest to the state.

The fixed amount of grain for the mouth was pretty generous. It was more than five hundred *jin* per person, I remember. And the amount was the same for adults as children. In our village at the time, one family did not have any small children and everyone in the family was a working adult. This family did not like the policy of regarding children and adults as the same. The mother of that family said that if anything that had a mouth, eyes, and nose was considered a person, could we put black beans onto a pumpkin as mouth, eyes, and nose and turn it into a person for grain? Very soon after that, the equal treatment ended. Replacing it was a scaled system in which active laborers, children, and older persons who were no longer engaged in field labor were assigned different amounts of grain.

At the same time the "Three Fixes" policy came out, grain coupons were introduced and allotted monthly to those who lived in urban areas and who were non-agricultural workers. My husband was a non-agricultural worker and received such coupons to buy grain-based food. After that, all store goods that contained grain had to be purchased with not only money but also grain coupons. My grandmother could no longer line up in front of a noodle-making store and buy noodles with money.

In the winter of 1955, we decided that it was time for me to stop

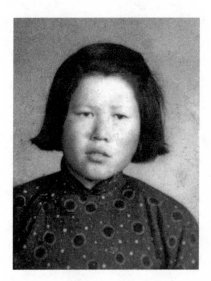

4.2 Chen Huiqin, 1955

breastfeeding Shezhen. It was our local traditional practice that the
mother went to stay in a relative's home for a couple of days in order
to break the breastfeeding habit. I went to urban Shanghai for the
first time and spent two nights at a relative's home. Meifang, the wife
of one of my cousins, went with me. While in urban Shanghai, we
visited the Great World Amusement Center. We went into a photo
studio and each of us had a photo taken just for fun. In the photo (fig.
4.2) I wore a traditional jacket that buttoned down the side instead of
in the middle. When I came home on the third day, Shezhen was no
longer interested in my breast milk. My mother had trained her to eat
regular foods.

HIGH-STAGE COOPERATIVE (*GAOJISHE*)

In 1956 we joined a high-stage cooperative and the initial-stage cooperative disappeared. Dawn became the name of our new cooperative.

As members of Dawn High-Stage Cooperative, we gave up our
titles to the land and our income became solely dependent on the
work we did in the fields. When the high-stage cooperative was first
established, landlords, rich peasants, counterrevolutionaries, and bad

elements were not allowed to join. It was an honor to be a member of the cooperative. We knew that we had to give up the land we had worked so hard to earn because it was the right thing to do. In Wangjialong, no eligible family refused to join Dawn Cooperative.

Our land became collective property and our income was determined solely by the work-points we earned in working on the collective land. In my family, I was the only work-point earner. Father was now an accountant in a local soy-sauce factory; as a non-agricultural worker he received a monthly salary and grain coupons. Mother stayed home to take care of Shezhen. My work-points had to pay for the grain and fuel we took from the cooperative. I worked hard throughout the year, never missing any opportunity to earn work-points. At the end of the year, if the work-points I had earned were not enough to cover the cost of the grain and fuel we took from the cooperative, my father, who managed the family finances, paid the difference to the cooperative. If my work-points exceeded the cost, we received a small dividend. My husband gave half of his salary to my father and used the other half to pay for the daily meals he ate at the town headquarters or at meetings. He was also a smoker and had to buy his own cigarettes.

My husband was seldom home. Even when he was not out of town attending training courses or meetings, he was often attending meetings at the town office in the evenings. These meetings would end late in the night and he would just sleep in his office. I prepared bedding for him, including a pillowcase onto which I embroidered a huge red peony with two green leaves, two swallows on the upper left corner, and three Chinese characters, Chen Huiqin, on the upper right corner. I embroidered the pillowcase when I was pregnant with Shezhen.

Families that had adult sons and daughters benefited from the work-point system. The family that had earlier complained about the equal amount of grain for children and adults had five adult persons and all of them were earning work-points. This family, which had been one of the poorest in Wangjialong before Liberation, was now the highest work-point-earning family in the village.

Each family was allotted a small plot of land (*ziliudi*), whose size was determined by the number of people in the household. Non-agricultural people, such as my husband and my father, were not entitled to such land. I grew things such as bok choy, beans, and sweet potatoes on our family plot. I tended the plot in the early morning before the cooperative work started, during my lunch breaks, and in the evening after the work-point-earning day was over.

In the evenings and on rainy days when we could not work in the fields, I made shoes for the entire family. For shoe making, we saved all the worn-out clothes and bedsheets. I would cut them into pieces and stack the pieces together to about half an inch thick to make soles. Covering the stack of old cloth would be new cloth. The soles had to be tightly stitched line by line and stitch by stitch. It took a whole day, including the evening, to stitch one pair of soles. For shoe tops, I used either homemade cloth or store-bought cloth, cut out the shoe top according to a pattern, and stitched it to the sole. For winter shoes, I padded the top and the sole with cotton before they were sewed together.

I also knitted sweaters. When we didn't need sweaters, I would undo them, have the yarn washed, and knit it together again. I made aprons for Shezhen and embroidered them with flowers and birds. I wrapped the collars and sleeves of Shezhen's cotton-padded clothes with protective covers, which could be taken off and washed very often, because cotton-padded clothes were not easily washable. I also embroidered head coverings that I wore to shield me from the sun while I worked in the fields.

Our grain now included various kinds of grain. Each grain we grew, such as rice and rye, was proportional to the total, so we had no choice what to plant. When we owned our own land, we could decide when to plant rice and how much to grow so that we always had rice to eat. Now, just like every other family in the village, we had a limited amount of rice and had to cook rice mixed with flattened rye. When Mother cooked, she would bring the rice to a boil and then gently add flattened rye at one side in the wok. That way, when the rice and rye finished cooking, one half of the mixture was whiter, with more rice than the other half. Shezhen's lunch would come from the

4.3   Shallow earthen container, for making fresh pickles

whiter part while my mother would get her lunch from the darker part.

We made our own condiments. During the rainy and damp season in the spring (*huangmei*), we made wheat flour dough with green broad beans, shaped the dough into cubes, and steamed them. The cooked cubes were placed in bamboo baskets lined with dry crop straw and covered with wet cloth for fermentation. When the hot summer days arrived, we washed the cubes clean and soaked them in boiled, then cooled, water with salt and ginger. We then put the mixture into a shallow earthen container (fig. 4.3), which rested on a wooden structure outdoors in the sun. The sun would turn the mixture into a salty and tasty paste, into which we put fresh tender cucumbers and squash picked from our family plot. In a few days, we would have fresh pickles (*jianggua*) to accompany our porridge for breakfast and supper.

The homemade paste produced more pickles than we could eat during the summer. We sun-dried what we could not eat and pressed them into earthen jars or glass bottles. So pickles were available most of the year as a condiment.

Another vegetable we pickled was turnip that we grew in our

family plot and harvested in late fall. We cleaned them, cut them into thick slices, put salt on them, and then lay them out on a reed mat to dry. When they were damp dry, we mixed some sugar in and pressed them into earthen jars or glass bottles. Preserved turnips would serve as our year-round condiment at breakfast and supper.

We also made fermented soybeans. Soybeans were cooked until they were soft and tender and then put in bamboo baskets lined with damp rice straw. The soybeans would go through a fermentation process, which turned them totally black. After washing off the mold and drying them in the sun, we prepared a sauce with soy sauce, cooking wine, sugar, and ginger. We soaked the dried beans in the sauce for a week or so, then we had another condiment.

In 1956, I gave birth to a baby boy who lived only one day. This is what happened. There was a local tradition that a newly born baby should get its first milk from a woman who was not the mother. But my family did not follow that tradition when Shezhen was born, nor when my first child was born. This time, one of my cousin's wives was breastfeeding her own son and so she was asked to give my baby boy his first milk. It was a hot summer day and my cousin's wife had been working in the fields. She had returned home to have lunch when she came to feed my baby.

Her breasts were swollen with milk. Right after the breastfeeding, my baby was sick, throwing up the milk. Milk came from his mouth and his nose. A doctor was called for immediately. We were told that milk had gone into the baby's lung. The doctor said that he could not save the baby. So I lost another child. That was the only time we called someone to breastfeed my babies.

From early on, Shezhen was quite a determined child. I remember one time she acted very willfully. She was about three years old. That day, I decided to run some errands in urban Jiading. After breakfast, I changed into some clean, presentable clothes. Shezhen sensed something was up and asked me. I told her that I was going to Jiading Town. She said she wanted to go with me. I told her that it was too far for her to walk, that she was to stay with Grandma, and that I would be home soon. She did not listen to me and started to cry, saying that she wanted to go with me. My mother told me to go and said that Shezhen would calm down soon.

I left. Shezhen struggled away from Grandma's embrace and ran after me. I quickened my steps, hoping that she would give up. But she ran on her little legs, crying and screaming. Since my mother had bad eyesight, she could not keep up with Shezhen, who kept running on the front road and turned onto the Big Official Road and showed no sign of giving up. I finally turned back, picked her up, and brought her home. I cried, my mother cried, and Shezhen continued crying. I canceled my trip to urban Jiading that day. Shezhen was willful, but I knew I was willful, too.

COLLECTIVE LIFE

In the middle of the 1950s, the "big belly" disease was recognized as the result of a blood-sucking parasite called schistosoma. The government used various ways to cure patients and to eliminate the parasite. Testing stations were established, including one in North Hamlet, inside a confiscated house. We were all required to give stool samples for tests and the station provided us with wax papers to collect samples. Local young people with some education were trained as lab workers for the stations.

Schistosoma lived in tiny snails that inhabited rivers and ponds, so an effort was made to get rid of these snails. Each cooperative contributed young people to work in snail-eliminating teams. They rowed small boats along the banks of rivers and ponds, looking for tiny snails. My cousin Zhongming was thirteen years old in 1957 and worked in a snail-eliminating team during his summer vacation.

Those who tested positive were given free treatment to get rid of the parasite inside their bodies. My mother tested positive and was given the treatment. The medicine was taken orally and daily and was either delivered to the house or the person could go to a local station and take the medicine there. I remember they delivered the medicine to my mother because her poor eyesight made it difficult for her to walk to the station in North Hamlet.

Another way to eliminate the cause of the disease was to stop human feces from going directly onto the land and into the water. The blood-sucking parasite reproduced inside the human body and its eggs came out through human feces. Since we used night soil as a natural fertilizer, the eggs would get into water through land, find housing in tiny snails, and develop into blood-sucking flukes. They would then get into human bodies as people worked in rice paddies, fished, washed, or swam in rivers and ponds.

The cooperative built a night soil collection station. It had a concrete pit to store night soil. This was covered with a lid, and a chemical was put into it to kill the eggs and to make it ferment. After the treatment and fermentation, the night soil was used as fertilizer free of parasite eggs.

Every morning, families put out their chamber pots and able-bodied women took turns collecting all the chamber pots in the village, emptying them, and cleaning them. The pots were no longer cleaned in rivers or ponds; they were cleaned in concrete water tanks that drained into the concrete pit.

These measures were very effective. At first, many people in our village tested positive for schistosomiasis, and all of them were treated. Into the 1960s, there were fewer and fewer people whose test came out positive. In the mid-1970s, it was announced that the disease had been eliminated in our area. After that, we continued to have our chamber pots emptied and cleaned collectively. But the stool testing stations closed down.

Collective life brought about other changes. After I had my first child, I stopped going to the night school. Many people who were about ten years younger than I was went to formal schools. Young people from our village went to a school inside the Yan Family Temple, which had grades from one to four; after that, they went to the school in Zhuqiao Town. The new government encouraged all school-age children to attend school. If children did not attend school, somebody from the government would come and ask why the children were not in school.

My cousins, Kaiyuan, Huijun, and Zhongming, all went to school. They were all good students. Kaiyuan went all the way up to college, became an engineer, and worked in Beijing. Huijun had enough education to be an accountant. Zhongming was good at making things with his hands. He made bamboo baskets and straw sandals when he was very young. He made a Chinese violin (*huqin*) with bamboo sticks and snake skin. He was enrolled in a school in Shanghai, where he learned to play the Chinese violin, and made a living by playing the violin in urban Shanghai all his professional life.

In the 1950s, local performing troupes were organized and they delivered performances to local communities; men and women went out to see performances in the evenings. People felt safe going out at night because criminal elements were under control. People who were ten or so years younger than I, especially single or childless people, enjoyed these times.

The local performing troupes were made up of amateurs, who rehearsed and performed in their spare time. A number of young men and women from Wangjialong belonged to a performing troupe and put on several plays. One of the plays told the story of He Wenxiu, a kind and honest young man who had a beautiful wife. A despot wanted his wife and so had He Wenxiu put into jail. With help from kind people and with his own effort, He Wenxiu became an official and finally brought the despot to justice. Huijun, my female cousin, played the role of Yang Mama, a courageous and kind woman, in the opera. After that, she was known to people as Yang Mama.

In the old days, people tilled their own land and never left their villages. A matchmaker was necessary to introduce a boy or a girl for possible matrimony. Now, the performing troupes got young people from otherwise disconnected villages together. With the protection of the new marriage law, some of the performers from Wangjialong found their spouses within the troupe. Aibao, who played a flower-selling girl in the story of He Wenxiu, fell in love with Sun Zhongxian, who acted as the main character in the play and was from another village. They got married in 1957. In the same year, Xiaomei, another young woman from our village, married a man from another village. Both Xiaomei and her husband played characters in the play.

Young people with some education were also given opportunities to make a living in other ways than tilling the land. Taiying was trained as a tractor driver and Meiying, whose mother died of a fatal illness and who was brought up by her grandmother, went to school after Liberation, received medical training, and became a midwife in 1957. Xiuqin was an accountant in a cooperative in North Hamlet and later became a teacher at Liming Elementary School. Chen Daxi went to a teacher's college in the 1950s and returned to teach at Liming Elementary School.

My husband also benefited from the opportunities made available in the 1950s and became an educated man. When we were first married, he did not write very good Chinese characters. He had had three years of formal education when he was a little boy. His mother died when he was thirteen years old. After that, he worked as a carpenter with his father and brother. He did not have any opportunity to use the little he had learned from that old-fashioned school. He admitted that at the time of Liberation, he had forgotten most of what he had learned. After Liberation, he participated in political activities and realized the importance of education. My father said that he was a very serious student at the night school and a fast learner.

After our marriage, my husband went to a number of training courses. He said that the seven months he spent in Nanjing when Shezhen was a little baby, he was a full-time student and really learned a lot. After that, my family continued to give him full support. We never asked or expected him to do anything at home. The family support and the opportunities provided by the new system combined to make him an educated person.

As a member of the cooperative, I personally participated in collective projects. My first experience living away from home and working on a public project was in early 1958. I went with a team of able-bodied men and women to help build an irrigation canal in Malu Commune. We packed our own bedding and clothes, pooled together rice and cash, and brought along a cook, who was a nice older man from South Hamlet. We slept on the floors of local people's guest halls. We used dry rice straw to cushion our cotton-quilted bedding.

We moved a lot of earth in building the canal. We first built a raised dike. On the raised dike we dug a canal. Only a raised canal could deliver water to nearby rice fields. Equipped with electrical pumps, such a canal made it possible to irrigate rice fields with as much water as was needed. Irrigation canals helped increase rice yields. The canal we built in 1958 was the first irrigation canal in Jiading County.[8]

When working on this project, Wang Xi'e, a fellow villager, and I were dealing with pregnancies. I could not eat preserved turnips or pickled cucumbers. If I ate porridge with these condiments at breakfast, I would throw up all my food and have to work on an empty stomach the whole morning. The cook was a nice man. I gave him some money and he bought a *jin* of soybeans and cooked them in soy sauce for me. I ate the soybeans at breakfast. Wang yearned for preserved bayberries and the cook bought her some when he went to the local market to shop. We worked during the day. For our evenings, we brought with us our needlework or knitting. After dinner, we sat in our beds and did our handiwork while chatting.

Some traditions and customs continued in this period. In South Hamlet, a childless old man died and his nephew, who inherited the old man's house, sponsored a funeral service that featured a day of chanting by Daoist priests. Incense, ceremonial candles, and paper money were still commercially available and were all used at the funeral service. The dead body was put in a coffin and buried underground right away. Since most land was no longer privately owned, the coffin was buried on the nephew's family plot.

There was also a wedding in 1957 in South Hamlet. The bride came from the same family as the groom's mother, so it was a marriage between two cousins. The wedding was a one-day affair that took place in the East Compound. We were distant relatives of the family as well as neighbors and attended the simple banquet. Shezhen was four years old at the time. To save a seat at a banquet table, we brought our own small bamboo chair for her. She sat in the bamboo chair and ate at the bench where my mother and I were seated. When a dish came out, we would take a little with our chopsticks and put it in her little bowl.

Some simple furniture such as a chest, a chamber pot, a basin, and quilts and clothes came around late morning. The bride arrived in a chimney sedan chair in the late afternoon. A few firecrackers were set off and there was a beanstalk bonfire. This was the last time a sedan chair was used to fetch the bride in our village.

This was a close-relative marriage, which had been accepted in our area and was even considered to be "adding love to a loving relationship." We learned gradually that such a marriage was not good, scientifically speaking, because it was more likely to produce unhealthy children. This marriage between the two cousins proved that the scientists were right. The married couple had two sons. The first one was a weak and sickly boy. Although he did reach adulthood, get married, and produce his own son, he was very small in size and was never physically strong. The second son developed a brain tumor and died in his teens.

Having learned the scientific theories about marrying close relatives, people avoided such arrangements. In the early 1980s, a young man from North Hamlet got married. He and his wife had a son, but soon they realized that the boy was deaf and mute. They applied for permission to have another child because the one-child-one-family policy was already in effect. Meiying, who was in charge of family planning in our village, gave the couple permission. Another son was born, but this boy was also deaf and mute. Meiying then said that there might be family history that would explain why both boys were born deaf and mute. She asked the mother of the two boys if any of her family had married close relatives. It turned out that this woman's mother and father were close relatives. This example convinced people further that marrying a close relative was not a wise practice.

NOTES

1 "Zhongguo gongchangdang zhongyang weiyuanhui guanyu fazhan nongye shengchan hezuoshe de jueyi" [Resolution of the Chinese Communist Party's Central Committee concerning development of agricultural production cooperatives], Dec. 16, 1953. In Zhonggong zhongyang wenxian yanjiushi, ed., *Jianguo yilai zhongyao wenxian xuanbian* [Selected important documents since the

founding of the People's Republic of China], vol. 4 (Beijing: Zhongyang wenxian chubanshe, 1993), 661–81. The *chujishe* in Wangjialong was an experiment and thus its organization preceded the issuing of the resolution.

2   Meimei is a local way for older people to address young women.

3   The two Chinese characters meaning "dawn" should be *liming* in Mandarin pronunciation. But in Jiading or Shanghai dialect, *limin*, benefit the people, and *liming*, dawn, have exactly the same pronunciation.

4   The elections were held in April 1953. *Jiading Xianzhi* [Annals of Jiading County] (Shanghai: Shanghai renmin chubanshe, 1992), 657.

5   Mama is a respectful way for a younger person to refer to a married woman who is usually of the parents' generation. Panjia means Pan family.

6   "Zhongyang renmin zhengfu zhengwuyuan guanyu shixing liangshi de jihua shougou he jihua gongying de mingling" [Directive of the State Council of Central People's Government to implement planned grain collection and planned marketing], Nov. 19, 1953. In Zhonggong zhongyang wenxian yanjiushi, ed., *Jianguo yilai zhongyao wenxian xuanbian* [Selected important documents since the founding of the People's Republic of China], vol. 4 (Beijing: Zhongyang wenxian chubanshe, 1993), 561–64.

7   "Nongcun liangshi tonggou tongxiao zanxing banfa" [Provisional methods for unified purchasing and marketing of grain in rural areas], Aug. 5, 1955. In Zhonggong zhongyang wenxian yanjiushi, ed., *Jianguo yilai zhongyao wenxian xuanbian* [Selected important documents since the founding of the People's Republic of China], vol. 7 (Beijing: Zhongyang wenxian chubanshe, 1993), 123–33.

8   In 1958, Jiading County government decided to "electrify the rural areas." *Jiading Jianshezhi* [Jiading construction annals] (Shanghai: Shanghai shehui kexue chubanshe, 2002), 621.

5

The Great Leap Forward

I N mid-1958, a kindergarten was established for Wangjialong
children inside a confiscated house in Bai Family Hamlet (Baijiazhai). All families were required to send their children there. This
was intended to save mothers and grandmothers from taking care of
children so that they could all go to work. We sent Shezhen (fig. 5.1) to
the kindergarten. Mother could not understand it. Her eyesight was
already very bad and she was no longer able to work in the fields. She
asked, "Why can't I take care of my granddaughter since I am home
anyway?" My parents missed Shezhen so much that several times
they went to see her in the kindergarten. They would say to the care-
givers that they would not take the child away. They would just stay a
while and hold Shezhen for a few minutes.

The kindergarten in Bai Family Hamlet did not last very long.
Replacing it was a kindergarten/nursery in each natural village, including one in South Hamlet. But there was no requirement for all children
to be sent there. Mother was happy to keep Shezhen under her care.

The kindergarten was the beginning of a crazy period. On a summer day in 1958, cadres in our village went to a "ten-thousand-people

5.1   Shezhen, late 1950s

meeting" in Jiading Town and said that at the meeting, representatives from various villages pledged a per-*mu* rice yield of 80,000 *jin*
and a per-*mu* cotton yield of 10,000 *jin*. These pledges were called
"welcoming challenges" (*baileitai*) or "launching satellites" (*fangweixing*). These were unrealistic figures, for the per-*mu* rice yield had
never been higher than 1,000 *jin* and the per-*mu* cotton yield never
exceeded 500 *jin*.

I was pregnant with another child at the time, but continued to
work in the fields. When the "ten-thousand-people meeting" took
place, I was working in an experimental cotton field. My uncle had
been named a "cotton expert" and was in charge of the experimental
field. He received this title because the cotton fields under his care
had yielded exceptionally good harvests in the previous couple of
years. The experimental cotton field I worked in that year looked
very promising, with tall and healthy cotton plants. Each plant hosted
layers of branches and each branch held several big cotton balls.

After the "ten-thousand-people meeting," an inspection team
from urban Shanghai came to our village. These inspectors were not

peasants and spoke the urban Shanghai dialect. Among them was a woman called Wu Mei. She lived with a family in our village and went into the fields with us.

The Liming High-Stage Cooperative now became part of a huge entity called Waigang Commune. Wangjialong and several nearby villages became an administrative section inside the big commune. My husband became a cadre in Waigang Commune and was gone even more often than before. There was a kind of crazy enthusiasm among people at that time. We worked day and night and attended a lot of meetings. The higher-ups told us what to do all the time.

One day Wu Mei, the inspector from urban Shanghai, was working in the experimental cotton field with us and asked my uncle if the cotton yield could reach four thousand *jin* per *mu*. Uncle, a very honest and straightforward man, replied, "Four thousand *jin* of cotton, if spread out to be dried, would need a space bigger than one *mu*." In other words, four thousand *jin* of cotton per *mu* was absolutely impossible and the question was just ridiculous.

That same evening, a meeting was called and we were all notified to attend. The meeting was to be held inside the house confiscated from the Pan family in North Hamlet. Around suppertime, I saw Uncle, who asked me if I was going to the meeting, and I said yes. We had no idea why the meeting had been called. It turned out that the meeting was to criticize Uncle for what he had said that afternoon. His words were considered a sneer at the enthusiasm for higher yields. He was labeled a "white flag," or a "backward element," and immediately removed from his position as a cotton expert and leader of the experimental field.

After that, nobody said anything; we just followed. Urban people who could not even tell chives from the blades of wheat plants were now in control. One day after Uncle was labeled a "white flag," Wu Mei said that according to the weather forecast, a typhoon was moving in our direction. She demanded that bamboo sticks be harvested from private bamboo groves to support each cotton plant in the experimental field.

That same fall, we pulled up ripening rice stalks from six *mu* of rice paddies and squeezed them into one *mu* for higher unit yield. When the cramped rice withered due to lack of air circulation, big fans, pulled by draft animals and human beings, were used to blow air into the crop. A well was dug in the middle of the field. We used buckets to get underground water to cool the rice plants. Finally, the uprooting and the piling up stopped the rice from growth at its critical stage. We harvested only rotten stalks with empty rice husks.

Unscientific farming methods continued to be implemented after the fall harvest in 1958. We were told to dig crop land three feet deep to bring up the unused soil. More bamboo sticks were cut down and bamboo craftsmen were mobilized to work day and night to divide bamboo culms into slivers and split the slivers into layers to make bamboo ropes. We then used the bamboo ropes to pull plows for the deep digging. After the deep digging, we were told to put dry rice straw on the soil and set fire to the straw. This was to burn the sticky, unused soil into top soil.

When we sowed wheat, we were told to put down two hundred *jin* of wheat seeds in a *mu* of land for high yields. Normally, twenty-five *jin* of seed was sowed in a *mu* of land. We were even shown the way to put down two hundred *jin* of wheat seed evenly: first we put sticky paste on old newspapers, then we spread wheat seed on the sticky papers, and finally we covered the prepared fields with these "wheat" papers. The papers would be removed when the wheat seeds had fallen off into the soil.

We continued to work day and night into the winter months. Gas lamps were strung over the ground outside our compound in the evening. We made soil cakes, baked them in the improvised furnaces erected in the field, and then crushed them into powder to spread onto the wheat as fertilizer. The brick stoves in our houses were torn down in order to get to the dirt that served as the stove's foundation. The theory was that because the stove had cooked food for many years, the foundation dirt had been so baked that it must be good fertilizer. We were also directed to scrape the top layer of our kitchen and guest-hall floors as fertilizer for the wheat crop.

During that period, we were organized to wipe out all the sparrows. The birds were considered pests because they ate our grain; therefore they had to be eliminated. The method was to deprive sparrows of any opportunity to rest so that they would be exhausted and drop dead. Young people were assigned to stay on house roofs and beat wash basins to prevent sparrows from perching and resting. Others stationed in the fields about twenty meters apart carried tall bamboo sticks to prevent sparrows from perching and resting. Further, grains of rice soaked in poisonous liquid were spread on the ground to kill sparrows that slipped through the network of people. This was all done on one day. We were required to get up and to our assigned positions before dawn, to bring our own food for the long day, and to remain at our positions until it was completely dark. We scared all the sparrows in the area and killed a few that day, but most sparrows survived and have continued to live in our midst.

TRYING TIMES

In the fall of 1958, we started to eat in communal dining rooms and had to hand in all grain at home and all of our cooking woks, which were melted to make iron and steel in peasant-run furnaces. Our family plots were taken away. Some of us became "iron and steel workers" and worked in a peasant-run furnace in Loutang Commune, another huge entity in our area.

At that time, our family again had surplus rice. When we were told to hand in our surplus grain, we had about one hundred *jin* of rice in our house. Having learned from the previous experience, my mother filled various available containers such as empty glass bottles and small earthen jars with the rice and stored them under our beds. We kept these containers when we handed in the rest of the rice. Father made a stove out of an empty kerosene container and gathered scraps of crop stalks and dead wood. When neighbors were out in the fields, Mother would cook two small bowls of rice on the improvised stove, one for Shezhen and the other for me. Mother said that I was pregnant with a child and needed more food. Shezhen was a good child. We told her not to tell anybody that Grandma cooked rice for her at home; she listened and never did.

My second daughter was born during this crazy period. I worked until the day of the birth. It was an autumn harvest day. I was on the threshing ground doing the lighter task of stretching big hemp sacks while others poured harvested rice into the sacks. In late afternoon when we had a break, I went home and told mother that I felt unusually heavy in the lower body. Mother suggested that I walk to the maternity ward in North Hamlet without telling anyone else. It was believed that the more people knew about your labor, the more pains you would suffer during labor.

I walked to the maternity ward, which was in the side rooms of the confiscated compound from the Pan family. Less than two hours later, the baby was born. The maternity ward cooked food for new mothers, but we had to bring our own material. I borrowed some rice from a woman who had given birth to a baby two days earlier. The midwife cooked the rice for me and that was my supper.

That evening, Zhu and Wang, two women peasant cadres from South Hamlet, were attending a meeting in the guest hall of the Pan compound. I asked the midwife to call them in. They came and were surprised that I had already given birth, because several hours before, I had been working with them on the threshing ground. I asked them to let my parents know that I and the baby, a girl, were doing well. I added that my parents needed to go to the dining room and get ten *jin* of rice and bring it to the ward. I also needed personal items such as a toothbrush and toothpaste, a change of clothes, a thermos, a wash towel, a wash basin, and diapers for the baby. I told Zhu and Wang to let my parents know that they did not have to come right away and that they could bring the things to me in the morning.

Mother and Father brought me what I needed early the following morning. At that time, my husband spent most of his days and nights in Waigang Town, the headquarters of the commune. He came home one day and found out that his second daughter had been born. He came to the maternity ward and the midwife showed him the new baby. The midwife referred to the new baby as a "thousand pieces of gold." My husband took a look, smiled, and left again for his work.

My father gave a name to the new baby and it was Shezhu. The first character, *she*, is the same as Shezhen's and *zhu* means pearl, another way to say that the child is precious.

During my stay at the maternity ward, eating in the dining room was free, but this lasted only a few days. While lying in bed, I heard loud and chaotic noises from the big dining room, which was inside the guest hall of a house right next to the maternity ward. I heard people breaking a bamboo fence outside the maternity ward to create a shortcut to the dining room.

I stayed in the maternity ward for five days. Besides the ten *jin* of rice we obtained from the dining room, I received coupons for one *jin* of sugar and one *jin* of cooking oil. These were special coupons for women in maternity confinement. My father bought the sugar and oil and brought it to the ward. Every day, the new mothers ate rice and preserved vegetables (*meigancai*) cooked with the sugar and oil bought with the special coupons.

When I returned home, the free dining experience ended. We still were not allowed to cook at home, but got our food from a kitchen inside our neighboring East Compound. People did not eat there but took the rationed portions according to the number of people in the household and ate the food at home.

The cook in our village kitchen was a kind old man. Every day, he would call out through the rear window to my mother before official mealtime so that Mother could get the food while it was hot. Also, that way, Mother did not have to stand in a queue. Mother would take our own food containers and get the food through the rear window. The cook would say to Mother: "Linshe is in confinement and should not eat cold food."

The new baby was assigned a food ration of six *jin* of rice per month. When she was big enough, we used the pestle and mortar in the Fortune Gate Room of the East Compound and pounded the rice into powder to make a baby paste. Sugar was very difficult to find at the time and my husband and father tried their best to get it.

Once, they brought home a box of cube sugar, which we had never seen before. I continued to breastfeed her, but the rice-powder paste, sweetened, was an important element in a healthy baby diet. We again had to cook the paste on the makeshift kerosene stove because we had no other cooking facility.

Food rationing and the lack of fat in the diet led to hunger. Villagers planted sweet potatoes and beans in unaccounted-for pieces of land or along roads and footpaths and the kitchen cooked them. But only those who were engaged in field labor had access to the supplemental food. After twenty-six days of staying home following the birth, I decided to return to work in the fields. Mother was not happy because she thought it was too early for me to be engaged in field labor. But I insisted because I was hungry and wanted to have access to the supplemental food.

Before Shezhu was born, Shezhen slept with me and her father in the same bed. After the birth of Shezhu, Shezhen slept with my mother. My father moved to sleep in the thatched house behind our main house. The thatched house was divided into two sections. The western section had been a pigsty; however, at that time, no individual families were allowed to raise pigs. The eastern section was used to store crop stalks for cooking fuel. We moved the crop stalks to the western section and cleared the eastern section and turned it into my father's bedroom.

The thatched house had bamboo-laced walls. We made mats of dry rice straw and hung them over the bamboo laces to shield the house from rain, snow, and wind. When father moved to sleep there, he cut a hole in the east-facing wall of the house and put a piece of plastic sheet over the hole. After he did that, he called me to see the plastic opening. He said, with a smile on his face, that he now had a window in his bedroom. Father loved me deeply. It had been his decision to keep me at home. He had to sleep in the pig-raising hut, yet he never complained or regretted.

My mother's health was poor. Every time she menstruated, she lost a lot of blood and was in pain. Around the time of Shezhu's birth, my mother went through menopause. When Shezhu was several months old, mother became weak and had to lie in bed due to heavy bleeding. When mother was bedridden, I put Shezhu in a cradle. The cradle was placed right in front of my mother's bed. A piece of brick was put under one of the legs of the cradle so that it would rock. A bamboo stick was attached to the side of the cradle that faced mother's bed. When the baby cried, mother would use the stick to push and rock the cradle.

One day, I returned home from the fields around three o'clock in the afternoon to find Shezhu crying in the cradle while my mother was sobbing in bed. Mother said she wanted to get up and hold the baby, but she was too dizzy to get up. I helped her get up to use the chamber pot. Blood came out in big chunks and would not stop. I was scared and went out to call for help. Neighbors came and suggested various folkways to stop the bleeding. My father went to Loutang Town and called for a doctor, who came on a bike. Father took the doctor's prescription to a pharmacy in Zhuqiao Town and got the herbs. We immediately brewed the herbs. Mother took the liquid of the brewed herbal mixture and gradually the bleeding stopped.

In the summer of 1959, before Shezhu reached her first birthday, she got chicken pox that spread quickly from her face to the rest of her head. I took her to Loutang Town to see a special doctor, who made an herbal paste for her and told me to put it on the affected area when I got home. On my way home, I had the urgent need to pee. But there was no bathroom on the road and my little baby could not stand on her own feet. The need became so bad that I had to find a way to relieve myself. I went into a corn field beside the road, put the cloth bag I was carrying down on the ground, and then put the baby on the bag. I relieved myself right there in the field.

The herbal paste worked wonders. Each time I applied it, the chicken pox dried a little. I was worried that the festering chicken pox would leave scars or marks, but the medicine was so good that it not only cured the problem, it also produced fresh, smooth skin. When the bark-like crusts fell off, my little girl's face was as smooth as a hard-boiled egg with its shell off.

When Shezhu had chicken pox, the kitchen in the East Compound had closed down and we had to go across the Zhangjing River (Zhangjing He) to North Hamlet to fetch food. Normally, I would fetch supper after I finished work in the fields, or my father would do so after he returned home from work. A few times, when I had to work in the fields late and father had to work in the evening, my mother sent Shezhen to fetch supper from the kitchen.

Shezhen was about six years old. One late afternoon, Mother sent her on that errand. Father had tied a rope onto the two ears of the pot so that Shezhen could carry the pot in one hand. As it grew dark, She-zhen was probably looking elsewhere when she stumbled at the head of the bridge spanning the Zhangjing River and spilled most of the supper, which was rice porridge, onto the ground. When I got home from the field, Shezhen, Mother, and the little baby Shezhu were all crying. There was only a little porridge left in the pot. Mother and I told Shezhen it was not her fault and tried to persuade her to eat some of the porridge. She refused to eat any, saying that it was all her fault. Mother refused to eat it, because she reasoned that she stayed home all day and was not hungry. Finally, the four of us shared what was left in the pot. That was our supper for that day.

The collective kitchens were again re-arranged sometime after Shezhen's accident. For South Hamlet, the kitchen was now in one of the side rooms of the East Compound. I became one of the two cooks working in the kitchen. The other cook was Xingying. We found a way to increase the portion of the rationed food by adding turnips and carrots, which were grown mainly as animal feed and were not considered grain, so we were not required to sell them to the state.

We experimented a number of times and finally came up with a recipe to cook carrot rice or turnip rice. Every morning, Xingying and I would wash and chop eighty *jin* of carrots or turnips, used on alternate days. We greased the big wok with a little cooking oil and put the eighty *jin* of carrots/turnips into the wok, put in some salt, cooked and stirred them for a few minutes to get some water out of them, and then put in the rationed amount of rice on top of them. Our hamlet had around thirty households and about one hundred people at that time. For lunch, the amount of rice for the entire hamlet was around twenty *jin.* Without any additional water, the liquid from the carrots/turnips moistened and cooked the rice.

In normal cooking, one *jin* of raw rice, with water added, produced two *jin* of cooked rice. With carrots or turnips, one *jin* of raw rice produced four *jin* of cooked rice. It doubled the amount of food for the hungry people. Everybody in the hamlet was happy. Cooks from other villages came and watched us cook and went home and copied our method.

At this time, each month, families were given coupons to get food from the kitchen. It was up to each family to decide how much food it would take from the kitchen at each meal. Every evening, each family would tell the hamlet accountant how much food it would take from the kitchen the next day. The accountant would then write on a blackboard the names of the heads of households and how much food each household was to take at each meal the next day. At mealtimes, each family would send one person to fetch the food from the kitchen.

I was able to recognize all the names and would use chalk to cross out the amount written on the board as food was served out to each household. Although Shezhen was not yet going to school, she had learned quite a few characters from her grandpa, my father. So I gave her the task of crossing out the amount on the board as each family took its food. She was so happy to help and took the task very seriously. She stood beside the board and crossed out each amount until all families had claimed their food.

I was pregnant again in the latter part of 1960. Unlike today, women then did not talk about pregnancies. Only when a woman's body became abnormally big would villagers find out that she was pregnant. After I realized that I was pregnant, I continued to go into the fields. It was the beginning of a cotton-picking season. One day, like everyone else, I fastened a bamboo basket to my waist and went into the fields. The cotton balls we picked that day were at the bottom of the cotton plant and did not get enough sunshine and were not expected to open up naturally. We collected them and put them out in the sun for drying. That way, the cotton inside them could be saved. If we did not collect such balls, they would rot away.

A basket full of such cotton balls weighed about twenty *jin*. This weight hung at my waist, pressing against my body. When I returned home from the field that day, I told my mother that I felt pain in my lower body. Both my mother and I realized something was wrong. I had a miscarriage.

RETURN TO NORMAL LIFE

The huge communes lasted only a few months and were soon replaced by smaller communes. Wangjialong now belonged to Zhuqiao Commune, with its headquarters in Zhuqiao Town. My husband now worked as a cadre in Zhuqiao Commune. Below the commune was an administrative unit called a brigade and below the brigade was the production team. The name Liming was retained, so we now belonged to Liming Brigade, which contained eleven production teams. Wangjialong was divided into three production teams, with South Hamlet as Production Team One.

In 1961, we had the family plots back.[1] One spring day, my husband brought home four *jin* of little taro. I was very happy and planted them in our family plot and had a good harvest of taro that autumn.

Individual families were also again encouraged to raise pigs. My father moved out of the thatched house and slept in our guest hall. My husband bought a piglet and we raised it in our thatched house. A pig had to be 100 *jin* in weight for it to be sellable to the government-run collection station in Zhuqiao Town. After several months of feeding the pig, I used the pull-trailer, which was collective property belonging to the production team, and took the pig to the station. But it weighed less than 100 *jin* and I had to take it back. It was very disappointing and I realized how inexperienced I was. Fortunately, that was the only time that I had to take back a pig from the collection station.

We were now encouraged to raise pigs and given incentives to do so. When we sold a pig, we received special coupons, which could be used to buy candies, sugar, meat, and other foodstuff beyond the rationed amount. We also received industrial coupons, which were for things such as socks, towels, cotton cloth, and other clothing materials beyond the rationed amount, and toiletries such as soap. In those days, practically everything required coupons for purchase.

Another incentive given to us for raising pigs was 0.2 *mu* of land for growing pig feed. This was in addition to the family plot allotted to us according to the number of people in the household. One year I grew Chinese cabbage on the 0.2 *mu* of land allotted to us because we raised a pig. I took good care of the cabbage and it yielded a very good harvest. At the time, male peasants regularly rowed boats to urban Shanghai to fetch urban kitchen waste, which was used as fertilizer on the collective land. Families could use the outbound empty boats to sell surplus produce in urban Shanghai.

I loaded the cabbage onto the empty boat before I went to bed one night and went with four men to urban Shanghai in the wee hours the next day. I sold several hundred *jin* of cabbage in the city at a wholesale market, earning seven yuan. This was a lot of money, for my husband's monthly salary was only forty-eight yuan. After I sold the cabbage, I thanked the men who rowed the boat by buying each of them a steamed bun (*baozi*) with meat fillings, which were half a yuan each.

While in urban Shanghai, I went to a public bathroom near the wholesale market. In the public bathroom, a woman asked me if I had grain coupons to sell. The woman added, "You people in the countryside must be doing better because you can find various substitutes for food. But we city people cannot grow anything on cement." This was right after the disastrous Great Leap Forward and there was still a severe shortage of food. I did have grain coupons with me. Both my husband and father received grain coupons as their food rations and I always carried some just as I carried some money. But I did not want to sell them. I was also afraid of being robbed and cheated in the city. In fact, I was scared and so replied that I did not have any and rushed out of the bathroom.

Several other women also went with the boat and sold vegetables in Shanghai. After we returned home, one of the women proposed that we should celebrate the result of our hard labor by going to urban Jiading for a dinner together in a restaurant. We did go, but when we found out how expensive restaurant food was, we each ate a steamed bun instead as our way of celebration.

The work-point reward system continued under the commune-brigade-team structure.[2] We elected a production team leader, usually a skilled farmhand, who decided what to do each day and rang the bell to call every working adult into the fields. The bell was fixed high on a tall wooden pole in the center of the village so that every household could hear the ringing.

On most days, there was division of labor. The team leader assigned various tasks. Some tasks, such as carrying wheat or rice on stalks to the threshing ground in harvest seasons or carrying bundled rice seedlings to the prepared rice fields in planting seasons, required more physical strength and were thus usually assigned to men in their prime. We women threshed wheat or rice, weeded rice paddies, picked cotton, and did the tasks that required less physical strength. Men and women joined together in cutting wheat or rice with sickles and transplanting rice seedlings. Older people were assigned even lighter tasks such as weeding cotton fields and separating chaff from grain on the threshing ground.

Different people doing different jobs were rewarded differently. Physically strong men earned the most, women in their prime came second, and old people earned the least. For example, ten hours of work done by a strong man was worth twelve work-points and the same number of hours by a strong woman earned ten work-points, while the same hours by an old person or a teenager learning to farm was only worth eight work-points.

Work-points were determined through a process called "self-appraisal and mutual assessment." The team leader would choose a day or an evening to call a meeting of all working adults for the purpose of assigning work-points to the recorded work hours. Such a meeting usually took place at the end of a season, so we had to evaluate if we worked in the past season as a strong laborer or a not-so-strong laborer. People who were sick or were getting old and did not work with the strong men or women would self-appraise themselves as belonging to a less worthy category. After the self-appraisal, there was the mutual assessment. In most cases, there was no difference between the self- and mutual assessment. In very rare cases, somebody would say that a certain person had been avoiding demanding tasks and therefore half a point or a point should be deducted from the self-appraised category. This would result in tension, so people usually tried to avoid such a situation. Self-appraisals therefore were usually well-considered and appropriate.

At the end of each calendar year, the team accountant would put up two posters, one to show how many work-points each person had earned, and the other to show how much money the production team had earned from selling grain, cotton, oil-bearing products, and cash products such as garlic, and from sideline production such as pigs raised collectively. We would keep 5 to 8 percent of the total income as collective funds. The remaining income would be divided by the total work-points to reveal its monetary value. Better collective income naturally resulted in a higher value for each work-point.

Each team had its own warehouse. I became the warehouse keeper in Production Team One. I took care of harvested crops of grain and cotton. On sunny days, early in the morning, I would get a few hands to help get the grain outside onto the cement ground and the cotton onto the reed mats for drying. After sunset, I would have people help me get the grain and cotton back into the warehouse. We did this until the moisture in the harvested crops dropped to the level stipulated by the state collection stations. We used boats to deliver them to the grain warehouse and cotton collection station in Zhuqiao Town. The payment we received was our collective income.

The grain we ate every day came from our own harvested crops. Each family also got an amount of crop stalks determined by the size of the family as cooking fuel. Each person was allotted one and a half *jin* of ginned cotton and we made cloth out of the cotton for our everyday wear.

The warping shop Big Aunt and I ran was closed in the early 1950s. When sideline production was allowed again, one man in our hamlet proposed that Big Aunt and I open a warping business to make money for the team. The team leaders consulted with us and we agreed to do it. The team paid a family to use its guest hall as our warping shop. The family house was right beside the Big Official Road so it was easy for customers to find us.

We charged a fee for the warping service, which we handed over to the production team, and gained work-points. In winter, when there was not much to be done in fields, the warping business was good. We worked fifteen or sixteen hours a day and earned between seven and eight yuan each day. For every two yuan we handed to the production team, we earned ten work-points. Eight yuan would be worth forty work-points, twenty for Big Aunt and twenty for me. The average monetary value of each work-point, determined by the total annual income of our team, was less than ten cents. Thus, Big Aunt and I received back less than half of the eight yuan per day we gave to the team. The rest of the warping shop service fee became collective income and was shared by everyone in the team.

After we started to run the shop, I worked day and night throughout the year. I worked together with everyone in the fields or on the warehouse grounds in the busy farming seasons. I worked in the warping shop in slack farming seasons when other people stayed home and relaxed.

It was around this time that Shezhen reached school age. She loved the idea of going to school. In the summer of 1961, her father took her to Zhuqiao Central Elementary School to register for school. In those days, children went to school when they were eight years old if they were born in the early part of the year or nine years old if they were born in the latter half of the year. While at the registration, when the teacher found out that Shezhen was eight years old, she asked if Shezhen was born in the early half of the year. Her father answered "yes," but Shezhen quickly corrected her father by saying that she had been born in July. The teacher smiled and said that Shezhen was too young for school and would have to wait until the next year. Shezhen was so disappointed that she cried.

MODERNIZATION

In the fall of 1959, construction of an electrical pump station, located at the west end of South Hamlet, began.[3] A woman from North Hamlet cooked lunches for the construction workers and technicians and used our village kitchen for the cooking. When the pump station was completed, it was powered by the electricity transformation station established in Zhuqiao in 1958.[4] Just as we went to help dig an irrigation canal in Malu in 1958, people from other villages came and helped us dig our first irrigation canal. The canal and electrical pump delivered water to our rice fields and the traditional waterwheel was now useless.

The two technicians working at the pump station married two young women from Wangjialong. One of these girls was Meiying, who had received medical training and was working as a midwife. Meiying's house was at the west end of South Hamlet, next to the irrigation station. Meiying had gotten to know the two technicians and fallen in love with one of them.

The other technician, surnamed Chen, married Hongying from our village a couple of years later. Chen was from a very poor family. When he wanted to marry Hongying, Hongying's father refused him because the Chen family was too poor. Chen did not give up easily. Adult villagers who knew Chen talked to Hongying's father, pointing out that Chen was a capable and caring young man whose love for Hongying was serious and committed. Chen's persistence finally won. Hongying's father agreed to the marriage.

In the early 1960s, tractors came to plow land for us. We would take our crops away from the land before we went to sleep. Throughout the night, we would hear the pong-pong-pong as we slept. When we got up the next morning, our harvested land was all turned over.

The tractor drivers were young men and women selected from among peasants. From Wangjialong, Taiying, a young woman about twenty years old with education, was selected to be a tractor driver. That both young men and young women were trained as tractor drivers provided another dating opportunity. Taiying's husband was a fellow tractor driver. She not only found her own husband that way, she introduced another male tractor driver to my female cousin Huijun. Both Taiying and Huijun married their chosen men in the early 1960s.

I do not remember that any of these young people were married with any formal wedding ceremony. There was still a food shortage so putting on a wedding banquet was difficult. These young people just obtained marriage certificates at the commune headquarters and moved in together as husband and wife. After my cousin Huijun was married and moved in with her husband, her parents did not know how to get to her home. When Huijun gave birth to her first child, we relatives went to present her with maternity gifts. All of us, including her parents, had to ask for directions several times along the way.

During the Great Leap Forward, Wangjialong hosted three "sent-down" cadres (*xiafang ganbu*),[5] young salaried workers from urban Shanghai. At the time, the difference between the rural and urban areas was huge. Urban workers and government employees received secured salaries and lived with modern conveniences such as electricity, while people in the countryside were totally exposed to natural elements and made a living with back-breaking labor. We rural people thus envied urban people.

Consequently, three mothers in Wangjialong found many opportunities to invite the three bachelors to their houses for meals and showed motherly care to these young men who were away from home. Gradually, the daughters got to know the sent-down cadres from Shanghai, and eventually they became three married couples. Instead of the traditional practice of moving to the husband's house, these three married couples established their homes and raised their children in Wangjialong. But unlike matrilocal marriages, in which children took the mother's surname, the children from these three families all took their fathers' surnames.

Tradition was also broken in burial matters. During the Great Leap Forward, even our family plots were taken away from us. For Liming Brigade, there was a piece of land, next to the Big Stone Bridge, reserved as a collective burial ground. My maternal grandmother, who died in this period, was buried in that collective burial ground.

Also in this period, the Big Official Road between Jiading Town and Zhuqiao Town was widened and paved with coal cinder. The bridge over the Zhangjing River was rebuilt and widened to match the new road. People from other villages came to help us with the project. Some of them slept in our guest hall. The new road, known as Coal-cinder Road, made it possible for people to ride bicycles to Jiading or Zhuqiao regardless of weather conditions. I never learned to ride a bike, but it was much easier to walk on the coal-cinder surface during or after a rainfall.

Modern roads and modern facilities saved lives. In the early 1960s, my uncle's second son, who was a teenager at the time, complained about bellyaches. When the traditional ways did not stop the pain, he was rushed to Jiading People's Hospital in an ambulance. He had appendicitis and underwent immediate surgery. The surgeon said that the appendix was about to rupture and the surrounding area had been infected. The surgeon not only cut out the appendix, he also cut off the infected area and put in about two inches of goat intestine as a repair.

We also had mechanical threshing machines. In the past, we threshed wheat and rice on threshing beds made of wooden frames with bamboo sticks as ribs. We used our muscles and beat wheat or rice stalks against the ribbed beds to loosen grain from stalks. Now we had threshing machines powered by foot pedals. The threshing machines were far more efficient than the threshing beds.

There was a famous ditty describing modern life at the time: Pong-pong-pong (motorized boats) in rivers, chimneys (tractors) in fields, downstairs and upstairs (modern buildings), and electrical lighting and telephone (in the home). The ditty summarized the aspirations of us peasants.

Life had been hard, but it seemed to be turning for the better.

NOTES

1   On November 3, 1960, the Chinese Communist Party's Central Committee issued "Guanyu nongcun renmin gongshe dangqian zhengce wenti de jingji zhishi" [Urgent directive on problems in current policies concerning rural people's communes]. The directive said that family plots should be given back to peasants. The document can be found in Zhonggong zhongyang wenxian yanjiushi, ed., *Jianguo yilai zhongyao wenxian xuanbian* [Selected important documents since the founding of the People's Republic of China], vol. 13 (Beijing: Zhongyang wenxian chubanshe, 1996), 660–76.

2   "Nongcun renmin gongshe gongzuo tiaoli xiuzheng caoan" [Revised draft of regulations on the work of rural people's communes], Sept. 27, 1962. In Zhonggong zhongyang wenxian yanjiushi, ed., *Jianguo yilai zhongyao wenxian xuanbian* [Selected important documents since the founding of the People's Republic of China], vol. 15 (Beijing: Zhongyang wenxian chubanshe, 1997), 615–47.

3   Sixty-six electrical pump stations were built in the county between 1959 and 1960. *Jiading Xianzhi* [Annals of Jiading County] (Shanghai: Shanghai renmin chubanshe, 1992), 227.

4   *Jiading Jianshezhi* [Jiading construction annals] (Shanghai: Shanghai shehui kexue chubanshe, 2002), 622.

5   "Zhonggong zhongyang guanyu xiafang ganbu jingxing laodong duanlian de zhishi" [Directive of the Central Committee of the Chinese Communist Party concerning sending down cadres to do physical labor], Feb. 28, 1958. In Zhonggong zhongyang wenxian yanjiushi, ed., *Jianguo yilai zhongyao wenxian xuanbian* [Selected important documents since the founding of the People's Republic of China], vol. 11 (Beijing: Zhongyang wenxian chubanshe, 1996), 193–200.

6

"No Time for Meals All Year Round"

WAR and revolution prevented us from building new houses. The new house my father wanted to build for me never materialized. The land on which the homesite was prepared became collective land when we joined the high-stage cooperative. By 1962, my family had outgrown our living space in the West Compound and my father had been sleeping in the guest hall. In the spring of 1962 when I became pregnant again, Shezhen and Shezhu (fig. 6.1) crowded my mother's bed every night. To prepare for the arrival of my third child, Father decided to build an extension to our existing living quarter.

The extension would be built on the land right outside our east-facing door. The land used to be our neighbor's ox pen before Liberation. During the Land Reform, that piece of land was taken away from our neighbor and became collective land. Surrounded by houses and a bamboo grove, the land was not cultivable or used for any other purpose.

In front of our West Compound there was a bamboo grove and we owned a piece of it. The piece was a little bigger than the piece of

6.1 Shezhen and Shezhu,
early 1960s

land outside our living quarter. My father applied to Liming Brigade
to exchange our piece of the bamboo grove for the piece outside our
own living quarter to build an extension. The brigade authorities
came and carried out an on-the-spot investigation. They approved the
application and told my father that the exchange was not necessary,
since the land outside our house was practically wasteland.

Father, however, insisted that it be an exchange. Just as he did not
allow me to buy any confiscated furniture during the Land Reform,
he would not take the land without an exchange. So we gave up the
bamboo grove and prepared the wasteland for house building.

House-building materials were very difficult to obtain at that time.
We obtained building materials in an interesting way. Four years
earlier, in 1958, during the "communist wind" period, a two-room
brick-and-tile house belonging to my husband's native family was torn
down and the building materials were taken to be used in building a
collective pig farm. My husband's family received some token money
for the building materials. In 1960, a new policy came out,[1] saying that
private property taken away during the "communist wind" period

should be returned. We redeemed the building materials from the brigade with some payment and used them to build the extension.

The extension was built in a traditional way. The walls were built with bricks. Five wooden beams were horizontally placed, that is, in the east-west direction. Rafters were nailed onto the five beams. Ceiling tiles were whitewashed first and then put over the rafters. Roof tiles were then put on top of the ceiling tiles.

Shezhen was nine years old at the time and wanted to help when we built the house. We gave her a small stack of ceiling tiles and showed her how to brush white liquid onto the tiles. She sat on a little stool and worked enthusiastically at it.

The extension stretched out directly from our main living quarter. The width and depth of the new house were determined by the sizes of the used beams and rafters. We divided the extension into a closed-in room and an open corridor. My father said that our neighbors had been using the stone steps to access the water behind our house and that our extension should not block their way to the steps. The corridor was thus our neighbors' passageway to the stone steps.

We hired a local carpenter and a couple of brickmasons. Neighbors and relatives helped in building the house. We offered simple food to the carpenter, the brickmasons, and those who helped. The house was built quietly with no traditional or celebratory ceremonies such as holding a banquet on the day we raised the roof beam.

After the extension was built, my family used the corridor to air our laundry in rainy weather. Before the extension was built, we had to air our laundry in our guest hall. The corridor provided more moving air and so our laundry dried more quickly. That was an improvement in our life. The closed-in room was divided into two sections with a wood partition. One section was for a bed and a desk and the other section was to store our annual allotment of grain. My parents moved to sleep in the extension. The wood partition in the bedroom inside our main quarters was removed and the two beds were now in one room. Shezhen and Shezhu slept in one bed, and my husband and I slept in the other bed.

CHILDREN AND FAMILY PLANNING

During my pregnancy in 1962, I went to see a movie that featured Monkey King and White Bone Demon. The movie was in the evening and I went with several women in the village. When I realized what the movie was about, I regretted having gone to it, yet I did not dare to go home alone in the darkness. I closed my eyes most of the time, trying not to look at the screen.

I regretted going to the movie because I had heard a story from my uncle's wife about somebody who gave birth to a baby without ears. This was in the 1940s when she worked in a shoe factory in urban Shanghai. A woman from her native village was working with her at the same factory. They went to see a play about the road to hell, where people had their ears, hands, and feet cut off. It was believed that her seeing the play caused the baby to be born without ears.

I did not completely believe in such a thing, but I was a little worried throughout my pregnancy. I feared that my baby could be born missing something now that I had gone to a movie with monkey-like human beings and scary demons.

I again worked until the day the baby was born. It was in September and the weather was still warm. This time, my husband happened to be home. Panjia Mama was called in when I gave birth. Right after the baby came out, I asked the midwife to check and see if the baby was missing any parts. She replied that not only was the baby not missing any part, it had an extra one, which was the penis. She said to my husband, "This time you are lucky." She told us that the previous night, a family in North Hamlet had given birth to a baby girl. The family already had two daughters and wanted a boy, so they were disappointed. The baby girl was later adopted by another family. Two years later, the couple had another baby and it was a boy. Many families preferred boys to girls. I agreed with my father that both girls and boys were precious.

My father named the baby boy Shebao. The first character was the same as the first character in Shezhen and Shezhu's names. *Bao* means "treasure." The three children were now named "Precious," "Pearl," and "Treasure."

After Shebao was born, we were encouraged to take contraceptive measures and the most common one was for the woman to wear an intrauterine device. That was what I did. Soon after that, my husband had a vasectomy. He was one of the first men in the village to do so. Because he was a member of the Communist Party and worked as a cadre in the commune, he needed to take the lead in such a matter. Gradually, more and more men of my generation in Wangjialong had vasectomies.

My family did not celebrate the birth of Shezhen, Shezhu, or Shebao in any way. They were all born in times of food rationing. Father loved all my children dearly, but he did not like the idea of holding a banquet and asking relatives to bring their own food. He preferred to do things within his means.

Some families, however, held celebratory ceremonies. West River Aunt's daughter and her husband held a banquet to celebrate the first birthday of their first child and invited us. I went and brought one *jin* of rice in a bag. Some people brought a coupon for one *jin* of grain to the banquet. At the banquet, instead of the usual white rice, we ate carrot-rice, the kind we cooked in our village kitchen during the Great Leap Forward.

MODERN CONVENIENCES

In July 1962, electricity, which had already been used to power the irrigation station, became available to us in our daily life. This was very exciting because it provided much convenience in our daily life. Before this time, we had used kerosene lamps for lighting. When I breastfed Shezhen and Shezhu and had to change diapers at night, my husband bought a battery lamp. It was easier and safer because we could turn on the lamp without having to strike a match.

Our hamlet was one of the first in the area to have access to electricity, because we were the closest to the pump station that was wired to the electricity transformation station in Zhuqiao. At first, several houses shared one electricity meter. At the end of the month, the electricity bill was divided according to the number of bulbs each household had. We cut a hole in the partition that separated the bedroom from the kitchen-dining room. A wire ran along the ceiling and dangled a bulb down to the hole. That way, we used only one bulb for both sections of our living quarters. The bulbs used in the village were all fifteen watts.

Over the next few years, electricity became widely available. We no longer had to pedal the threshing machines with our feet—they were now powered by electricity. A wired loudspeaker system was set up in our area. Small loudspeakers were installed at every house and big ones were put up on tall poles that stood in the fields and on the threshing ground. We could turn the loudspeaker in our house on and off anytime we wanted or needed to. Three times each day—morning, noon, and evening—the wired loudspeaker gave us daily news; made announcements; discussed new and innovative farming methods; introduced new farm tools, fertilizers, insecticides, and seeds; and played music and local operas. All those programs came from a radio station run by Zhuqiao Commune, and a young woman from South Hamlet worked as an announcer at the station for several years.

When the first loudspeaker came to our village, it was set up in Yang Ji'an's guest hall, the place where we held village meetings at the time. The coming of the loudspeaker was an exciting event, so I took Mother to experience it with me. The loudspeaker was a bowl-like metal box. When it started to play a local opera, Mother asked if the opera singers were hiding in the next room. When I told her that there were no opera singers present in the house, she wondered where the voices were coming from. We were all amazed at the bowl-like metal box that emitted voices.

On the National Day (October 1) of 1962, a public bus started to run on the Coal-cinder Road between Zhuqiao Town and urban Jiading. Although I was in confinement after the birth of Shebao, I went to the stone steps behind our house and from there I saw the bus running on the Coal-cinder Road. Some people in our village paid to take the bus to and from urban Jiading, just to experience a ride in a motor vehicle. There were several fixed stops on the bus route and Wangjialong was one of them.

With electricity, we were now able to have rice unhusked or to have rice turned into flour at a processing plant at the brigade head-quarters, about one *li* from our village. Before electricity was available, we had to take harvested rice to Zhuqiao Town by boat for unhusking. The nearby processing plant made things easier for us. We used our production team's pull-trailer to take rice to the plant for unhusking. If we only needed a small bag of glutinous rice turned into flour for rice balls with meat or sweet fillings, we took it over on our shoulders. We no longer used the pestle and mortar in the Fortune Gate Room to pound rice flour.

WORK AND CHILDREN

My husband continued to devote his time and energy to his work (fig. 6.2). For about two years, from early 1963 to late 1964, he was sent to work in Jinshan, another suburban county in Shanghai, as a member of a Siqing, or Four Clean-ups, work team. The Four Clean-ups Movement was to investigate whether cadres, accountants, or warehouse keepers had done anything wrong historically or had abused power and taken what was not theirs.[2] While my husband was in Jinshan and lived in local peasant houses, a Siqing work team, made up of people we did not know, came to our village. Zhang Zhigao was one of the team members. He was assigned to eat lunch at our house.

When my husband worked in Jinshan, he came home for short visits. One day, my father took Shezhu to Jiading Town for a visit. When they got to the bus terminal in Jiading Town to return home, Shezhu saw a food stand selling sugarcane sticks. She wanted one, so my father went to buy it while Shezhu got onto the bus. She saw two men sitting and talking on the bus. She thought one of them looked like her father. Shezhu timidly approached and called, "Diedie, Diedie." The man did not respond. When my father got onto the bus, Shezhu pointed at the man and asked Grandpa in a low voice if that was her father. Grandpa accompanied her to find out. Indeed, it was her

6.2   Chen Xianxi in a rice paddy, 1960s

father. My husband said that he had not expected to see his daughter on the bus and he had been engaged in a conversation. Shezhu was so unsure of herself that she might have just whispered from a distance, so her father did not hear her calling voice.

Another time when my husband came home from Jinshan for a short visit, I was working on the threshing ground and Shezhu and Shebao were playing around. Someone noticed that my husband was entering the village and said to my children, "Your father is coming home. Go quickly to meet him. He must have brought you treats." Shezhu and Shebao did not move right away, so I said, "Their father is not in the habit of bringing treats to kids." When I returned home that evening, I found that my husband had brought something home this time. It was four-horned water caltrop (*sijiaoling*), a Jinshan specialty.

My husband did not have any weekends or any fixed days off work to come home. Even when he did come home, sometimes our children had already gone to sleep. When he came home before they had gone to sleep, one of them would shout, "Dad is home" when they heard the ting-ting-ting of his bicycle. He had to dismount from his bike outside the compound and push the bike through the dark alley. As he pushed it, the bike made the ting-ting-ting sound.

The Siqing Movement did not find any corruption in our production team. But our production team leader had participated in a local defensive corps before Liberation.[3] He was thus considered a person with a historical problem and removed from the leadership position.

While working as a Siqing work-team member in Jinshan, my husband himself also underwent an examination. He said that there were cadres who were called back from their assigned work-team positions because they themselves were found to be guilty. My husband was found to have a clean historical record, to have led an upright lifestyle, and to be clean in economic matters.

In the fall of 1962, Shezhen started to attend the Zhuqiao Central Elementary School, which was in Zhuqiao Town, the same place my husband's office was located. For her first semester, Shezhen would ride on her father's bike to school if her father had spent the previous night at home. Most of the time, she went to school with her little friends. In the Western Compound, two other children were of the same age and so they kept each other company.

My husband made an arrangement for Shezhen to have lunch at the dining room of the commune headquarters. The cook was a middle-aged woman, and we told Shezhen to call her Granny (Ah Po). The dining room kept a tab of everybody's meals, and my husband paid for Shezhen's as well as his own meals at the end of each month.

This lunch arrangement lasted only one semester. When her father went to Jinshan, we prepared a lunch box for Shezhen every school day. My mother would wash some rice and cut a carrot into little pieces and put them, with a little salt, in the lunch box. Shezhen would bring the box to school and have it steamed-cooked at the school kitchen as her lunch.

When it rained in the afternoon, somebody in the hamlet would take umbrellas to all of the hamlet's children in school. Adults with schoolchildren took turns volunteering for the job. On her way back from school, some kids, usually boys, would bother Shezhen. Usually her cousin Ah Xing from North Hamlet, my husband's nephew, protected Shezhen. Ah Xing was one year older than Shezhen, and a husky and daring boy.

Shezhen loved school, brought perfect scores home, and received awards for excellent school performance every semester. She also won awards at Mandarin-speaking contests (*Putonghua bisai*). We spoke a local dialect at home while schools taught children to speak Mandarin, so the contests were platforms for children to show how well they had learned Mandarin. We were all very proud of her school performance. My father put Shezhen's awards, which were colorful certificates, on the main wall of our kitchen-dining room.

When Shebao was born, there were more preventive vaccines given to babies. These vaccines were free and they worked well. While both Shezhen and Shezhu suffered from measles, Shebao did not. Shezhen was about three years old when she had measles. It was winter, and we kept her in bed under a heavy cotton-padded quilt. We knew that when a child got measles, the illness had to come out. Shezhen was covered with little red dots. We had to keep her from scratching, because too much scratching would lead to infection and leave scars. At one point, she could not even open her eyes. Measles came out from her eyes. I remember somebody brought us red eggs to celebrate the birth of their new baby, and we showed one to Shezhen, asking her if she could see the pretty color. She replied, "No." We were very worried.

When Shezhu had measles, it was in summertime. The hot and humid climate made it more difficult for the illness to come out. For the illness to run its course, we had to keep Shezhu from being exposed to wind. Her rash was much worse than Shezhen's. We also realized that the rash was a combination of measles and heat rash. It took a long time for the rash to disappear.

Shezhu suffered from joint dislocations several times when she was little. At the time, my grandmother lived independently in one big room partitioned into a bedroom section and a kitchen-dining section. Grandmother loved children and did not mind having them play in her room or on her bed on cold and rainy days. One time, while playing with another girl, Shezhu suffered dislocations at the shoulder, the elbow, and the wrist. We took her to the woman who cooked meals at the commune headquarters. She was a local expert in putting back a dislocated joint. She fixed the dislocations and told us to be more careful from now on because once a dislocation happened, it was possible that it would happen again. She was right. No matter how careful we were, Shezhu had more joint dislocations. Fortunately, although it was painful when it happened, it was easy to correct them with the help of that expert.

Shezhu also suffered from asthma when she was little. During asthma attacks, she would breathe with difficulty. There were times that her face turned blue. Asthma attacks were usually activated by catching a cold, so she learned to stay warm. In summer, after supper, my mother and father would take the children out to cool down on the ground in front of the compound. Shezhu would bring a piece of clothing with her. Neighbors noticed it and commented that this little child acted like an adult who had the sense to care of herself.

After my husband returned home from Jinshan, he learned about a medicine to cure asthma and bought some for Shezhu. It was a yellowish powder and an over-the-counter medicine. We explained the reason for the medicine to Shezhu and instructed her to take it. This was before she started school, but she acted like an adult, taking the medicine herself three times a day without ever forgetting about it. Since the medicine was in a powder form, it was not easy to swallow. But Shezhu never fretted about it. She was also smart and saw the result—there were no asthma attacks. She was so afraid of the stifling attacks that she was willing to do anything to stop them from coming. After about three months, we stopped the medication. Her asthma problem never came back again. She was cured of the illness before she started school.

After Shebao was born, my mother's eyesight deteriorated further, although she continued to do house chores. When Shebao was learning to walk, she was worried about his falling and bumping into dangerous objects without her being quick enough to protect him. So we decided that when no other adult was around, she would keep Shebao in a "standing bucket." We told Shebao, "When Grandpa comes home, you will come out and walk." The "standing bucket" was designed to support and protect kids when they were strong enough to stand until they were fully independent walkers. The bucket was round, about three feet high, with a two-and-a-half-feet diameter opening at the bottom and a one-and-a-half-feet diameter opening at the top. Inside this cone-shaped bucket, there was a removable board for the child to stand on. The board could be taken out and washed. The board was located about one and a half feet above the bottom rim. In winter, a foot warmer filled with warm ashes would be put on the ground and under the standing board so that it would be warm for the child standing inside the bucket.

Every day, Shebao would wait for Grandpa to come home. Looking at his little shoes hanging from a bar below the dining table, he would tell everyone, "When Grandpa comes home, I will put on my shoes, walk, and play." When he saw Grandpa come home, he would jump in the standing bucket and shout joyfully, "Grandpa is home, Grandpa is home."

My mother was very patient with her grandkids. Just like most children, my kids did not like to eat while sitting down. My mother had to feed them mouthful by mouthful. Shebao was the most troublesome of the three. My mother found all kinds of ways to feed him. She would allow him to run around while she fed him food. When he was three years old, he ran so fast that sometimes Mother could not catch up with him. She would follow him, food in hand, to the ground outside our compound, trying to feed him. I told mother that she did not have to do so, and that when he was really hungry, he would eat. But Mother replied, "Don't mind my business. I have all the time under the sun to do so and I do not mind doing so."

This was during the Siqing Movement and Zhang Zhigao was eating lunch at our house. He was a young man who ate a lot and was a fast eater. When Mother was feeding Shebao, she would say, "You are also a big man and should eat food like Zhang Zhigao." This was

6.3   Shebao, mid-1960s

one of the ways Mother coaxed her grandson to eat. Our neighbors
and villagers heard my mother, and so Shebao got the nickname "Big
Man." Even today, some villagers refer to Shebao as "Big Man."

In those days, in winter, we would use electrical pumps to dry village ponds to get silt for fertilizer as well as to harvest the fish. The harvested fish would be allotted to families. When the ponds were pumped
dry, adult men in the village would put on rubber shoes and get down
to the bottom to get fish. This was usually around Chinese New Year's
Day and a festive event. Women and children would go to watch.

When Shebao (fig. 6.3) was about three years old in the winter of
1964, I took my children to see the fish that had been caught and were
kept in big bamboo containers. It was a cold and gray day and I held
Shebao in my arms. We approached a container of fish and one huge
black fish flipped over and splashed drops of water and mud around. I
took a step back. Shebao was so shocked that he pressed tightly against
my chest. I quickly returned home. That night, Shebao ran a fever. He
uttered "pong, pong" and indicated that there was something in the
bedroom that was frightening him.

To calm him down, I tried a folk method. I filled a bowl with raw rice, put a silver ring in the rice, and then wrapped the bowl with a handkerchief. I then put the bowl of rice, handkerchief side down, on his chest. I kept the bowl of rice there for the whole night and watched him without sleep. He calmed down as time went by. It was believed that silver helped to calm disturbed nerves. The next morning when I lifted the handkerchief from the bowl, the silver piece was in the center and on the surface of the bowl of rice.

One harvest season, when I was working on the threshing ground, Shebao played with another boy in piles of newly threshed wheat stalks. They climbed up to the top of a pile and jumped down. Shebao hurt his leg on one of the jumps. A barefoot doctor, who was a peasant with some medical training, took a look and said that he had just sprained it a little, and that it was not serious.

A doctor from urban Shanghai was "receiving re-education" in our neighboring Dongfeng Brigade. Every day, he would bring a medicine box and walk the villages to provide medical service and advice. The day after Shebao's incident, the doctor came to our village, and I asked him to take a look at the leg. He felt it and said that a minor bone had been broken. He recommended that a plaster cast be put on the leg to help heal it. Or, he added, if the child was not a restless one and would listen, he could use two bamboo sticks to keep the leg in a straight position. Shebao would be required to sit and rest until the bone was healed.

I told the doctor that my child would listen to me and could sit well, so the bamboo-stick method was used. Shebao listened and did not complain, but lay on the little reclining rattan chair under my mother's care during the day until the bone was healed.

When the children were small, in winter, my mother would prepare a foot warmer with warm ashes after cooking breakfast. She would then put the children's clothes on the foot warmer so that when they got up and dressed, the clothes would not be damp and cold. In the evening, she would stuff the foot warmer with warm ashes from cooking supper and warm the beds for the children.

In summer, I worked in the fields until dark. During harvest seasons, I had to work day and night, until nine or ten o'clock in the evening. Father worked in a factory and usually returned home earlier than I did. He helped Mother take care of the children. They fed the children supper. After supper, Mother used an oil lamp, which had a chimney-like shade, to kill mosquitoes inside the mosquito nets over our beds. Since her eyesight was poor, she asked the children to find mosquitoes for her. When they pointed at a mosquito, she put the chimney-like shade under it to catch and burn it. She then drew close the net openings and tucked them under bamboo mats to stop any bugs from entering.

In the evening, Father took benches and chairs out to the ground in front of our compound for cooling down. He and Mother warmed water on our brick stove and poured it into a wooden basin for the children and themselves to wash and clean one after another. Afterward, they all went out to the ground.

Our house was in the northeast corner of the West Compound and summer winds in our region usually blew from southwest or southeast directions; so we rarely got any natural wind. In those days, natural wind was the only way for us to cool down after having cleaned ourselves in the evening. My children were not very brave when they were little. They would come home through the dark alley between the East Compound and the West Compound holding Grandpa or Grandma's hands or clutching onto their clothes.

We had no disposable diapers when the children were growing up. We cut worn-out bedsheets into small pieces and sewed several pieces together as diapers. Such a diaper had to be washed every time it was wet. When it rained three days in a row, our guest hall, or our corridor after the extension was built in 1962, would be full of washed diapers and we would be out of dry ones. Mother would use the foot warmer to dry the washed diapers piece by piece. When the sun came out after several days of sustained rain, we would get all the washed diapers out to dry in the sun. At the end of the day, Mother would happily say, "Now we have enough dry diapers to last another few rainy days."

From time to time, my father would buy fruits and sweets. If it was an orange, he would ask the children to peel it and then divide it into several portions for everyone in the family to share. For an apple, he would peel it, cut it into pieces, and again ask the children to divide and share. They were also asked to divide sweets into equal portions for sharing. Every time, after dividing and handing a portion to every member in the family, Mother and Father would give their shares to the children as a reward for a well-done job.

Father prepared brand new money for the children at Chinese New Year. These were ten-cent bills. Each child got one yuan, or ten ten-cent bills. The ten bills were numerically connected. He was able to make them connected because he was an accountant and dealt with the bank. These bills were so new and pretty that the children would keep them as souvenirs, not as money. In summer, when a store clerk brought popsicles on a bike to sell in the village, we asked them to use the money to buy popsicles for themselves. But they would not use their bills because they were too pretty to surrender.

After the Movement to Learn from Dazhai started, we planted three crops each year, instead of the two traditional crops.[4] The additional crop was the early rice, with seeds sowed in April, seedlings transplanted in early June, and ripened rice harvested in August. We started late rice seedlings in July and transplanted them right after the early rice was harvested. Late rice would be harvested in late October.

Every year, between April and late October, I was busy, just like everyone else, either working in the fields or on the warehouse grounds. At harvest times, so long as there was grain on the warehouse grounds, I could not take the lunch break everyone else took. My mother asked my children to deliver food to me, or sometimes the children came and stayed on the grounds so that I could run home and eat a quick meal.

Both Shezhen and Shezhu wore braids. In the morning, after they got up, they would bring a comb and come to the warehouse grounds so that I would do the braids for them. They did not want to have Grandmother do it because Grandmother was too old fashioned. I had too much to do at the warehouse and could barely find the time for them. I tried to persuade them to have their braids cut off, but they refused. I finally made the decision and cut their braids off. They were both upset. Shezhu accepted the situation better than Shezhen, who was so upset that she cried and screamed, stomping her feet on the ground.

In the summer when I got home from the fields, I had to wash all the clothes for the family. In those days, there were no mosquito-repelling measures. My legs would be covered with mosquito bites when I was done with the washing. I would ask my children to scratch for me. They would work so hard that the skin of my legs would be scratched white.

In slack farming seasons, I was still busy, working in the warping shop. When business was good, people would come before daybreak for service. Many customers returned year after year and so knew where I lived. They would come and knock on our bedroom window to let me know that they had arrived and were already waiting. I would get up and start right away. Mother sent the children to the warping shop to call me back to eat. When customers begged me to finish the job for them before I took a break, I usually told my children to tell Grandma that I would come home later.

My children lost patience a number of times while encountering persistent customers. One morning before dawn, a customer knocked at the window and Shezhen was awakened. She responded rudely, saying, "It is not even dawn. My mother has just gone to sleep. You are so unreasonable." The customer responded, "Meimei, I am not asking your mother to get up. I am only letting her know that I have arrived."

One day, Shezhen came to the shop to call me home for lunch. A customer begged me to finish the job before I took a lunch break. I agreed. Shezhen went into a rage. She grabbed one of the essential tools in the shop and threw it into the nearby rapeseed field. I took the break. The waiting customers went into the field and retrieved the tool.

Customers were even more afraid of Shebao. When he was little, he found a way to stop my work instantly. He would come, get inside the wheel, and sit there. The wheel had to have the right amount of weight as pressure as I combed and reeled the warp threads onto the weaving beam. When Shebao got into the wheel, he added extra weight so the wheel was no longer workable. I had to stop right there.

BEGINNING OF THE CULTURAL REVOLUTION

In the latter part of 1966, there came another movement, the Cultural Revolution. Red Guards, made up of young, daring people, came into our houses and dismantled family altars and took away our ancestral tablets. They came into our bedroom and scraped off the various figurines carved onto the front wooden board of our beds. They also took down the balls of baby hair hanging from the bed frame. They said the figurines represented feudal ideas and that hanging balls of baby hair was an old custom. They said that anything that was feudal or old was bad and had to be destroyed.

Tablets and altars from every household were piled up on the production team's threshing ground and a fire was set to burn them all. Shezhen went to see the burning and stepped onto a very rusty nail from an altar. The nail went deep into the sole of her foot. A barefoot doctor said that the nail could be hundreds of years old and the rust could cause tetanus. I asked somebody to take Shezhen on a bike to the commune medical center and there she received a tetanus shot. Red Guards knocked down bodhisattvas and gods and goddesses from Yang Family Temple and Yan Family Temple.

All schools were closed, so Shezhen started to learn farm work and earned about eight hundred work-points that year. Now that our family was bigger, with three children, and we took more grain from the production team, my work-points were barely enough to cover our expenses. If they were not covered, my father would pay the balance to the team accountant. At the end of 1967, the work-points Shezhen earned brought us out of the red and we received about eighty yuan of dividends. I used part of the money to buy Shezhen one *jin* of wool yarn and she knitted a sweater for herself.

Shezhen had learned to knit sweaters when she was very young. She not only helped me with the knitting work, she also helped neighbors knit. One of my cousins living in the West Compound had two boys and no girl, so Shezhen knitted a sweater for this family and my cousin bought Shezhen a pair of nylon socks. One of my distant cousins was a bachelor and his mother was old-fashioned and never learned to knit. Shezhen knitted for him and his mother spun cotton into yarn for us in return.

Shezhen learned to appreciate things early. In summer, the production team grew sweet melons and watermelons. They were allotted to families according to the number of people in each family. At the time of the allotment, the accountant would be there, recording the amount each family actually took. Since this was usually done on the warehouse grounds, I helped to load and weigh melons for each family. At the end of the allotment, there were usually some melons left. Families competed to get more and children begged their parents to get more. But Shezhen was the opposite. Sometimes I wanted to get some, but she would stop me from getting them, saying that they would put us in the red.

Schools opened again after about one year. Shezhen did not go back to the Central Elementary School. A school was established in North Hamlet for kids in the vicinity. Shezhen told me she did not like this school. Students from two different grades were combined in one room. The teacher would teach one grade at a time and then assign one grade some work to do. Then the teacher would teach the other grade in the same room. Local people who had less than a middle-school education were recruited to teach at such schools. They were known as peasant teachers (*minban laoshi*). They kept their peasant status and taught in local elementary schools. It was right at that time that Shezhu started school. She went to the school in North Hamlet with Shezhen every day.

Red Guards and rebels attacked cadres and school principals, calling them "authorities taking the capitalist road." One day, my husband came home and said that he wanted to use our home to temporarily store important records and files from the commune. I was afraid and at first did not agree. My husband said it was an urgent decision made by the leaders in the commune and the archival materials would arrive at our house around midnight that same day. He added that rebels had completely taken over. If the archival materials were not taken away from the commune office, they would either be destroyed or used for the wrong purposes. He further said that it was his responsibility to protect the archival materials.

I accepted the reality. That night, we did not sleep. We turned our lights off as we waited, for we were afraid that someone might become suspicious of us if we had lights on after the usual bedtime. We waited in the dark. Around midnight, there was a knock on our window. Three men came with more than ten boxes of material on a boat. They moved the material up from the stone steps behind our house and stored it in the attic of our main living quarter. I shivered with fear and wondered what would happen to us if somebody saw this. I cooked some rice and some egg soup for them. They ate the food sitting on the footboards in front of our beds.

Later, the government issued a policy to specifically protect government records and files. The men rowed a boat to our house again one night and took the material back to the commune office in secret. Only then was I able to take a deep breath.

The rebels accused my husband of being one of the "authorities taking the capitalist road." The rebels found out about the storing of archival material in our house and accused him of obstructing the Cultural Revolution and of distrusting revolutionary rebels. This was one of his "crimes." Another crime was the names we gave to our children. They said that using the characters of "Precious, Pearl, and Treasure" in the names showed that my husband harbored bourgeois ideology. But they did not say anything about the fact that the other character in our children's names was in praise of the cooperative. My father quickly changed the names to Shedong for Shebao, Shefang for Shezhu, and Shehong for Shezhen. The three characters behind *she*, which were *dong fang hong*, meant "The East Is Red," the title of a popular song in praise of Chairman Mao.

My husband was later "united into" the Revolutionary Committee at the commune. He was considered a "reformable capitalist roader."

We peasants now had to "ask for directions" in the morning when we started the working day, "evaluate our behavior" at noon, and "report our performance" at the end of the working day. We learned to dance the "loyalty dance" and were instructed to remember Chairman Mao's quotations. Since most people of my generation or older were illiterate, the production team leader would call a meeting when a new quotation from Chairman Mao was issued. At the meeting, an educated person would read the newest quotation and ask us to repeat it and remember it. We pinned Chairman Mao's badges onto our clothes every day. My father wrote one of Chairman Mao's quotations onto the east-facing wall outside our main living quarter with red paint and a Chinese brush.

NOTES

1 This was the same policy that gave back family plots to peasants. See the previous chapter for more information about this policy.

2 "Zhonggong zhongyang guanyu muqian nongcun gongzuo zhong ruogan wenti de jueding (caoan)" [Draft resolution of the Chinese Communist Party's Central Committee on some problems in current rural work], May 20, 1963. In Zhonggong zhongyang wenxian yanjiushi, ed., *Jianguo yilai zhongyao wenxian xuanbian* [Selected important documents since the founding of the People's Republic of China], vol. 16 (Beijing: Zhongyang wenxian chubanshe, 1997), 310–29.

3 Local defensive corps were organized in the 1940s by the government to stop the spread of Communist influence.

4 The movement began with a news report titled "Dazhai zhilu" [Dazhai road] and an editorial titled "Yong geming jingshen jianshe shanqu de haobangyang" [A good example in using revolutionary spirit to develop mountainous regions] in the official newspaper *Renmin Ribao* [People's daily]. See *Renmin Ribao*, Feb. 10, 1964.

7

Years of Ordeal

THE Chinese New Year's Day of 1968 was at the end of January. In preparation for the most important festival, we made six big rice cakes. Making rice cakes was a traditional family activity. It involved all family members and had a festive atmosphere. We chose a Sunday, a day off work for my father. The day before, I washed and prepared ninety *jin* of rice. On Sunday morning, my father took the washed rice to the brigade processing plant and had it ground into flour. I took the afternoon off from the warping shop and helped my father make rice cakes.

We mixed the rice flour with sugar water. When sugar water was poured into the flour, many balls were formed. We used our hands to break the balls. Shezhen, Shezhu, and Shebao all joined in breaking the balls. We had told the children not to talk about the balls, for if the cake fairy heard us talking about them, she would prevent the steam from penetrating the cake. I sifted the mixed flour into the cake steamer and my father placed the steamer onto the brick stove. My mother fed the stove with firewood. We watched the steam gradually penetrate the cake mix. The cake was done when steam had penetrated the entire surface. My father lifted the heavy steamer and poured the cake out onto the prepared rice straw.

When all six cakes were made, my mother roasted peanuts in the shell over the remaining embers in the stove. Embers provided the most balanced fire for roasting peanuts. We grew peanuts on our family plot, and roasted peanuts were our typical New Year's treat. So that day, mother was behind the brick stove, feeding it for more than three hours.

By evening, when the cakes were cooled enough, Father cut off big pieces and gave one to each of our neighboring families to share. Sharing special foods with neighbors was a customary practice. When neighbors made special foods, they also shared some with us.

The next morning, I got up early and went to work in the warping shop. Father was in the guest hall cutting the cakes into pieces. Mother prepared some soybeans and asked Shezhen to exchange them for tofu at the brigade tofu shop. Shezhen took the soybeans and a cooking pot and brought the tofu back in the pot. When Shezhen got home, her grandma was in her bedroom using the chamber pot. Grandma called Shezhen in and told her to fetch Grandpa, because she was feeling dizzy. Shezhen went quickly to the guest hall and brought in Grandpa. Grandpa helped Grandma to bed and asked Shezhen to run and bring me home. Shezhen ran fast, and I got home immediately.

My mother was still conscious. She grabbed my hand and said, "My dear, I will now become a burden to you." Then she became unconscious. White foam appeared around her mouth. Before I arrived, she had told my father that she felt numbness in one of her hands. My husband's father had suffered from a hemorrhage of the brain more than ten years earlier and had to be helped with everything in life after that. My mother realized that she too had suffered a brain hemorrhage. At a time like this, she did not think of herself, but of me. I held her hands and said, "M'ma, don't say such a thing. You will be all right."

I went outside and called for help. This was the traditional day to send off the Kitchen God. The Cultural Revolution, however, had condemned this practice as "feudal superstition." We no longer had a portrait of the Kitchen God on our brick stove, nor was there any place to buy candles or incense for the ritual. Besides, no sensible person wished to get into trouble by performing the ritual. But we were peasants and this was the least busy season of the year. The production team leader had not rung the bell to call people into the fields that day. So when I cried out for help, my cousins and neighbors were all home and rushed to help immediately.

My cousin Hanming went quickly to the brigade office, the only place nearby that had a telephone. There he called Jiading People's Hospital for emergency help. He also called the Lixin Brigade office, where my husband was stationed at the time, to ask them to let him know the emergency situation at home. An ambulance came quickly and took Mother to the hospital. My father and I went in the ambulance to the hospital. My husband arrived at the hospital later on bike.

Doctors at the hospital told us that Mother had a massive hemorrhage of the brain. She was put on oxygen and measures were taken to restore her. By noon, the doctors told us that Mother's heart had stopped beating.

This was a thunderbolt out of blue skies. Darkness fell over me and I passed out. I could not imagine how I could live my life without my mother. Mother had been taking care of everything for me at home. I did not even know where rice was stored. I was able to earn work-points to cover the family expenses only because Mother took care of the children. At the time, my youngest, Shebao, was only seven years old and needed my mother's care. Whenever I was not feeling well, menstruating, pregnant, or nursing, Mother took care of me. She would cook something, sometimes just a bowl of sugar water, and ask one of my children to take it into the fields for me. I worked hard outside, but when I returned home, I could relax in a loving atmosphere.

Mother lived a hard life. When I was little, she worked during the day as a hired hand and spun or wove into the night to help provide for the family. She suffered severe headaches, which finally made her eyesight poor. After I was born, her menstruation was always painful and heavy. Several times, she lost so much blood that she passed out.

Her poor eyesight limited her mobility and slowed her movements. But she managed to do household chores for me. During the days of scarcity, she starved herself to save every little bit of food for me and for my children. She refused to accept any new clothes, insisting that whatever she had was enough. She would say, "I am not going anywhere and so do not need new clothes."

The bond between my mother and me was strong. Mother had been willing to shield me from possible bullets with her body during the war years. I was the only "flesh and bone" for my mother. But she disagreed with my father about keeping me at home, for she did not want me to live my life in clan controversies. When she realized that she had had a stroke, she did not think of herself. Her last words showed her concern that she would become a burden to me. Mother loved me selflessly.

I lived my thirty-seven years of life with my mother. We never quarreled, not even once. She only complained about my willfulness, but even then she did it in a loving way. I was not only practically dependent on Mother because she took care of the house for me. I was emotionally dependent on Mother, too. I confided everything to Mother. Mother was my strength. Without concrete words, Mother cheered me on. I wished that Mother had survived the hemorrhage so that I would at least have had an opportunity to carry out my filial duty by taking care of her. That would also have helped to prepare me for the breaking of the bond.

Mother passed away during the crazy period of the Cultural Revolution. All dead bodies had to be cremated and all traditional funeral practices were forbidden. Mother's body was shipped directly to West Gate Cremation Station from the hospital. I do not remember how I got home.

At home, Father wept. He said that he had been to many places and met all kinds of people, yet he had never seen anybody like my mother. Father said that Mother lived her life thinking of others only, never of herself. Despite all the knowledge of traditional funeral practices, Father could not do anything for Mother. He sobbed, shaking his head. Little Aunt came and wailed. She was eleven years

younger than Mother. When Mother married into the Chen family,
Little Aunt was still a little girl. Mother combed Little Aunt's hair and
made braids for her. When Little Aunt got into trouble while working
at Jiafeng Textile Mill (Jiafeng Fangzhi Chang), Mother supported
Father in asking her to quit the job. Whenever Little Aunt needed to
confide in somebody, she came to talk to Mother.

We wept and remembered Mother during the night, without
a memorial table or Mother's remains with us. The next morning,
Father decided to create a memorial table. We placed a table in our
guest hall, made a bamboo arch over it, and hung white cloth over
the arch. Incense was considered superstitious material so there was
no place to buy it. We lit two white candles, which were made for
lighting purposes and so were still available. It was a simple memorial
table, but at least it was a symbol that allowed us to express our grief.

Father gave money to my cousins who did the shopping and
cooked lunch for our relatives and neighbors. One of my cousins
rode a bicycle to the cremation station and carried clean clothes with
him, including a blue-colored (shilinbu) long gown, and the staff at
the station put the clean clothes on for Mother. When Mother had
been rushed to the hospital, she was wearing very old clothes. The
long gown we sent was relatively new. Because cremation had been
arranged for that afternoon, we did not have time to make Mother
any new clothes. After lunch, our neighbors and relatives who had
bicycles went to the cremation station. Each rider took another person
on the rear seat.

Before we left for the cremation station, we kowtowed to the
memorial table. At the station, Mother was pushed out on a flat cart
into the room where we had gathered. Since she passed away so
suddenly she looked as if she were just asleep, wearing the long blue
gown. When the station staff pushed Mother into the crematorium,
I wanted to go with her. Many people pulled me back. I remember
seeing the crematorium door close. After that, I passed out. I do not
remember what happened next.

I carried the box of my mother's ashes back home, riding on the
rear seat of my husband's bike. I placed Mother's box in our extension

house. There was no incense or paper money to burn for Mother. I wept before Mother's box many times. I remembered Mother every seventh day for seven weeks. This was a traditional practice that should involve food, candles, incense, and paper money. However, in that political atmosphere, I was only able to offer Mother simple food, without incense or paper money.

For many months after Mother passed away, when I returned home from work, I would have an illusion that my mother was coming out from the pigsty with a pig-feed bucket in her hand and walking toward me with a smile on her face. When Mother lived, she made sure that she had cooked the meal for the family and fed the pigs before I returned home. That way, I could sit down and eat right away.

A THEFT

About three weeks after Mother passed away, during the Lantern Festival, an old man who lived in the East Compound died. This man only had one child, a daughter who had been married out. Under the New Marriage Law of 1950, his daughter had the right to inherit the family house and one of her sons had moved to live in the old man's house. But the boy was still young, so the old man's daughter came and sponsored a simple funeral ceremony in the guest hall of the East Compound. We neighbors helped.

In the evening of the funeral day, while we were all in the guest hall of the East Compound, my husband came home. He had been to urban Shanghai to see an agricultural exhibition during the day. He had never suffered from motion sickness before, but that day he did. He said that while sitting on the bus from Shanghai to Jiading, he had been so sick that he had to vomit. He stood up, rolled down a bus window, and put his head out to vomit. Shortly thereafter, he realized that his wallet, which had been in his pants' rear pocket, was gone. In his wallet were his entire month's salary and all the coupons for the month: on that particular morning, before he left for Shanghai, he had received his salary and all the coupons.

My husband was very depressed when he came to the East Compound and told me the bad news in a low voice. I went home and wept. We now had to dig into our savings to cover the losses. It seemed to me that we were having an unlucky year.

A NEAR-DEATH EXPERIENCE

I had not been feeling well the whole spring of 1968. In May, my husband finally persuaded me to see a doctor in Jiading People's Hospital. The doctor said that my bad health was caused by hookworms inside me and prescribed medicine to kill the worms. I took the medicine and had a bad reaction that almost killed me. I passed out at home and was rushed to the emergency room of Jiading People's Hospital in an ambulance. Doctors there did not know what to do with me other than give me an IV drip. Dr. Chen Long, who had been president of the hospital, was sweeping the floor in the emergency room because Cultural Revolutionary rebels accused him of being one of the "academic authorities of the bourgeois class." My husband had met Dr. Chen at meetings before and they were acquaintances. When my husband told the floor-sweeping Dr. Chen about my sickness, he was very alarmed and immediately wrote a note and told my husband to give it to the doctors as quickly as possible. Having realized what was wrong with me, the doctors in the hospital consulted with Dr. Chen, brought in an expert from a Shanghai hospital, and took measures that finally saved my life.

We learned that Jiading People's Hospital had seen a few cases of bad reactions to the hookworm medicine before me and that none of those patients had survived. I believe that without Dr. Chen Long's timely intervention, I would not have survived, so I am very grateful to him. Not long ago, my husband read in the newspaper that Dr. Chen had died. He lived to be ninety-some years old and totally deserved it, because he was a good man. I wished that I could go to his funeral and kowtow to him.

ANOTHER DEATH

My father-in-law had suffered a brain hemorrhage when I was still breastfeeding Shezhen. My husband's biological mother, a very hard-working woman, died in the 1940s. My father-in-law got married again, to a woman who was very nice but not very capable. He worked as a carpenter during the day. After he returned home, he had to take care of the crops on their own land. One spring in the mid-1950s, while working on their own land, he felt dizzy and fell to the ground. We took him to a hospital where traditional Chinese medicine was prescribed for him. His wife brewed the herbal medicine for him, and he recovered. Then he went into the fields again. This time, he was putting down sweet potato plants. He had to bend over to do this, and he suffered another, more severe, brain hemorrhage. He fell down and was unconscious. He was hurried to the People's Hospital in Jiading. He survived, but lost the ability to speak and to use his right hand and right leg.

His wife was very good to him and took meticulous care of him. At mealtimes, she put food on his spoon so that he could use his left hand to get food into his mouth. She helped to clean him. From time to time, after a busy planting or harvesting season, she would ask me to go to their house and make sugar or scallion pancakes for him. Such pancakes, kept in a bamboo basket hung in a drafty place inside the house, could be kept for at least two weeks without going bad. My father-in-law liked this snack very much.

He lived with his partial paralysis for more than ten years. His health gradually deteriorated and he became bedridden. In July 1968, he passed away. Again, there was no traditional funeral service for him. A very simple service, with white candles, was held at home. He was taken to West Gate Cremation Station. My husband's elder brother took the ash box home with him.

ACCUSATIONS

By the latter part of 1968, the Cultural Revolution had entered a phase called "cleansing of the class ranks." In early September, I went to a meeting at Zhuqiao Commune headquarters. In the evening when I returned home, I saw my husband was already home. Also at my home was a Cultural Revolutionary rebel chief. He was there to take my husband away to a "study course" (*xuexiban*). In those days, entering a study course meant political trouble.

My husband had come home by himself earlier that afternoon. He had to get bedding and clothes, for he would not be allowed to return home during the study course. He promised the rebel chief that he would return to the commune headquarters as soon as possible. He got the bedding and clothes and was waiting for me to return home so that he could inform me about the study course. This delayed return caused the rebel chief to come to our house.

My husband was accused of being part of a counterrevolutionary organization. My husband firmly assured me that he had never belonged to any counterrevolutionary organization and that the facts would help to clear him of the accusation. With me, my father, and our children watching, my husband pushed his bike out through the dark alley that connected the West Compound with the East Compound and rode away. On his bike were his bedding and clothes. The rebel chief followed my husband on his own bike. My husband's departure that evening was the beginning of an ordeal that lasted twenty-two months.

The so-called counterrevolutionary organization was known as Jifei Agent Organization. Jifei refers to the Ji brothers, the famous local despots and anti-Communists.[1] The Ji brothers had been arrested and sentenced at the time of the Land Reform. Their followers had also been arrested and prosecuted. Now, in the Movement to Cleanse Class Ranks, the rebels claimed that more local people were members of the organization and had been "hidden class enemies." Many uneducated peasants, including some in Wangjialong, had been accused and most of them "confessed." For many of those who confessed, the evidence for membership in this organization was that they received free rice from somebody around the time of Liberation. At the time, they said, they did not know where the rice was coming from. Now they realized that it was the rice the Ji brothers and their followers had obtained by robbing grain warehouses.

The rebels at the brigade and the commune were very happy about the "discovery" of this counterrevolutionary organization. For them, this was a major achievement in "finding class enemies." It showed that they had worked hard and that they had been highly vigilant in guarding against enemies of the revolutionary cause. As the slogan went at the time, "class struggle has to be talked about every year, every month, every day." The discovery proved the correctness of the slogan.

Yet finding enemies among peasants was not significant enough for the rebels, who were interested in power. Therefore, they pressured those who had "confessed" to expose Jifei agents among cadres. My husband was the "biggest class enemy" they found.

The study course for my husband was first held at Zhuqiao Commune headquarters. My husband refused to admit or confess. He said that the Ji brothers' organization had been thoroughly investigated and those who had participated were dealt with in the early 1950s. He added that the uneducated peasants who had "confessed" confused relief grains from the new government with the grains the Ji brothers and their followers stole from grain warehouses and distributed among themselves.

The rebels would not accept my husband's argument. They continued to hunt for more Jifei agents. One day, after my husband had been taken away to the study course, I heard that they had found another "big fish." This time, it was the head of Liming Brigade.

One midnight, about ten days after my husband was taken away, I heard a knock on the door. I went to open the door and found my husband. I shivered when I saw him. He said that he had put a pair of shoes outside the mosquito net of his bed and slipped out when everybody was asleep. Unless somebody actually looked inside his bed, he or she would think that my husband was sleeping there. While working as a commune leader, he had visited many places and so was very familiar with the landscape. He did not walk the major roads; instead, he took the narrow paths in crop fields to avoid running into people who would recognize him. Because the study course had been moved from the commune headquarters to Dengta Middle School, it took him an hour to walk to our house.

He came home to tell me to dispose of a pack of bullets inside our house. In the mid-1950s, my husband had worked in the public security department of Waigang District. He had been equipped with a pistol and bullets for his patrol duties. Later on, when he stopped working in the public security department, he handed in the pistol and most of the bullets but kept a few as souvenirs. After more than a week of the study course, my husband realized that the rebels were determined to bring him down and condemn him as a counterrevolutionary. He was afraid that they might search our house. If they did, they would find the bullets. Since private families were not supposed to keep weapons and ammunition, the discovery of the bullets would get him and his entire family into big trouble.

Thus, my husband had to come home and tell me to dispose of them. He also reaffirmed that he had never participated in any counterrevolutionary activities. He firmly believed that he would be cleared of the baseless accusations. Then he left. I did not sleep at all that night. Early the next morning, I got up, took up a hoe and a bamboo bucket, and went to our family plot. I had put the bullets in the bamboo bucket. When I got to our family plot, I threw the bullets into the river. I worked in the plot a bit to cover the purpose of my trip and then returned home.

After the October 1 National Day of 1968, the rebels proclaimed that they had "solid evidence" to prove my husband was a Jifei agent. The so-called solid evidence came from my husband's elder brother, who worked as a carpenter in Nanjing. Three rebels journeyed there and ran a special "study course" for the brother. The course lasted seven days, during which the rebels pressured my husband's brother to admit that he had joined the Jifei organization and had introduced his younger brother to it. His brother at first denied the accusation, but finally he succumbed to the pressure and put his fingerprint on the so-called confession notes.

With the "confession notes" in hand, the rebels declared my husband a counterrevolutionary. They came to our house and painted the big slogans, "Down with Jifei agent Chen Xianxi" and "Down with counterrevolutionary Chen Xianxi" onto our east-facing wall with black ink. They took my husband to more than forty mass meetings where he was denounced as an enemy of the people.

One of those mass meetings was held on the grounds of the Liming Brigade office. They raised a platform. There, my husband stood with his hands tied behind him. Two rebels stood beside him. They were responsible for pushing down my husband's head. I also stood on the platform as my husband's companion. My husband's brother's son-in-law was one of the rebel leaders of Liming Brigade. He led the shouting of "Down with Jifei agent Chen Xianxi; Down with counter-revolutionary Chen Xianxi" and the crowd on the grounds followed. Another rebel read aloud my husband's alleged crimes.

Before the rebels took my husband to Liming Brigade, they had talked with me, trying to persuade me to "stand out and expose" him. But I refused. I said that he told me that he had never participated in any counterrevolutionary activities, and I believed in him. My refusal made me "a stubborn woman and a dependent of a counterrevolution-ary." That is why I had to stand beside him on the raised platform.

After my brother-in-law's confession, I wondered if my husband had told me the truth. But how could I find out? Many people in Wangjialong said that he had participated in the Jifei organization. In North Hamlet, one man who was two or three years older than my husband refused to say that Chen Xianxi was a Jifei agent. I was afraid to visit him openly because in those days anybody who was in contact with me might get into trouble.

So I decided to visit this man at night. One night, after most peo-ple had gone to bed, I went to his house and knocked on his bedroom window. He and his wife quickly ushered me into the bedroom. I begged him to tell me the truth. He said that Chen Xianxi was a good, honest man. He said the two of them grew up together and he told me firmly that he had never participated in any Jifei organization, nor had Chen Xianxi. He believed that those who accused my husband either had some grudges or were ignorant people. His words were very reassuring to me in those days. He was a man of integrity and honesty. I will be grateful to this man forever.

My husband's study course was now moved to Baiqiang Brigade, about four *li* from our village. As the weather turned chilly, he sent home for some warmer clothes. On my way to Baiqiang to bring him clothes, I ran into my husband's brother's son-in-law. He dismounted from his bike and walked with me for some time. He asked, "Do you think my father-in-law would hurt his brother? He put his fingerprint onto the confession notes because that is the truth." He tried to persuade me to convince my husband to "confess." He said that "confession leads to lenient treatment, while confrontation leads to harsh treatment." He also tried to persuade me to take a stand against my husband, saying, "The facts prove that he is a class enemy." I told him that I could not do what he asked me to do and that I believed what was truth would come out as truth in the end.

When I got to Baiqiang Brigade, the rebel leader took me into a room and said more or less the same things as my brother-in-law's son-in-law had, asking me to talk my husband into a "confession." When I told him that I could not do so and that I believed in my husband, the rebel leader said to me that in the whole commune, he had not seen "a more stubborn woman." Because I refused to do what they wanted me to do, the staff at Baiqiang study course did not allow me to see my husband. They took the clothes and said that they would give them to him.

As the weather got colder, my husband also sent home for a heavier quilt. I prepared it and Shezhen took it to her father on a bike. When Shezhen got to the study course, they took the quilt and felt all over it for any possible secret note sewed into it. My husband at the time was under "isolated examination." They were worried about any outside information passing into his hands.

The rebels did allow Shezhen to see her father. After they had examined the quilt, Shezhen took it into the room where her father slept. Shezhen told me that she saw her father's makeshift bed with a mosquito net. Onto the mosquito net were hung big-character posters accusing him of being a Jifei agent. Shezhen's father told her to be careful of the posters. Shezhen said she understood that any tear or damage would be an act of defiance or confrontation and would be an added crime for her father. Shezhen came home, told me her experience, and cried. I cried with her. I did not know how to comfort her.

The staff at the Baiqiang study course had to take two days off for the New Year's Day holiday. They sent my husband home for the two days and put him under the surveillance of the rebel leader in our village. On New Year's Eve, when my husband arrived home, the village rebel leader came and told my husband to empty and clean chamber pots the next day, New Year's Day. At the time, this job was always given to landlords, who had been the biggest class enemies in a village. Clearly, my husband was now considered a worse enemy than the landlord in our village. My husband replied directly to the rebel leader, "I will not do that." My husband was so firm that the rebel leader could not do anything to force it. For two days, nobody dared to visit us, for nobody wished to get into trouble.

After New Year's Day, it was the Chinese New Year. This time, they did not allow my husband to come home. The staff took turns on duty at the study course. Besides my husband, there were three other men in the study course. My husband spent the Chinese New Year holidays with them. They made rice-stalk ropes for the local production team. My husband became very good friends with one of the three men and stayed friends with him for a long time. This friend came from a landlord family, was educated, and worked as the vet in Zhuqiao Commune.

In the spring of 1969, the study course ended. My husband, who still denied any connection with the so-called Jifei Agent Organization, was sent to work under surveillance at Lijiang Brigade's pig farm. The pig farm was about ten *li* north of our village. He was not allowed to come home.

In late May, Yan Shoufu, who was working at the commune pig farm, went to visit Lijiang Brigade's pig farm. My husband asked him to pass a message to me. My husband said that if it was possible, he wanted me to send him some grain coupons. He relied on his monthly allotted coupons for the three meals in the dining room on the farm, but they were not enough, so he was often hungry. Besides conveying the message, Yan Shoufu gave me directions to get to the pig farm.

The next day, I got up before dawn and walked for an hour to get to the pig farm. I had to ask for directions only once. When I got there, it was before breakfast. A woman was cooking in the kitchen for the workers on the farm. I asked her if Chen Xianxi worked there, and she said yes and showed me where my husband was working at the time. Across a field in which wheat had just been harvested, I saw one man on the top of a pile of crop stalks and another man standing below throwing bundled crop stalks to the man on the top. The woman said the man standing below was Chen Xianxi. I told her that I was his wife and had brought some grain coupons for him. She said she could run and call him back. I thanked her and said no. I gave her the coupons and asked her to give them to him. She told me that he was doing fine and that people at the pig farm and in the surrounding villages respected him and got along very well with him. She said that sometimes villagers and workers at the pig farm brought him homemade foods. I thanked her again and told her to let him know that everyone at home was doing well and that all he needed to do was take care of himself. The woman sent me off with tears in her eyes.

I returned home and went into the fields on time. I did all of this before the day's field work started and nobody knew what I had already done that day.

Summer came and went. As the weather was getting cold again, I prepared another heavy quilt and asked Shezhen to bring it to her father on a bike. I described the way to Lijiang Brigade's pig farm. Shezhen remembered it and got there fine. There at the farm, Shezhen saw her father. On her way back, a quick storm wetted the dirt road she rode her bike on. She was not very good at controlling the bike and so fell on the slippery road a number of times. When she got home, she was covered with wet dirt. She sobbed and said that she could hardly recognize her father. She said that he had long hair and a long beard. He was thin and his face was dark.

My husband returned home from the pig farm in the summer of 1970. He was cleared of the accusation of being a Jifei agent, as were

CHAPTER 7

all the others. Just as my husband had said, the Jifei organization had been thoroughly investigated and those who were involved had been dealt with in the early 1950s. Afterward, my husband was assigned to work as a cadre in Chengdong Commune, which was located southeast of Jiading Town. It took more than an hour for him to ride a bike from our village to his new job. He again devoted himself to work. He came home even less frequently due to its distance from home.

SUICIDE ATTEMPT AND DEATH

When my husband was shut up in the study course at Dengta Middle School in September 1968, my father was also called away to a study course inside Zhuqiao Middle School. My father's position as hamlet head before Liberation was now deemed a crime. But more seriously, the rebels also accused him of being a member of the Jifei Agent Organization. The rebels pressured him to "confess" his involvement in the organization as well as to say that he knew my husband was also a member. After the October 1 National Day holiday, there were big banners inside the Zhuqiao Middle School declaring Chen Xianxi a Jifei agent, a counterrevolutionary, and the biggest and most deeply hidden class enemy in Zhuqiao Commune.

My father denied any involvement with the counterrevolutionary organization. He said that it was impossible that Chen Xianxi had supported any anti-Communist organization, because he worked for the new system from the very beginning. My father said that since Liberation, he had been watching how whole-heartedly Chen Xianxi had been working at his job, which was in the service of the people. My father asked, "How could such a person be a counterrevolutionary?"

Father had witnessed the irrational craziness of the past two years. The traditional customs he was familiar with had either been destroyed or condemned. He had seen his son-in-law taken away. He had now been accused of being a counterrevolutionary and was shut up in a study course. He could not see any way out of such a mess. He was totally disappointed and decided to end his life.

144

The following is what my father told me afterward.

One late night after everybody had gone to bed, my father went out to the middle school grounds and tried to electrocute himself by unscrewing a light bulb on a post and putting his fingers into it. He was repelled by the electricity. He then climbed over the middle school wall and got into a cotton field.

At the western edge of the cotton field was Xijing River (Xijing He), a major river in our area. This was the river in which Little Aunt, Father's little sister, did her washing every day. Father chose Xijing River to drown himself so that his sister would identify his body and take him home.

In the darkness, Father groped his way between fully grown cotton plants toward the river. When he got to the edge of the river and tried to jump in, he tripped on a trailing weed, fell down, and became unconscious. (I believe it was our ancestors who stopped him from taking the action.) When he woke up, it was dawn of the next day.

He could hear people walking and greeting each other on the road. This was a major dirt road connecting Little Aunt's village and villages beyond to Zhuqiao Town and to the Coal-cinder Road leading to Jiading Town. Father did not jump into the river then because he was afraid that he would be saved by people walking by and his "crime" would be doubled. At the time, an attempt to commit suicide was considered "stubborn confrontation" with the revolutionary cause. He decided to stay in the cotton field, wait for another night to fall, and then jump into the river.

That morning, I got up and went to work in the warping shop before breakfast. This was a slack farming season and people were using the time to do their needlework, to spin, and to weave. The warping shop was busy. Little Aunt's husband appeared at the warping shop on his bike. I was a little surprised and said, "Gufu [Uncle], is there anything wrong? This is very early." Uncle replied, "Your father has disappeared." I said, "My father is in the study course." Uncle said, "It is the study course people who said that your father has disappeared. The staff at the study course center are out looking for your father. We live nearby and heard the news." I put down my work and walked toward home. Before I reached home, I fell down to the ground and passed out.

Uncle cried for help. Villagers rushed out. They helped Uncle get me home. Very soon after that, the study course sent a staff member to see if my father had taken the liberty of coming home. The staff member comforted me, saying that I should not think the worst yet. I asked him to take me to Zhuqiao Middle School on his bike, which he agreed to do. At this point, the staff at the study course center were also worried. They were responsible for the personal security of those people under their control.

On the way to the middle school, I tried to think logically. I knew my father. *Mianzi*, or "face," was very important to him. Throughout his life, he lived properly and behaved reasonably. He had never done anything that caused gossip. He was a man of principle and of integrity. If he decided to do something and believed that was the right thing to do, he would not waver. He had now escaped from the study course; returning on his own would totally contradict my father's personality.

My world had collapsed once more. Father had kept me at home because he loved me. He gave whole-hearted support to my husband because he believed that the new system was good for the poor and the majority. Now it was my husband and his position as a commune leader that had brought trouble to my family. Without my husband, my father would not have been noticed and would have escaped the study course and the ordeal.

When I got to the middle school, they still had not found my father. They were using various ways to comb the river behind the middle school for the body. I tried to jump into the river, believing that was where my father was. Too many people were present and they stopped me. I cried loudly, calling my father and asking him why he had left me and why he had not taken me with him. I rolled on the ground and fainted many times. Crowds of people watched. The staff members finally persuaded me to return home to wait for further news. Somebody took me home on a bike.

In early afternoon of the same day, Little Aunt's husband came to my house on his bike again. He told me that my father was alive and had now returned to the study course. I replied, "Uncle, I know you are trying to comfort me, but this is no use. I do not believe it." Uncle said he was telling the truth and offered to take me to his home so that I could talk to Little Aunt. Uncle said, "Your Little Aunt saw your father herself and would not deceive you." I sat on the rear seat of Uncle's bike and went to his house immediately.

This is what happened. As my father sat in the cotton field waiting for night to fall, he heard people walking on the road say that what had happened to the Chen family was a tragedy. They said Chen Zhengqi, my father, was a nice man. He had a wonderful family before this Jifei event. Now this family is broken. Chen Zhengqi has now committed suicide. His son-in-law is shut up in a study course and has been accused as a counterrevolutionary. The saddest of all is his daughter. She has been crying and rolling in the dirt since early morning. She fainted many times. They also said that she may not survive such a blow and, unless guarded day and night, she could easily find a way to end her life. People sighed and said, "What would happen to the children? They are not old enough to take care of themselves."

Such talk awoke my father to an important reality: it was easy for him to end his life, but his death would kill me and ruin our family. He knew his returning alive would ruin his "face," but compared to his love for me and his family, his own "face" was less important. He decided to return and live for the sake of me and my children. With his face, hands, and clothes covered in dirt, he walked out of the cotton field, crossed the bridge, and went directly to Little Aunt's house, which was just on the other side of the river.

When Little Aunt saw him, she could not believe he was real. She said to herself that she had been crying since early morning and now must be deluded and seeing the ghost of her big brother. The sister and brother embraced each other and wept together. Little Aunt warmed some water and my father cleaned himself and changed into clean clothes, which belonged to Uncle. He then walked back to the study course in the middle school. Little Aunt convinced me that my father was alive and had returned to the study course. I went there, asking to see him, but was refused.

After this event, my father was sent to the soy-sauce factory where he used to be an accountant. He was no longer trusted, so he now worked in a soy-sauce bottling workshop. He worked under surveillance and had to write "thought reports." Father told me later that he did not mind the work in the workshop.

The soy-sauce factory, a commune-run business, had expanded and also made chemical fertilizer. The rebel leader at the factory was a vicious man. He made my father stand in the downside of the wind when a load of chemical fertilizer was being emptied out. Workers at the fertilizer section wore special masks provided by the factory when the hot, steamy chemical fertilizer came out; it was known to be poisonous and had a strong, choking odor. The rebel leader made my father take in the odor as his punishment. The process of emptying out the load took about forty-five minutes and my father had to stand for forty-five minutes and take in the poisonous, choking odor. This treatment lasted a whole month. During the month, my father was not allowed to come home and so I had no idea that this was happening.

During that month, I went to Zhuqiao Town for various things several times. I usually went early in the morning before field work started. On my way to Zhuqiao, I would go past the factory where Father was. A couple of times, I saw him standing inside the factory gate looking out. I saw him and he saw me. I did not go in, nor did he try to come out to meet me. I knew any meeting would cause more trouble for him. I continued walking, but could not help having tears in my eyes.

When the whole Jifei fiasco came to an end, Father returned to his accountant position. This time, he was assigned to work at the Zonghe Factory of Zhuqiao Commune. The major product of the factory was bean noodles.

By June 1971, Father was complaining about an uncomfortable stomach and began to throw up whatever he ate. I urged him and finally accompanied him to see a doctor in the People's Hospital. A gastroscopic exam determined that Father had stomach cancer, which was already at a very late stage. He was operated on and three-fourths of his stomach was cut off. But the doctors said that the cancer had already spread to the remaining portion of the stomach. At that time, radiation treatment was available, but we were told that it could not be performed on the stomach. The doctors said that if Father was taken good care of he could live one to two more years. They added that the best way for me to express my filial piety was to buy and cook whatever Father wanted to eat.

I did my best to take care of Father. Exactly one year later, in July of 1972, Father started to complain about stomach problems again. We consulted with specialists at Shanghai Tumor Hospital as well as doctors at the People's Hospital. They all concluded that Father could not be operated on again and advised us to resort to traditional Chinese medicine for help.

By mid-August, Father said that he did not want to take the herbal medicine anymore because it did not help at all. After that, one day, with me present, he said to his mother with a smile on his face, "Lin-she represents me. She will take care of you on my behalf. When we came to this world, we already knew that we would leave this world one day."

To me, Father said, "I suggest you do not go into the fields. Keep me company and we shall spend some time together. I have lived a complete *jiazi*, a sexagenary cycle,[2] and I am very content with my life. Your mother was a good and kind woman. You make me happy. I have no worries or concerns." He smiled a little and added, "I don't want to see tears. Life is a natural process and it ends one way or another."

On September 30, 1972, Father did not get out of bed at all. That was the only day in which he did not leave his bed. Before this, I would help him get up in the morning. I would get him water and he would wash his face and rinse his mouth. He would then lie down on a makeshift bed in a cool, breezy spot in our house during the day. That morning, he had become very weak. I sat at his bedside. He told me that something inside his stomach was exploding. I used my hands to stroke his stomach area. I wished I could take away some of his pain.

CHAPTER 7

By late afternoon, Father said that he was feeling hot and asked me to help take off a knitted wool vest he was wearing. I did so. Right after that, he gasped for air and passed away.

I realized that the last request Father had made in his life was not due to feeling hot, but because he knew that after he passed away, the knitted vest would have to be cut open in order to be removed. Once a knitted piece of clothing was cut, the wool thread was no longer useful. In the last moment of his life, Father thought of saving the wool thread of the vest he was wearing.

Again, the world had fallen apart for me. I cried and screamed, "Diedie, Diedie" and passed out.

This was still during the Cultural Revolution and all traditional funeral practices were forbidden. Father had performed many funeral services for others in his earlier life. Yet the one for him was void of any formal rituals and of incense and spirit money—the most basic funeral ritual items.

Father's life was cut short by the cancer. After Father passed away, I wished that his ghost would haunt the rebel leader in the soy-sauce/chemical fertilizer factory and make him suffer.

My father had been in charge of the family finances. Before he passed away, he took out all the bank deposit certificates and gave them to me. Altogether it was more than seven hundred yuan, a lot of money at the time.

NOTES

1   See chapter 2 for more information on the Ji brothers. According to *Jiading Xianzhi*, during the Movement to Cleanse the Class Ranks, 430 people were accused of being Jifei agents and thirteen people in the county died as a result of the accusations. *Jiading Xianzhi* [Annals of Jiading County] (Shanghai: Shanghai renmin chubanshe, 1992), 625.
2   The sexagenary cycle derives from Heavenly Stems, which are associated with yin and yang and Five Elements, and Earthly Branches, which are connected with the Chinese zodiac. Since the first Heavenly Stem is *jia* and the first Earthly Branch is *zi*, the cycle is known as a *jiazi*. A *jiazi* is also popularly known to be a full lifespan.

8

Reaching beyond Peasant Life

W HEN my husband was condemned as a counterrevolutionary, I
was the warehouse keeper of our production team. Ever since
the establishment of the high-stage cooperative in our village,
I had been in that position. After my husband was condemned, I
became worried that this position made me more vulnerable to unreasonable charges. Somebody could deliberately sabotage the warehouse and put the blame on me because I was now the dependent
of a counterrevolutionary and had the motivation to harm collective
property. So I talked to the team leader and begged him to replace me
with someone else. At first he refused, saying that he trusted me. A
little bit later, he was told by the brigade that I should be replaced. I
was really thankful when I was relieved of the responsibility.

The person who replaced me as warehouse keeper ran into
problems, and she resigned. The same thing happened to the second
one. They complained about the non-stop responsibilities, on the one
hand, such as having to open the warehouse when somebody needed
to get pig-feed grain during off-work hours. On the other hand,
villagers complained about the warehouse keeper's failure to take

care of harvested crops whenever there were instances of rotten grain because it had not been dried properly in sunny weather.

When the warehouse was under my care, I also ran into such problems. Yet I dealt with the problems differently. First, I did not complain about the responsibility of having to work during off-work hours. I was nice to the people who needed to get the pig-feed grain they deserved. Second, I tried my best to take advantage of sunny weather to dry harvested grain. There were still instances of rotten grain, but most people showed their understanding. If a few complained, I did not react emotionally. I understood that harvested grain was the result of collective sweat and it hurt to see the stores become rotten.

When the Jifei event was over, the team leader begged me to take over the warehouse again. The warehouse keeper at the time was reacting strongly to complaints and most people were not happy with her. I thanked the team leader for his trust but told him that I did not want to do it. I said to the team leader that now that I no longer had my mother's help, I was needed at home and did not have the time and energy to do a good job as the warehouse keeper. I also said that I had served already and that there were many capable people in the team who could do the job.

The team leader then called a meeting of all adults in the production team. At the meeting, he asked people to nominate a warehouse keeper. Many people nominated me. I thanked them and explained why I could not accept the nomination. The team leader then asked for an open vote at the meeting. He said, "All those who want Linshe to be the warehouse keeper, raise your hand." Everybody present at the meeting raised his/her hand. Taking care of the warehouse thus became my responsibility again. I served in the position until the Family Responsibility System was introduced to our production team. Under the Family Responsibility System, the warehouse was no longer necessary, because each family took care of its own harvested crops.

One year after I took over the warehouse-keeping job again, I encountered a serious problem. That year, our production team was required to send a certain number of able-bodied people to a river-widening project sponsored by the commune. Normally, such a project was popular because it was in a slack season and an opportunity for people to earn work-points. This particular time, however, the team leader had difficulty finding enough volunteers for the project. This was in the latter part of the 1970s, and many younger people were working in local industries. Workers for a public project usually brought along their bedding and a cook and stayed at the project. Those who could do so were usually unmarried or did not have children to look after at home.

That year, to fulfill the quota given to our team, the team leader asked me and three other women to work at the project. The four of us all had children and a house to take care of. Unlike the others, who slept in local people's guest halls, we came home every night. The project was in the Waigang direction and it took us about forty-five minutes to walk there in the morning and another forty-five minutes to walk home after the day's work.

Before I accepted the job at the commune project, I told the team leader that the surplus grain in the warehouse had not been dried enough. I said a few more sunny days were needed to dry it. The team leader and his associates said that the project would take only a couple of weeks and that a couple of weeks would not create a problem.

While I was away working at the project, it rained a lot. The rain created much dampness on the cement floor inside the warehouse. After the project was over, I immediately went to the warehouse and put my hands into the grain pile. I felt it was warm inside the pile. When I shoveled to the bottom of the pile, I saw that dampness had ruined a thick layer of the grain. I wept and was ready to take the responsibility. But the team leaders comforted me and said that the problem was not due to my negligence. At that time, such incidents had to be reported to the brigade or the commune authorities and those who were responsible would be criticized. But the team leaders did not report this incident to the authorities. They simply threw the rotten grain into the team's ponds as food for fish.

CHAPTER 8

SHEZHEN

When my husband was shut up, my children, particularly Shezhen and Shezhu, who were going to school at the time, were confused. Slogans of "Down with Chen Xianxi" were painted and hung everywhere—on the walls of public buildings such as pig farms, bridges, brigade and commune offices, schools, and stores. Everywhere my children went or looked, that was what they saw. They had become "son and daughters of a counterrevolutionary." While other schoolchildren wore armbands indicating they were Red Guards or Little Red Guards, my children were rejected by such organizations.

Shezhen went to school intermittently while working in the fields for work-points. One day in the autumn of 1969, she returned home from school very excited. She told me that on her way home through Zhuqiao Town, she had seen sewing machines on sale in a store. She was told that in order to buy the machine, we had to get a letter from the brigade authorities. We also had to use "industrial coupons" for the machine. We had enough industrial coupons for the machine from our rations and from selling pigs. I went to the brigade authorities for the letter. A brigade leader asked me why we needed such a machine and I replied that my elder daughter wanted to learn to sew. He was not happy and asked further why my daughter did not concentrate on schoolwork and instead wanted such an expensive machine. He even lectured me on how to raise a child properly. He said, "Kids are unreasonable. You should not buy what a kid asked you to buy." I waited in the office patiently. He grudgingly wrote the letter and stamped it with the official brigade seal. I walked out with tears in my eyes. I knew he had treated me this way because of my husband's status.

My father and I carried the sewing machine home on a shoulder pole. We did not know anything about the machine. Shezhen read the instructions and started to sew on old cloth. The machine had a foot pedal. When Shezhen first pedaled the machine, it jammed quite often. She had to learn to coordinate her legs and hands.

One day around the Chinese New Year of 1970, Shezhen tried to take care of a jam by taking off the tiny screw on the bobbin case. The

154

tiny screw dropped from her hand and disappeared. It was so small that we could not find it, even though the whole family helped to look for it. The machine was in our bedroom, where the floor was made of wood planks. We suspected that the screw could have slipped through the cracks and fallen under the wood floor. We took off one plank of the wood floor where Shezhen had dropped the screw, but did not find it there.

I took Shezhen to a tailor in our village. He worked in a tailor shop in urban Jiading, but was home for the holidays. I thought he might have extra screws to share with us or that he could tell us where to buy one. Surprisingly, he told us that there was no replacement for the screw and that the machine was useless without it. Shezhen cried hard, for we had paid more than 160 yuan for the machine and it had not done anything useful.

I wondered about what the tailor said. Why would manufacturers not sell replacement screws? It did not sound right. The next day, we went to Zhouqiao Comprehensive Store in Jiading Town. A shop assistant took out a tray of bobbin case screws. Each screw cost three cents. We were so happy that we bought several in case we dropped one again. Shezhen learned to use the machine quickly. She sewed shoe soles at first. Then I cut simple patterns of short underwear and she sewed them together.

Shezhen graduated from middle school in 1970. There was no high school at the time, so she became a full-time peasant. Working in the fields had proven to be very challenging for her. She did not complain and tried hard. She sweated profusely. In summertime, sweat could soak her clothes entirely, leaving no dry spot. She also attracted bugs like a magnet. In early morning and evening when we worked in the fields, she was bitten so badly that her face was swollen with bug bites. She was also afraid of snakes and leeches. I remember the first time she found a leech hanging on one of her legs. She jumped out of the rice paddy and cried out loudly. Some villagers still remember this incident today. They say, "How could this kid who was frightened by a leech be so daring as to live and work in a foreign country?"

In 1971, Zhuqiao Commune opened a clothes-making factory. The factory was housed in a confiscated house in Wangjialong. The old house had been renovated and an extension was added to the original house. The new factory was looking for people who had sewing machines or sewing experience. I talked to Shezhen about the factory. When she said that she was interested, I asked the team leader to consider Shezhen as a candidate, and she was recruited into the factory.

At the time, I had not thought that Shezhen would have any opportunity other than working in the fields. The trade of tailoring at least would keep her away from the harsh labor in the fields. After she entered the factory, I talked to an experienced tailor who was working in the same factory. He agreed to accept Shezhen as his apprentice. I bought some meat and cookies and Shezhen presented them as gifts to recognize this experienced tailor as her master.

Her work at the clothes-making factory earned work-points. Just as in the production team, her working hours were recorded. Apprentices were assigned lower values for their working hours than those of experienced tailors. They were then paid accordingly at the end of the year. What Shezhen earned from the factory helped to keep us in the black.

In the clothes-making factory, Shezhen worked on an assembly line, with each person making only a part of a piece of clothing. In her spare time Shezhen learned from her master how to sew together a shirt or a pair of pants. Since the factory had electric sewing machines, she did not have to bring her own machine to work. Her master cut cloth into patterns for her and she sewed them together. Very soon, she was able to sew together the most complicated clothes such as a man's Zhongshan jacket.

Shezhen had Sundays off from the factory. On her days off, she followed her master and worked in private homes. At that time, people in our area still depended on homemade cloth for their clothing. Once a year, families asked tailors to their homes and had their clothes made that way. At the customer's house, while Shezhen's master measured and cut, she sewed on the machine he carried to the house on his bike. The customer family provided lunch, afternoon snacks, and supper for Shezhen and her master. In addition, the family they worked for paid each of them two yuan for a day of service. During the Cultural Revolution, young people from urban areas were sent out to the countryside and two girls from Jiading Town came to our hamlet. In 1973, one of these girls went to the Shanghai Foreign Languages Institute. At that time, those who attended colleges had to be recommended by ordinary people in various walks of life, so college students were called "worker-peasant-soldier students." In 1974, recommendations for colleges were taken again and the clothes factory recommended Shezhen. When she filled out the application form, we told her to put in Shanghai Foreign Languages Institute simply because her friend was there. Because Shezhen was a country girl and had never lived away from home, we thought it would be better for her to go to a place where she already knew somebody. For her choice of a major, her father said that the English language was used by many countries. So although her friend majored in Spanish, Shezhen put English down as her preferred major.

Shezhen took a written test at Zhuqiao Commune headquarters. Then she was called to urban Jiading for an interview. Her father accompanied her to the interview, which was conducted by teachers from Shanghai Foreign Languages Institute. In August, a letter informing Shezhen of her enrollment by the Institute was mailed to our home.

After Shezhen got the letter, she decided to make some shoes for herself. I helped her to prepare materials for the shoe soles. She sewed the shoe tops on the sewing machine, now that she was very good at using it. She learned to make "hundred-layer" shoe soles, which were the best kind but the most time-consuming. We used homemade paste to stick a few pieces of cloth together. When the cloth was dry, we cut it into pieces according to the pattern of her shoe sole. Then she used the sewing machine to sew pure white cloth onto each layer of the hardened cloth. These layers were then stacked up and stitched together into thick soles. While ordinary hand-stitched shoe soles did not show layers, the shoe soles she made clearly showed the layers, many of them. So they were called shoes with "hundred-layer" soles. The two pairs Shezhen made, with my help, were indeed very pretty.

Onto the "hundred-layer" shoe soles she sewed pure black Venetian cloth, manufactured particularly as shoe-top material. Shezhen wore the shoes she made with her own hands in college.

My husband asked somebody from Chengdong Commune to drive Shezhen and her bedding to the Institute and he went with her. Shezhen became the first college student in our family. I thought of my father then, wishing that he had lived to see Shezhen go to college. When Father heard that colleges were recruiting students again, he had said to Shezhen, "You should go to college, instead of being a tailor for life." Father believed in Shezhen's potential as a student and wanted her to get as much education as possible.

In college, the government provided Shezhen with grain coupons and a stipend. She was able to save money from the stipend to pay her bus fare for weekend visits home. But Shezhen told me that after evening studies and before she went to bed, she was always hungry. Sometimes she and her roommates would go out to a small convenience store and buy the cheapest food, such as pickled turnip, to eat. After I heard this, I thought of ways to prepare her some snack food.

I had raw rice ground to powder at the brigade processing facilities and then I roasted the rice powder on our brick stove over a low fire. I had to be patient because rice powder burned easily. I also roasted sesame seeds harvested on our family plot. I had to find a way to crush the roasted seeds. I thought of the brigade herbal pharmacy, which had a hand grinder that ground dry herbs into powder. The man in charge of the pharmacy learned to be a Daoist priest from the same master as my father did. Because of that relationship, I addressed him as uncle. I explained to him what I needed to do. He gladly helped me clean the grinder, and I used it to grind the roasted sesame seeds.

I mixed the roasted rice powder and sesame together and bought one *jin* of white sugar. Shezhen brought the mixture and the sugar to school. She could either eat the rice-sesame mixture directly, with some sugar added to it, or she could use some hot water to make a hot snack out of the mixture and sugar. She liked it very much and told me that she shared it with her roommates.

In those days, there was a saying about people who went from the countryside to the city. The saying went like this: "The first year, you are 'earth-bound'; the second year, you are foreign; and the third year, you refuse to recognize your father or mother." But this did not happen to Shezhen. She continued to wear clothes she made out of homespun cloth and homemade shoes. Her father and I wanted to clothe her with store-bought materials, for we did not want her to look so "earth-bound," but she said that she did not mind. She was good at learning the English language, which she said was more important than one's looks. When she returned home, she still spoke the village dialect. During her summer vacations, she returned home and went to work in the fields. Although she earned no work-points, she volunteered to help with farm work.

Shezhen graduated from Shanghai Foreign Languages Institute in the summer of 1977 and was assigned a job in Beijing. The job was to teach English. She was told that if she did not accept the Beijing assignment, she could get a job in Shanghai. Shezhen and her father thought that the job in Beijing meant honor and a brighter future. I really wanted her to stay closer, but her father persuaded me, saying that as parents, we should think of our children's future more than anything else.

My husband and I accompanied Shezhen to urban Jiading and bought her a pair of leather shoes, the first pair of leather shoes in her life. We bought cloth from the department store in Jiading Town, and she made shirts, jackets, and pants for herself. We also bought wool yarn and she knitted herself a new sweater. Her tailor master helped her make a new cotton-padded jacket.

I dug up a handful of second-layer soil from our production team's farmland, wrapped it in paper, and put the packet in Shezhen's traveling bag. I asked her to put it into the first cup of boiled water she would drink in Beijing, wait until the dirt sank to the bottom, and then drink the water. That would help her more easily adapt to the new "water and soil" environment.

On the day Shezhen left Shanghai for Beijing by train, her father again asked a driver from his commune to take her to the train station. This time, Shezhu, Shebao, my husband, and I went together to see

CHAPTER 8

Shezhen off at the station. We all rode in a pickup truck. We put
benches in the truck for us to sit on. We went onto the platform.
When the train pulled away from the platform, Shezhu burst into
tears. She sobbed all the way home on the truck.

It took more than a week for Shezhen's first letter to reach us. I was
really worried. My heart hung in the air. In those days, there was no
other way to get in touch. It was that long-awaited letter that finally
allowed me to put my heart back in the place where it belonged.

SHEZHU

Just like Shezhen, Shezhu was helpful around the house very early.
When Shebao started school at the end of the 1960s, Shezhu looked
after her little brother when the two of them went to school together.
She learned to knit and do needlework. Both Shezhen and Shezhu
learned the simple aspects of the warping trade and were able to
replace me when I went home to cook during busy business seasons.

During school vacations, I would prepare raw rice for lunch in the
morning before I went into the fields. Shezhu would cook the rice.
When I returned from the fields for lunch, I would quickly stir-fry a
simple dish and that would be our lunch.

This was the time that the two city girls came to our village. They
lived in the side room right next to our house. The ownership of the
side room was in dispute during the first few years of the Cultural
Revolution. Big Aunt's family said that during the Land Reform the
side room was allotted to them. But the rebel leaders in the brigade
did not agree. While the matter was being investigated, the side room
was considered collective property. The city girls also prepared raw
rice before going into the fields and Shezhu helped to cook the rice for
them during her school vacations.

Eventually, the investigation found that the side room had been
allotted to Big Aunt's family in the records. When her second son got
married in the early 1970s, the family took back the room, so the two
urban girls moved to another house, which used to belong to a man on
"five protections" welfare (*wubaohu*). This gave old people or children

who did not have family support help from the collective with food, fuel, clothes, education, and burials. After such a person died, their house became collective property.

The two young people kept each other company. Neither of them dared to sleep in that house alone, because they said that it was haunted. Whenever one went back to her home in urban Jiading, Shezhen or Shezhu would spend the night there with the girl who was left behind. One night, Shezhen went to sleep in that house. When we had all gone to bed, Shezhen and the city girl knocked on our door. I opened the door and they rushed inside, with pale faces. They said that they had heard a knock on the door. They asked who it was, but got no answer. They were so frightened that they ran to our house. That night, the city girl, Shezhen, and Shezhu squeezed into one bed in our house.

When Shezhu finished middle school, she attended high school, which had become available again. During her high school vacations, she learned to do farm work and worked on public projects, one of which was to dig a new canal, the Dianpu Canal (Dianpu He), to connect Dianshan Lake (Dianshan Hu) with Huangpu River. The section she worked on was in Meilong Town in Shanghai County, which was more than eighty *li* away from home. The project lasted about a month and Shezhu and other workers stayed there for the duration.

After the project was completed, Shezhu came home and told me the following story. The section of the project she had worked on was a very sandy place. The project had begun in the coldest month of the year in Shanghai. When it rained, the ground froze at night. In the morning the sun came up and melted the frozen ground. The sandy soil combined with melted ice was difficult to walk on. Bamboo platforms were put down on the mushy ground. But the platforms were limited, so they were only for the trip with full baskets. When they carried empty baskets, they had to walk on the mushy ground. Workers had to wear high-top rain shoes due to the dampness. After ten or so hours carrying heavy loads of earth and having to walk in sticky soil with heavy, boot-like shoes, Shezhu's feet were covered by many blisters.

One day after supper, Shezhu took off her shoes to get ready for bed in a collective bedroom. She looked at her blisters with many people around her. Somebody said, "Shezhu is going to cry." With her eyes already full of tears, she burst into real sobs. She was only eighteen years old at that time, still young and tender. My heart ached when I heard the story. Peasant life was too harsh.

Those were the years that we grew three crops each year. In the heat of the summer, we harvested the early rice and put down the late rice and worked from about four o'clock in the morning until ten or eleven at night. We pulled up late rice seedlings in the early morning hours, cut early rice and moved it to the threshing grounds before lunch, prepared rice paddies in early afternoon, put down rice seedlings in late afternoon, and threshed early rice on the warehouse grounds in the evening under very powerful electrical lights called "sun lights." All of this was backbreaking and heavy labor. At the end of the day, having spent many hours in water, our hands and feet looked as if they were parts of floating dead bodies. Blades of rice seedlings were usually tough and coarse, like files. The skin on our palms was rubbed off as we pulled the seedlings from beds and transplanted them in paddies. At the end of this busy season, nobody had much skin left on their hands.

Even worse than the field labor in the harvesting-planting season was the work of unloading urban kitchen waste from a boat in summer heat. We regularly sent our boat to urban Shanghai to fetch kitchen waste that we used as fertilizer in our farmland. During the harvesting-planting season, urban areas had to hold their waste, for we did not have spare labor to fetch it.

As soon as the busy season came to an end, Shanghai municipality would send us the kitchen waste that had been accumulated. The waste came in big vessels and each production team got one. When the big boat arrived, we had to unload it and pile up the waste on our land for further decomposition before it could be used as fertilizer. The untreated waste, which contained rotten vegetables and meats, produced a lot of heat, which was in addition to the summer temperature of thirty-eight or thirty-nine degrees Celsius. The freight compartment in the vessel held about fifty tons of waste and was deeper than the height of a man. As we unloaded the packed waste shovel by shovel, a terrible rotten smell steamed out.

It took several hours to unload a boatful of waste. Everyone working at the task would be totally soaked by sweat; no part of our clothes would be dry. We would smell like decomposing waste ourselves at the end of the task. It would take several washings for our clothes to be totally clean from that smell.

By the latter part of the 1970s, in addition to the clothes factory, a number of commune-run factories had been established. After Shezhu graduated from high school, she was recruited into the Zhuqiao Farm Machine Plant, which made and repaired farm machines. She was apprenticed to a female master, who had formal training and was an experienced lathe operator, and learned to work on a lathe. Workers in commune-run factories were still peasants. In busy farming seasons, she came back and worked in the fields. In winter, she participated in more river-digging or river-widening projects.

Dining-room food at public projects was usually not very good. One time when Shezhu left for a public project, I prepared some condiments for her. I washed and cut pickled turnips into small pieces and stir-fried them. I put them in a jar with a lid for easy carrying and storage. I knew this would add a little home flavor to her dining-room food. Another time while she was working at a public project, I heard that somebody from the project had come back to the village to fetch something. I quickly made some glutinous rice cakes and asked that person to take them to Shezhu.

Life was hard. I tried as much as I could to help lessen the harshness.

SHEBAO

When Shebao was growing up, he liked to play outdoors and do boys' things. When the long school summer vacation arrived, I worried about his safety. There were rivers, ponds, and uncovered irrigation canals that boys, including Shebao, loved to play in on hot summer days. When we first had the electrical pump station, our irrigation canals were uncovered. Later on, some irrigation canals were turned into covered ones, which were huge prefabricated concrete pipes buried underground. On top of the pipes were packed dirt roads for pedestrians to walk on or for bikes and farm machines to ride on. Irrigation water passed through the concrete pipes to rice fields. At the junction of an open canal and a covered one was a deep well of water. We called this a "hidden well" because it was at the bottom of the open canal and was submerged when the open canal had water. The hidden well was a vertically installed prefabricated concrete pipe.

Like other village boys, Shebao liked to catch crabs and fish. One time, Shebao and two of his little friends went into an open irrigation canal to catch crabs and fish. Shebao was almost drowned that day. He was about ten years old at the time. He told me the following story only after he had become an adult.

This was late in the rice-growing season and the irrigation station had already stopped pumping water. There was still calf-deep water in the canals and thus fish and crabs continued to live there. Shebao and his little friends got down into one of the open canals, looking for fish and crabs.

The boys saw some fish and tried to catch them. As the fish swam away, the boys quickened their steps, chasing after the fish. Shebao was ahead of his friends. As he bent over chasing the fish, he did not realize that he was approaching the junction between an open canal and a covered canal. All of a sudden, he stepped into a hidden well. The water in the hidden well more than submerged him. He had not yet learned how to swim. But he somehow struggled to the surface of the water and managed to grab the rim of the concrete pipe with his little hands. But he was not strong enough to lift himself out of the water. As he struggled, he fell into the deep well again and again he emerged above the surface of the water, his hands grabbing the rim of the concrete pipe. His life was at stake.

One of his little friends was so frightened that he ran away. The other one, who was two years older, stayed with Shebao. He realized that Shebao had fallen into a hidden well. He lay flat on the ground right at the edge of the irrigation canal, stretched out his hand, and grabbed Shebao's hair. As he pulled the hair, Shebao tried again to lift himself up. With the extra help of his friend, Shebao finally got out of the water. The two boys realized that they had just been involved in a life-threatening incident and decided not to tell their parents about it. They took off their clothes and dried them in the sun. When the clothes were dry, they put them on and returned home, pretending that nothing had happened.

After Shebao was married, he told his wife about this incident. One day, many years after we had moved to urban Jiading, our whole family went to a wedding banquet in Wangjialong. At the banquet, Shebao introduced a person to his wife, saying, "This is the man who saved my life." When I heard this, I asked Shebao about it. Only then did he tell me the above story. I am very grateful to this man. His name is Sun Yongqiu. He saved my son's life.

A few times during summer vacations, Shebao went with his father to Chengdong Commune and spent a few days there. His father said that Shebao was very good. He was quiet and played by himself most of the time. He visited the broadcast station when it was not on the air. He would touch the switches and buttons and ask the station master what they were used for.

On his father's office desk, there was a cute little clock, a gift from a Japanese delegation. Shebao loved it and asked his father if he could take it home. His father said no. Shebao came home and told me about the clock. He asked me why his father would not allow him to take the clock home. I talked to his father. I said, "The Japanese presented the clock to you as a gift. Why can't you take it home?" His father said, "Because it was a gift to me as a commune leader. So it belongs to the commune, not to me."

Another time, Shebao's father told me the following story about a different visit to Chengdong.

One day my husband went down to a brigade for a meeting. Shebao went with him, riding on the back seat of his father's bike. After the morning meeting, his father was invited by a local peasant family to have lunch with them. His father accepted the invitation and took Shebao along. Shebao said that he wanted to go back to the commune canteen for lunch. His father explained it was too far and he had other business to take care of in that brigade after lunch, so they had to eat lunch with that family. Shebao refused to eat. The host family offered everything they could think of, but he refused. His father explained to the family that his son refused to eat not because what they cooked did not meet his appetite, but because he was being willful.

After lunch, the host family cut a watermelon and offered a slice to Shebao. He took it, threw it onto the ground, and smashed the melon slice with his feet. His father was so enraged that he spanked Shebao, the first and only time he did so to any of our children.

Both Shezhen and Shebao carried a streak of willfulness. After Shebao was married, Xiao Xie, his wife, one day asked me, "Where did Chen Shedong get his stubbornness?" I replied, "From me."

Another time that Shebao went with his father to Chengdong, they came home with a bag of Chinese plums (*pipa*), a very expensive fruit, and some other fruit. I asked my husband, "Why did you buy such fruits today?" My husband replied, "Our son did a good deed." He explained:

Shebao went out to play while his father attended to his business. Across the street from the commune headquarters was the commune auditorium. Outside the auditorium, there was a square where an open-air movie had been shown the night before. While playing on the square, Shebao saw a wallet. He picked it up and handed it in to the office of the commune. When the owner got his wallet back, he was very grateful. He said that the wallet contained quite a bit of money and grain coupons. To express his gratitude, he bought the *pipa* and the other fruit and gave them to Shebao as a reward.

My husband was very proud of what Shebao had done. When we asked Shebao why he handed in the wallet, he said, "because it was not ours."

Shebao graduated from high school in 1978. Exactly at the time he was finishing high school, the government issued the 104 Document, which said that one unmarried child in each family could replace a salary-earning father or mother when he or she retired.[1] Fathers and mothers could retire before they reached their retirement age if they had health problems. Some salary-earning fathers and mothers took advantage of the new policy, took early retirement, and gave their position to a son or a daughter. In our village, a bamboo craftsman worked in a bamboo crafts shop in urban Jiading. His son was already married when the document came out and could no longer take the opportunity. The bamboo craftsman retired and gave the position to his daughter. She became a shop assistant in urban Jiading.

I talked to Shebao about using the opportunity, but he did not like the idea. After Shezhen went to work in Beijing, she wrote letters home. In almost every letter, she encouraged her little brother to study hard in order to go to college. Around the same time, colleges restored the practice of recruiting students by administering entrance exams.[2] I believe both Shezhen's letters and the opportunity to compete for college enrollment significantly impacted Shebao. In his senior year, he became a serious student and was one of the famous three high-score achievers at his school. This encouraged him further.

His father bought him a complete set of study guides, ten books altogether, for the entrance exams. In the last half-year before he took the college entrance exams, Shebao worked day and night, studying hard. At night, I would urge him to go to sleep. He would say, "Mom, you go to sleep. I will go when I am sleepy." I would cook something and leave it there for him to eat as a midnight snack. I would sleep and wake up, finding him still at it. Every night, he worked beyond midnight. When summer came, Shebao put on high-top rain shoes and wore heavy pants and a long-sleeve shirt to protect him from mosquitoes while he studied. At the time, our windows did not have any screens. Only our beds were screened by mosquito nets.

In July 1978, Shebao took the entrance exams. He did well in the exams and was enrolled by Shanghai University of Science and Technology to major in electrical engineering. At the time, the university was expanding by incorporating Shanghai Technical College, which was also located in Jiading Town. Shebao was informed that the start of his college classes would be delayed until the merge of the two schools was complete.

In October 1978, the Yunzaobang River–digging project, sponsored by Jiading County, was recruiting workers. The production team leader tried to recruit Shebao because he needed one more person to fulfill the quota given to the team by the county. I said that my boy had not done much manual labor. The team leader said that was not a problem. So Shebao went and worked on the river-digging project.

They were on the project site for about a month. The workers brought their own cook to the site. After the project was completed and they came back home, the cook told me the following story.

All participants put in the same amount of grain and money for his or her daily meals. The three meals were offered at fixed times and there was no food otherwise. The cook said that Shebao would only eat a little at mealtimes. In the evening, he would ask the cook if there was anything to eat because he was hungry. The cook told me that he felt bad for Shebao, that he thought that he was a silly boy, but could not help him. All he could do was tell Shebao to eat more when the next mealtime came along. I guess Shebao went to bed hungry many times during that month.

He was an innocent boy. In the days when food was rationed, people learned to eat as much as they could whenever they had an opportunity. Shebao was born in 1962, which was after the years of the Great Leap Forward, and did not experience the severe hunger. At home, although we were not any richer than other peasant households, he never experienced a shortage of food. I am glad that this collective project was the only one he had to work at.

Shebao finally received the notice to start his college career after the Chinese New Year in 1979. He became the second college student in our family. He worked hard and lifted himself out of the fate of being a peasant.

MOVING BEYOND THE ANCESTRAL COMPOUND

In 1968, my cousin Zhongming, my uncle's elder son, got married. Zhongming was working as a Chinese violinist in the Beijing Opera Troupe in Shanghai. His wedding involved new practices such as distributing "wedding candies." Both the bride's and groom's families gave candies to each person present at the banquet. Candies were also given to all households in the village and to colleagues and friends of the bride and groom. In fact, beginning in this period, when asking somebody when he or she was getting married, the question became "When will I eat your candy?" Since the sedan chair had been destroyed during the Cultural Revolution as an "old thing," the bride now got to the groom's house either on a bike or on a "sedan chair with a tail," which was a boat, whose propelling oar looked like a tail.

Zhongming's wedding continued the tradition of having unmarried girls as maids accompanying a bride. Shezhen served as one of the bridesmaids. The practice of giving gifts to the bride continued, too. Elder relatives presented meeting-ritual money at a ceremony where the bride was introduced to the groom's relatives. After the wedding ceremony, the bride presented appreciation gifts, which were face towels at that time, to the groom's relatives who had given her money gifts.

The wedding also retained the tradition of having a party in the bridal bedroom. At the party, people counted pieces of homemade cloth, pieces of clothing, and pairs of handmade shoes inside the furniture the bride brought with her. Zhongming's bride, Ah Juan, did exquisite needlework. Neighbors and relatives admired the shoes she made and sang her praises.

When Zhongming got married, his family's bedroom, which was in the southwest quarter of the West Compound, was partitioned into two rooms, one as the bridal bedroom and the other as the bedroom for Zhongming's mother and younger sister. His younger brother and father slept in the side room attached to the East Compound. That room had been my grandmother's living quarter. Grandmother now slept in the guest hall right outside our main living quarter.

By the early 1970s, my uncle's second son, Hanming, had started to date a girl and needed his own space. The family applied for a homesite and was granted one right in front of our West Compound. A three-room house was built. One of the three rooms was used as the bridal bedroom, the middle one as guest hall, and the other one as kitchen. Hanming got married and established a home in the new house.

Around the same time, the elder son of Ah Bing, who occupied the northwest quarter of our compound, was also old enough to get married. Ah Bing's family of five people—he, his wife, two adult sons, and a teenage daughter—all slept in one bedroom. The crowded living conditions made it very difficult for the sons to find wives. To make the situation even worse, Ah Bing's family had been categorized as "landlord" in the Land Reform. During the Cultural Revolution, landlords were regarded as "class enemies" and children of such families had difficulty finding spouses.

In 1974, Ah Bing applied for a homesite and was granted one away from our compound, on the west side of the production team's warehouse. At that time, it was a piece of cropland. About ten years later, that piece of cropland would be filled with new houses. There had been very little house building before the 1970s, so housing conditions had become very crowded for most families.

Ah Bing tore down the northwest quarter of the West Compound to get the building materials for the new house. Ah Bing shared the ownership of the guest hall with us, and this was also torn down. The guest hall had seven beams. According to tradition, beams should not be cut in half, for that would hurt posterity. Ah Bing's wife asked me if they could take four beams, while we took three. Her reason was that their class classification made it very difficult for them to get building materials, which were in shortage at the time, and that it might be easier for us to get them. I agreed. So they took four beams. Using the same reasoning, they asked for the wooden plaque that carried the *Dun Hou Tang* inscription. I also agreed to let them have that. The plaque was made of very good wood and was big enough to be turned into window frames.

Ah Bing built a seven-beam house that had three sections. The middle section was the guest hall and the two sections on the sides were partitioned into kitchen-dining rooms and bedrooms. The house would allow his sons to marry and establish families in the two sections while sharing the guest hall.

The new and bigger house helped Ah Bing's elder son to find a wife, a woman from Jiangsu. At that time, living standards in the Shanghai area were higher than in other places such as Jiangsu. Young women from poorer places tried to move into Shanghai through marriage and were willing to lower their criteria, which included tolerating the landlord class label.

After the guest hall was torn down in 1974, our main living quarter was very exposed on the west side. Since that wall was not meant to be an outside one, it was not as thick and solid. Northwest winds in winter made us very cold inside and heavy rain pounded the exposed wall and brought dampness into the house. When strong winds blew, we felt the wall shaking, as if it were going to fall down.

In the autumn of 1975, my husband and I built a two-story house on the site of our original guest hall. Since we only had one son, our old homesite was supposed to be enough, so we could not get any more land to build on, nor could we apply to move to a new homesite. We built a two-story house because living in the back of the compound all our lives had made us long for some living space that offered more sunshine in winter and more breeze in summer. We used the upstairs room as our bedroom and the one on the ground floor as our guest hall. We removed the partition in the extension and turned it into our kitchen and dining room. My grandmother started to sleep in our original living quarter, which was now between the two-story house and the extension.

In 1979, the side room, which stretched southward from our main quarter, was torn down. Kaiyuan, Big Aunt's second son, had returned from Beijing and now worked as an engineer in urban Jiading. He and his wife had two children, so the side room was no longer big enough for the family. He got a new homesite, tore down the side room for its building materials, and had a new house built at the east end of the village, near the Coal-cinder Road.

After the side room was taken down, it created an open space on our south side. We put in a window on that wall, which finally allowed sunshine to come into our old living quarter. Our compound had been torn apart. The remaining southeast and southwest quarters and the west side room would be torn down in the 1980s.

NOTES

1 The 104 Document is titled "Guowuyuan guanyu gongren tuixiu, tuizhi de zanxing banfa" [Provisional regulations of the State Council on retirement and resignation of workers], May 24, 1978. In Sun Wanzhong et al., eds., *Zhonghua renmin gonghegou ling: 1949 nian shiyue-2001 nian siyue* [Directives of the State Council of the People's Republic of China: October 1949–April 2001], vol. 1 (Changchun, Jilin: Jilin renmin chubanshe, 2001), 842–44.

2 See the front-page article titled "Gaodeng xuexiao zhaosheng jinxing zhongda gaige" [Important reforms for recruiting students into institutions of higher learning] and the editorial titled "Gaohao daxue zhaosheng shi quanguo renmin de xiwang" [To do a good job in college recruitment is the hope of the whole nation] in *Renmin Ribao* [People's daily], Oct. 21, 1977.

9

Changes in the Family

M Y grandmother passed away in 1979. She was eighty-nine years
old.

When Grandmother was young, she was a very active
woman. She had walked all the way to urban Shanghai. She was also a
curious person and would go long distances to visit places and attend
temple fairs. When Chairman Mao died in 1976, there was a funeral
meeting on the grounds of the brigade headquarters. We were told
that the brigade had a TV set from which we could watch the funeral
ceremony in Beijing. I asked Grandmother if she was strong enough
to go with me to watch the funeral on television. She said that she
would not be able to walk the distance, which was about one *li* away
from our house and would take a normal person less than ten minutes.

I went to the funeral meeting. When I came back, Grandmother
asked me how we could see an event happening in such a faraway
place as Beijing through a "land pool." She referred to television as
a "land pool" because the pronunciation of television in our local
dialect is *tian*, which means "land," and *chi*, which means "pond" or
"pool." I explained, "Television is a wired box with a screen. Just like

a movie screen, which you have seen, the television screen shows moving pictures of the event in Beijing." After listening to my explanation, Grandmother nodded.

Grandmother did not get out of bed much during her last two winters. She complained about cold and preferred to stay in bed. When the weather was warm, in spring, summer, and autumn, she lived a normal healthy life, getting up with us in the morning and going to bed at night. She took turns eating her meals with us or with my cousins, Zhongming and Hanming. In winter when she stayed in bed, Zhongming and his wife brought her food one day; Hanming and his wife brought her food another day; and I brought her food for two days. Every two weeks or so in the last two winters, Little Aunt would come to help shampoo Grandmother's hair, clean her and change her clothes, and cut her nails in the warm sun. We would offer to help Grandmother do those things, but she would say, "No. Wenlin [Little Aunt] should be coming." Little Aunt was a filial daughter, and Grandmother was never disappointed.

Grandmother had outlived her two sons. My father died in 1972 and my uncle died in 1975. Her elder daughter, Big Aunt, was sick with stomach cancer at the time and left this world soon afterward.

Grandmother was a strong, bold, and decisive woman. She was widowed in her thirties, but she did not get remarried and leave. Instead, she ignored the conventions that limited many women in that society by openly taking in a bachelor man. Together with that man, Grandpa Bai, she maintained the family and raised her four children. Grandmother lived a full life. She worked in the fields until she was in her seventies. She lived independently until she moved to our guest hall to make room when Zhongming got married. After that, she had to depend on me and on my cousins for food because she no longer had her own stove. She never had any major illness. In the last few days of her life, she ate very little and became very weak. She died like the flame of a lamp that had exhausted the oil in it.

When Shezhen left for Beijing after having spent the Chinese New Year of 1979 at home, Grandmother said to her, "Shezhen, I now say farewell to you. When you come back next time, I will not be around." Shezhen said, "Taitai, don't say such a thing. I will be back around next Chinese New Year to see you." Grandmother was right. In June of the same year, she passed away.

This was after the Cultural Revolution, so incense, ceremonial candles, and paper money were available again on the market, and some traditional practices had been restored. Grandmother's body was moved from our main quarter to our guest hall. A memorial table was set with incense and candles right next to her remains. Grandmother had her "longevity" clothes made when she was still strong. We cleaned her body and put the clothes on her.

Grandmother's body rested in our guest hall for two days. My cousins and our neighbors, who offered to help, rode bikes to various places to inform Grandmother's relatives of her passing away. As Grandmother's children, we stayed up the whole night. The women wailed, narrating Grandmother's life stories. Every time one of us wailed, paper money was burnt. Male relatives stayed up and played cards to kill time.

We mourned Grandmother by wearing a long piece of white cloth at the waist and a black armband. Great-grandchildren of Grandmother's, such as my children, wore black armbands with a piece of red cloth stitched to it. The red cloth was to show that Grandmother was very lucky, for she had a fourth generation to mourn her. The second day was the formal funeral service. Many relatives came to offer condolences. My cousins and I hired two professional chefs and sponsored a funeral banquet for all the relatives and neighbors.

Grandmother's body was cremated at the West Gate Cremation Station. I took back the ash box and put it in our extension, where my mother's and father's ash boxes were. I represented my father, who was Grandmother's eldest son. Grandmother lived her last years with us and died in our house. I did my share in taking care of Grandmother. I always remembered what my father had said to Grandmother before he passed away and I carried out the promise my father had made to his mother.

DAUGHTERS' ENGAGEMENTS

In 1979, both my daughters were engaged. My husband and I had confidence in both of them and did not try too hard to interfere with their spousal selection. When Shezhen was going to college in Shanghai, one of the teachers at Liming School expressed a desire to pair her with his son. The teacher asked Ah Juan, Zhongming's wife, to talk to me about it. I knew the teacher, a fine and kind man, and had heard that his wife was also a teacher in a school in urban Jiading. I also learned that their son was in military service at the time and afterward would be working as a salaried worker. At that time, a salary-earning person was much better off than a peasant, who earned work-points. So I talked to Shezhen about this. Since she did not outright reject it, she and I, accompanied by Ah Juan, went to visit the teacher's home in urban Jiading one evening.

We met the teacher's son, who was on a home visit from the army. He was a very quiet and reserved young man. After that, Shezhen and he wrote a couple of letters to each other. Then, one weekend, Shezhen came home from college and said that she was still young and had decided not to pursue the relationship any further. I was fine with that. I told Ah Juan to tell the teacher's family about Shezhen's decision.

This teacher really liked Shezhen. After that, every time my husband or I ran into him, he would inquire about how Shezhen was doing. He admired young people who pursued scholarly endeavors and praised Shezhen when he heard that she had become a university professor in Beijing and later on when she went to the United States for graduate work. When his younger son passed the college entrance exams and became a college student, he told me the news with pride in his eyes.

Sometime after Shezhen started working in Beijing, we could tell from her letters that a married couple, both of whom were teachers at her school, were very kind to her. She went to their home to watch TV. They invited her to their house for dinners on holidays. Later on, we learned that she was helping their daughter and son with their English lessons. I told my husband that the couple in Beijing had taken a particular interest in our daughter.

When Shezhen came home for the Chinese New Year in early 1979, I asked her about this particular family. She took out a photo and showed it to me. She said that the young man in the photo was Zhou Wei, and he was the elder son of this family she had mentioned in her letters. She told me that when she was planning her trip home, Zhou Wei went to a photo studio and had a photo taken for her to bring home and show us. She added that when he went to get it, he realized that the photo, only one inch in size, was too small for me and my husband, so he asked the studio to make a two-inch print. Listening to her explanation and holding the photo in my hand, I thought, "He is a thoughtful young man."

The following fall, my husband found a way to go to Beijing. At that time, he was one of the main cadres in Chengdong Commune and had some decision-making power. He had learned that Beijing Agricultural Exhibition Hall was having an important exhibition, and he decided to visit it. Part of the reason he wanted to go was to meet Zhou Wei in person.

My husband visited Shezhen in Beijing and met Zhou Wei and his family for the first time. He came home and told me that Zhou Wei was indeed a pleasant and thoughtful young man. It was Zhou Wei who gave detailed directions to my husband to get to the Agricultural Exhibition from Shezhen's school. My husband visited Shezhen's campus, ate meals at her dining room, and met some of her colleagues, who spoke highly of her. He came home and told me everything about her workplace.

That same year, Shezhu came home and told me that a young man working in the same factory, the Farm Machine Plant, had shown her a lot of unusual fondness. She told me who this young man was. Although I did not know the young man, I knew of his mother, who had the reputation of being a very tough woman. I told Shezhu that this was not a suitable family for her to marry into, because she had too soft a heart. When her feelings were hurt, all she knew was to cry. She would not fight back. I was afraid that she would be easily hurt as a daughter-in-law in that family.

A few days later, Shezhu's master came to visit me. The master said with confidence that the young man was smart and pleasant. She tried to persuade me to give my consent to Shezhu. The master added that Shezhu was also fond of the young man. That is, the attraction was mutual.

My husband was more open-minded than I. He said that we parents should leave such decisions entirely to our children. He added that our daughter was choosing to live the rest of her life with the young man, not the mother of the young man. I also realized that Shezhu was not happy with my decision, although she did not fight back or argue with me. So I gave in and told her that I was no longer blocking the development of the relationship.

Then on the first day of the tenth month on the peasant calendar (*shiyuezhao*), I held a ceremony to remember Grandmother. This is the day people make offerings to a loved one who died within the previous year. Little Aunt and some other relatives came for the ceremony. After lunch, at which we made offerings of food and burned paper money for Grandmother, I stayed home because I had relatives visiting. About mid-afternoon, I was making a snack for my relatives when one of my neighbors came and told me that somebody other than Shezhu was working in our family plot. It was her boyfriend, Ah Ming.

I had cut the rice on our family plot the day before and planned to bundle up the rice stalks and bring them to the threshing ground after my relatives left. Shezhu was aware of my plan when she went to work in the morning, so she brought Ah Ming with her to help bring in the rice. They rode their bikes straight from work to our family plot without making a stop at my house. After the relatives left, I joined them in the field. That was the first time I met Ah Ming.

BUILDING ANOTHER HOUSE

One day in November of 1980, I was working in the fields when my husband came on his bike to see me. This was unusual, so I was puzzled. He called me out of the field and told me that he thought we should raise our old living quarter into a two-story house in order to get another bedroom on the second floor. When I asked him why he was in such a hurry, not even waiting until I returned home in the evening, he said that he had received a letter from Shezhen that day, informing us that she and Zhou Wei planned to get married the following January and to come home together during the Chinese New Year holiday. My husband said that when Shezhen and Zhou Wei came home, we needed at least one more bedroom. He explained that it would take time for new walls to dry.

I agreed with my husband. He started to buy building materials such as bricks, pre-fabricated concrete beams, wood, and glass for windows. We hired brick masons and carpenters, and building began before the month of November ended.

We carefully took down the old house, which was between the two-story house and the extension, and re-used the bricks and wood beams in the new building. Although we did not tear down the two-story house, its roof was affected because it had to be connected with the new house. Consequently, our bedroom on the second floor could not be used during the construction. We closed the warping shop temporarily, removed the warping frame and its related equipment, and turned the guest hall into a big bedroom. We all slept on the floor with a thick layer of dry rice stalks as a mattress.

Ah Ming was of great help. He was a strong young man and attended to various matters on the site on our behalf. Our son, who was attending college at the time, came home during the weekend and brought some of his classmates to help. Many of our relatives, friends, and neighbors helped to mix mortar, to bring bricks and mortar to the brick masons, and to raise the roof beams. A few women helped me to prepare lunches, mid-afternoon snacks, and dinners for the artisans and helping relatives and neighbors. On the day when the roof beams were raised, we hired a professional chef, who cooked a banquet dinner for us.

House building is a very tense business. We hoped that Heaven would cooperate with us by allowing a span of days with no rain and that there would be no injury or accident. Every day, I worried about the safety of all the people helping and working for us. The most dangerous activities in house building were putting up the beams and completing the roof. When all the tiles were laid down on the roof, I took a deep breath. What was left was plastering walls, which was a much less risky job.

One afternoon after the roof was up, I was preparing an afternoon snack in Zhongming's kitchen and Ah Juan was helping me. I said that a stone had been lifted from my heart now that the building project was almost completed. Right after I said that, I heard some unusual sounds from the building site. I quickly stepped out of the kitchen and saw Ah Ming carrying a woman in his arms. The woman's hands and legs were limp and dangling as Ah Ming rushed out to the front road. It was a speechless scene of heavy steps and hurried activity. I quickly realized that it was Ah Du, wife of one of my husband's nephews. The limp body and the speechless scene suggested that it was a serious accident. Before I said or did anything, I fainted. I was carried to Zhongming's bed and then came to consciousness. My relatives tried to comfort me, saying that it would not be too serious, but to no avail. I fainted time and again.

Ah Du was rushed to the People's Hospital in Jiading in a truck that was helping with the house building. Every time I came to consciousness, I asked for details about the accident. This is what I gathered.

That afternoon, the brick masons were plastering the interior side of the roof. Wood planks were put up about two meters above the floor on the second level. Ah Du stood on the wood planks to pass up buckets of mixed lime mortar to the masons. The wood planks were not fastened and Ah Du knew that. She sat down on the wood planks after passing up one bucket. When the bucket was empty, she would stand up, get another bucketful of mortar from somebody below her, and pass it up again. She had been there doing this job for a couple of hours when she somehow got to a loose end of a plank, fell down to the floor, and became unconscious. Ah Ming was nearby and responded swiftly. He rode with Ah Du in the truck while my husband and several others rode their bicycles to the hospital.

By late afternoon, somebody came back from the hospital and told me that Ah Du had regained consciousness and had undergone several medical tests. Doctors said that she had no head injuries or broken bones, but she was asked to stay in the emergency room for the night for further observation.

I did not believe what I was told. I said, "You are telling me this just to comfort me." I said that I wanted to go to the hospital to see Ah Du personally. My husband and relatives realized that I would not believe them unless I saw Ah Du myself. So the truck driver made another trip and drove me to the hospital.

There, I saw Ah Du in the emergency room. She broke into tears and said to me, "Xin Mama, it was all my fault"[1] because she had learned that I passed out in response to the accident. I asked her how she was feeling. She responded that she was a bit dizzy. She said that the doctors told her that her dizziness should be temporary and would disappear gradually.

I was relieved a bit but remained worried for quite some time. For several months after the incident, I checked with her often, asking if she was still feeling dizzy. Indeed, she had not suffered any serious concussion or head injuries. In time, her dizziness disappeared. Only then was I totally relieved.

The house was completed by early December. In those days, both the interior and exterior walls were covered with lime mortar. It took a long time for the walls to dry. I remember that when Shezhen and Zhou Wei came home for the Chinese New Year at the end of January, the walls inside the new house were still a bit wet.

After the building was completed, we had two bedrooms on the second floor. I set up the warping shop again in the guest hall on the first floor. Parallel to the guest hall was another big room with a cement floor and big glass windows on both the north and south sides. Our kitchen and dining room were still in the extension we built in the early 1960s. On the second floor, we built a bathroom between the two bedrooms. Before this, the chamber pot had been placed inside the bedroom with no further privacy. Now the chamber pot was inside the bathroom. With the doors closed, we now had privacy while relieving ourselves.

9.1   Shezhen and Zhou Wei in the new bedroom, January 1981

For the new bedroom, Ah Ming put together a radio–tea table. Ah
Ming was very smart. He installed a radio under the tea table. We
bought two sofa chairs and placed them on each side of the radio–tea
table. Two people could sit down and enjoy music. We hired a carpenter to build a new modern bed (*Zhongshan chuang*). The modern
bed did not have a canopy-like frame to support a mosquito net, so for
the new bedroom, we put screens on the windows so no mosquitoes
could get inside the room. We also bought a nightstand and put it
beside the bed. This kind of furnishing was considered modern- or
city-style at the time. The bedroom was furnished for Shezhen and
Zhou Wei (fig. 9.1).

Outside the two bedrooms, we had a spacious balcony. Running water had arrived in the village several years earlier. Pipes were installed and we had a concrete sink built on the balcony so we had convenient access to running water upstairs.

WEDDING BANQUETS

Before the Chinese New Year's Day of 1981, Shezhen arrived home with Zhou Wei. They were really modern people and traveled from Beijing to Shanghai by plane. When Zhou Wei arrived at our house, many neighbors and villagers came to see him. It is the custom that villagers go to see somebody's bride or groom. That was also my first opportunity to meet Zhou Wei. I think he was surprised that so many people came to see him, but he did not seem bothered. He was a young man who had seen the world.

After Zhou Wei arrived in our house, my husband asked him to help plant two ginkgo trees behind our house. The piling of building materials, construction of scaffolding, and human activities during the construction had damaged the vegetation behind the house. After the house was built, we cleaned up the area and decided to plant a few new trees. At the time, the ginkgo tree was very popular. People believed that because the ginkgo tree provided a cooling effect, it was good for people with high blood pressure. My husband got two little ginkgo trees from one of his nephews in North Hamlet. Zhou Wei was given a shovel and he worked hard digging holes and planting the trees. The trees grew very healthily and rose straight into the sky.

Shezhen and Zhou Wei had already been officially married. Yet my husband and I still wanted to hold a banquet to announce their marriage to our relatives, friends, and neighbors and to provide an opportunity for everyone to meet our son-in-law. The wedding banquet was held on the fourth day of the Chinese New Year.

In preparation for the banquet, I made rice wine with the help of West River Uncle. We only made simple rice wine, not the raw sweet wine (*shengganjiu*) we had made for my wedding banquet, because the fermentation starter for the latter had to be made several months ahead of time. Zhou Wei told me that he loved the homemade rice wine. He said that it was one of the best wines he had ever tasted. After that, when I knew he was coming for a visit, I made rice wine for him. But during the hot summer months in Shanghai, the temperature is too high for rice-wine making. One time that he was coming for a visit in early June, I made rice wine in March. I squeezed and bottled the wine. When he came for the visit, the wine was still good.

We had seven tables of relatives and friends, about sixty people, at the banquet for Shezhen and Zhou Wei. I filled a water kettle with the homemade rice wine, warmed it on a coal stove, and asked Zhou Wei to pour wine for everyone at the banquet. My husband and I accompanied him and introduced him to all our relatives and friends. We also distributed wedding candies to everyone at the banquet and to all the families in the village.

My husband and I wanted to give Shezhen a special gift. She lived far away from us, so we could not buy her furniture, which was the most common dowry parents prepared for a daughter's wedding. My husband decided to buy a good wristwatch for Shezhen. A good watch meant a Swiss watch at the time. We had heard that Switzerland made the best watches in the world. My husband had been wearing a Swiss watch, which he bought secondhand, since the early 1950s, and the watch was still dependable. Imported watches, however, were not easily available. My husband sought help from a friend who had a relative working in a Shanghai watch shop. Through this connection, we bought a Swiss watch, which cost 190 yuan, as our wedding gift to Shezhen. At the time, my husband's monthly salary was forty-eight yuan.

The wedding banquet for Shezhu was in January 1982. In those days, young people in our area participated in collective wedding ceremonies, so that is what Shezhu and Ah Ming did. The collective ceremony, held in early October 1981, officially made them husband and wife (fig. 9.2). However, my husband and I still planned a wedding banquet for Shezhu, as we had done for Shezhen. We wanted our relatives, friends, and neighbors to know Shezhu was married.

With better living conditions, rural people were holding larger and fancier wedding banquets. As a result, the government issued policies

9.2   Collective wedding photo of Shezhu and Ah Ming, October 1981

that discouraged such banquets and the collective wedding ceremony was intended to replace the traditional wedding banquet. People, however, did not respond well to the government's call.

My husband was a commune leader at the time and was expected to follow the government policy and to lead by example. We decided that the wedding banquet for Shezhu would not exceed eight tables of guests, which for us rural people was already a small banquet. So my husband volunteered to pledge at a county-wide cadre meeting. His pledge drew derisive laughter from the audience, which included urban people, to whom eight tables of guests meant a grand banquet. They usually had one or two tables of guests for a wedding banquet. Following the meeting, the county authorities criticized my husband. Nonetheless, we still went ahead and held the wedding banquet for Shezhu with eight tables of guests.

Ah Ming's family brought over wedding gifts (*caili*), which included six hundred yuan and twelve pieces of homemade cloth.

His family also prepared the bridal bedroom with a new bed. We prepared a dowry for Shezhu, which included a wardrobe, a desk with a mirror, a quilt chest, a clothes trunk, a golden chest, two crimson-red square stools, two crimson-red benches, three wood wash basins, a chamber pot, and a bike. Bikes had become essential in young people's lives, because most worked in factories and depended on them for their daily commute. I helped Shezhu prepare several cotton-padded quilts for her new bedroom. She had new clothes made by a tailor, made new shoes for herself and Ah Ming, and knitted new sweaters. And, in the preceding years, she and I had made homespun cloth of various colors and patterns.

On the morning of the wedding day, Ah Ming's family sent a boat to fetch the furnishings, except for the golden chest. I boiled eggs, dyed them red, and put them in the new chamber pot, thus making it a "descendants' pot" (*zisuntong*). The cotton-padded quilts, with pretty satin covers, were strung over the two benches. Homemade cloth was put in the clothes trunk. Furniture drawers contained new shoes. The wardrobe contained new clothes and new sweaters. We put a handful of raw rice and beans into every other empty space in the furniture, to wish to the newlywed couple a plentiful life.

Before lunch, Ah Ming came, riding a brand-new bike, accompanied by his best men and several girls to escort the bride. At the lunch, Ah Ming was the guest of honor. My husband and I took him, accompanied by Shezhu, around the tables to meet our relatives and he poured wine for them. Senior relatives such as aunts and uncles gave him meeting-ritual money wrapped in red paper.

After the banquet lunch, Shezhu, dressed up in a red jacket, left for her new home, riding on the rear seat of Ah Ming's bike. She brought along several of her best friends as bridesmaids. She said goodbye to me and to her father with tears in her eyes. Shebao and Hanming, one of my cousins, went with Shezhu and carried the golden chest, which contained a few pieces of basic clothing for Shezhu and Ah Ming, nuts and fruits for the bridal party, and face towels for Shezhu to give as appreciation gifts to Ah Ming's relatives.

Sending Shezhu off to her new home was an emotional experience. Yet that experience was made much more emotional by the following incident. Shezhen had come home from Beijing right before her sister's wedding. We were very happy that she made it home for the event. The day after she arrived home, she went to Shanghai Foreign Languages Institute to get her college transcript. Shezhen wanted to go to the United States for graduate work.

Shezhen returned home that day and was very unhappy. The bureaucrats at the school said that they had not kept very good records during the Cultural Revolution and so in order to issue her a transcript, she had to obtain written letters of grades from all the teachers who had taught her. This was not easy, because the teachers had already started the school winter vacation. The only way to see them was to go to their homes, which were in every corner of urban Shanghai.

But Shezhen was determined. She decided to collect all the necessary letters and obtain the transcript before the transcript-issuing office closed for the Chinese New Year holidays. So, the next day, she went to urban Shanghai again. When she came home that evening, she was encouraged because the teachers she had seen all remembered her and gave her excellent grades in their written notes. But she had not been able to visit all of her teachers on that one day.

The next day was her sister's wedding day. It was also the last day before the transcript-issuing office closed for the holidays. She got up early and left for urban Shanghai again.

It was getting dark outside but Shezhen was not yet home. The last bus from Jiading to Zhuqiao was scheduled to stop at Wangjialong around 6:30 p.m. I went to the stone steps behind our house and saw the bus passing by. Then I went to the front road, hoping to meet Shezhen, who should have taken that bus home. It had become completely dark now, but she did not show up. I could no longer contain my emotions, and I went to the back of our house, away from all the guests, and burst into tears.

Shezhen had no place to spend the night in urban Shanghai and would have to come home that night. Now that she had missed the last bus, she would have to walk the eleven *li* from the Jiading bus station to our home in the dark. I discussed the matter with my husband and we decided to ask Qilong, one of my husband's nephews, to go and meet Shezhen. We told him that he should ride his bike slowly and watch out for Shezhen, who could be on the road anywhere between Jiading Town and our village. If he did not see her, he should go all the way into Jiading bus terminal and wait for the arrival of the last bus from urban Shanghai. Qilong finally came back with Shezhen, who had caught the last bus from urban Shanghai to Jiading Town. I will never forget that day.

Shezhen was disappointed because she had not come home with her college transcript. She did get the letters from all her teachers, but she failed to get the signature of the current English Department chair, which was needed for the office to issue her the transcript. It was only after the Chinese New Year holidays that Shezhen finally got her college transcript. I did not understand why she was so determined to study abroad. But I knew that once she decided to do something, she could not be persuaded otherwise.

VISITING FOREIGNERS

After Shezhu's wedding, Shezhen's foreign friends came to visit us. My husband made arrangements to have them picked up at their Shanghai hotel and driven to our home. Three foreigners came—a woman with the name of Annina and two men, one with a brown beard and the other with a black beard. Since the men had names that we could not pronounce, we referred to them as Brown Beard and Black Beard. Shezhen told us that Black Beard was from Pakistan and Annina and Brown Beard were Americans.

They did not speak a word of Chinese and we did not speak a word of English. Shezhen had to translate all the conversations during their visit. They stayed two nights and two days. Since this was in the middle of the winter season, we all wore cotton-padded clothing. But they did not. When we realized that they were not wearing enough clothes, we loaned them cotton-padded long coats, two of which were borrowed from our neighbors. We vacated the upstairs bedrooms for them and Shezhen. The rest of us put up temporary beds in the guest

9.3   Shebao and Shezhen on the balcony, early 1982. Photo by Annina Mitchell.

hall and slept there for the two nights.

They liked the food I cooked very much. I had kept some deep-fried pork and other meat dishes from Shezhu's wedding banquet and cooked fresh vegetables and fresh mushrooms we grew ourselves. They watched me cook and took pictures of our traditional kitchen with a brick stove.

We made several big rice cakes before Shezhen's friends came. When they were visiting, they helped to lay out the cake pieces on the balcony in the morning. I could see they really liked that, because they took out their cameras and shot quite a few pictures of the scene (fig. 9.3).

My husband arranged for Shezhen's friends to visit some factories and animal farms in Chengdong Commune one afternoon. The rest of the time, they went out walking in our crop fields. They toured our village and talked to people, with Shezhen translating. One old man, who had returned from Singapore before Liberation, still remembered a few English words and talked to them directly.

It was again my husband who asked a driver to take our foreign friends back to their Shanghai hotel. When they left, they told us, through Shezhen's translation, that they had visited many places in China, but their visit to our home had been the most interesting and meaningful.

BIRTH OF GRANDDAUGHTER

Shezhu was already pregnant when we held the wedding banquet for her. She continued to work in the Farm Machine Plant during her pregnancy. One morning before breakfast, Ah Ming came and told me that Shezhu had started contractions and was now on her way to the maternity ward in Zhuqiao Town. Ah Ming's brother was the tractor driver in his production team. In busy farming seasons, the tractor pulled a plow or a rake-roller that flattened rice paddies. In slack farming seasons, the tractor pulled a trailer and served as a transportation vehicle. Shezhu's baby was not due for another month, so they were unprepared. The only way Shezhu, who had already started contractions, could get to the maternity ward about four *li* from their house, was to ride in the trailer pulled by the small tractor.

I jumped onto the back seat of Ah Ming's bike and we rushed to the maternity ward. There, Shezhu gave birth to a baby girl naturally and smoothly. The baby was born one month before her due date. The nurse asked if we wanted to have her put in an incubator due to its early birth. I said no, because the baby came into this world with a loud and strong cry. We saw the baby after she was cleaned. She was tiny, but she was very active, with her legs and hands kicking and moving. Ah Ming and Shezhu trusted my opinion and did not put the baby in an incubator.

Before Shezhu breastfed the baby for the first time, I cooked some bitter herb (*huanglian*), dipped a cotton ball into its liquid, and rubbed it onto the baby's lips. We did that to all our babies when they were born. When a baby comes into this world, it should taste the bitter flavor first so that it won't be picky about food in the life that follows.

Shezhu's milk ducts were very tight. She had milk, but it would not come out. I asked Ah Ming to suck at her breasts. It was very painful and Shezhu cried. I told Ah Ming that it had to be done. He sucked until milk came out. At first, the milk was mixed with blood. Having a baby and raising a baby is not easy; it is quite a sacrifice. Shezhu produced very good milk. The baby was tiny, but healthy.

Ah Ming and Shezhu asked Shebao to come up with a name for the baby. Shebao came up with two names. One was the official name, Yang Xi, Yang being Ah Ming's surname and Xi meaning the morning sunshine. The other was a nickname, Beibei, which means "flower bud."

When Beibei was one month old, Shezhu brought Beibei to our house for the first time. According to local customs, as maternal grandmother, I was not supposed to be the first one to hold Beibei on her first visit. When I saw Shezhu approaching our house with Beibei in her arms, I asked one of our neighbors to take the baby from Shezhu. Only after that was I able to hold Beibei.

When Beibei was born, the government policy of "one child one family" was already in place. Being the only child, Beibei received much attention from her family. The family held a big banquet to celebrate her first birthday. In addition to the usual food for a banquet, Ah Ming also bought steamed buns (*mantou*) and sure-to-rise cakes (*dingshenggao*) for the occasion. Both were traditional foods carrying good wishes for the new baby. The common gift for a child's first birthday banquet was fresh noodles, which are symbolic of a long life. My husband and I brought ten *jin* of fresh noodles to the banquet in a big bamboo basket.

Ah Ming's family rented a big portrait of the Longevity Star. The portrait had one long-bearded smiling man sitting in the middle, with many plump-faced smiling babies surrounding him. On the morning of the banquet day, they placed a square table in the middle of their guest hall against the north wall. Above the table, they hung the portrait of the Longevity Star. On the table, they arranged piles of steamed buns and rice cakes and uncooked noodles and glutinous rice flour. Special longevity incense sticks and huge red candles were lit on the table.

Ah Ming helped Beibei kowtow to the Longevity Star on a soft mat while we and other guests gathered in the guest hall and watched. The table of food under the Longevity Star portrait remained there and incense and candles continued to be lit for the rest of the day.

Lunch followed the ceremony. The most important meal was the banquet dinner, which had many dishes, but the most essential one on a child's first birthday banquet was the noodle dish, again for the symbolic wishes for a long life. Bowls of noodles with glutinous rice balls were delivered to each family in the village as "helping-child noodles."

When I returned home after the banquet that evening, I brought back a basket of the longevity noodles. The next day, I cooked them with glutinous rice balls and delivered them bowl by bowl to the families in the West and East Compounds. This was to prepare our neighbors for Beibei's potential need for help when she came to visit us.

TRIP TO BEIJING

We learned from Shezhen's letters that she had been allotted an apartment right on the campus of her university. In September of 1982, I decided to visit Shezhen in Beijing. That same month, my husband was going to Guangzhou on a business trip. Today, we can buy a train ticket or a plane ticket in a travel agency just down the street, or our children can buy a ticket on the Internet. In those days, we had to go all the way to the train station in Shanghai to get a train ticket. So my husband got me a ticket when he got his. We also decided to leave on the same day. That way, I could go with him to the train station. At the station, he took a train going south while I got onto a train going north.

Shebao had written down Shezhen's Beijing address on a piece of paper, and I carried it with me. We sent Shezhen a telegram informing her of the train I was taking and the date and time it was scheduled to arrive in Beijing. The train coaches were numbered and the telegram also told Shezhen the number of my coach so that she would meet me on the platform inside the train station.

This was the first time I had taken a train. Since I had never traveled far away and alone, I was a little nervous. The train stopped at many places and the ride was more than twenty hours long. Whenever the train made a stop, people went down to the platform and bought local products from vending stands. Or they went onto the platform to stretch their legs. Since I was traveling alone and worried about losing my things, I did not dare to go onto the platform throughout the trip.

Among the things I brought with me was a bag of rice, about twenty *jin*. Beijing was in the north. I knew northern people received only a small portion of their monthly grain ration in rice. The rest was wheat flour and cornmeal. I planned to stay for two or three weeks and did not want to exhaust her limited supply of rice.

Sitting next to me on the train was a man traveling on a business trip. At mealtimes, he said to me, "You go ahead and eat. I will look after your things. When you come back, I will go and eat and you look after my things." He added, "You go first, because I want to have a beer with my meal and it will take me more time." That was a good arrangement. Other than going to the bathroom, the mealtimes were the only times I was away from my luggage.

Sitting on the train for more than twenty hours was very tiring. I was so tense that I did not close my eyes the entire night I spent on the train. When I got to Beijing, my legs were swollen.

When the train approached the Beijing train station, I became very nervous. I did not know if Shezhen had received the telegram. I thought to myself, if the train arrived and Shezhen was not on the platform, I would not know what to do. Although I had her address written down, I did not know how I could find the way to her place. I did not speak the Mandarin dialect, so I could not communicate with anybody in Beijing.

I had a window seat. As the train slowed down and approached the platform, I rolled down the window and stretched my head out to look. When the train stopped, I saw Shezhen jumping on the platform, having already spotted me. I was so relieved.

I was glad to see Shezhen's comfortable apartment with its own kitchen, bathroom, and little balcony. During my stay, Zhou Wei's parents invited me to their apartment and treated me to a dinner. One day, Zhou Wei's little sister came to Shezhen's apartment with a dish that their mother had cooked. I still remember the dish, which contained seaweed, peanuts, pieces of lotus root, and other items stewed together.

Shezhen and Zhou Wei took me to the Summer Palace, the Beijing Zoo, Tiananmen Square, and the shopping street called Wangfujing on weekends. At the zoo, we walked past a snake cage. Shezhen's face turned pale when she saw the snakes. It reminded me how frightened she was by snakes and leeches when she worked in the fields in Wangjialong. I was happy that she no longer had to deal with such things.

Zhou Wei bought me a ticket to take the train back to Shanghai. Shezhen and Zhou Wei accompanied me all the way to my seat inside the train coach. Zhou Wei was a very thoughtful person. He bought a padlock and a chain. He chained my travel bag to the seat and locked it. Zhou Wei said, "Now, Mom, you can move around in the train, get down to the platform if you want when the train makes a stop on the way, and go and eat your meals without having to worry about losing your bag." It worked very well. On my return trip, I was no longer nervous and moved around when I wanted.

When the train pulled into the Shanghai train station, I was not as worried. Shezhen had sent a telegram to her father, whose trip to Guangdong had been much shorter than mine, informing him of my arrival. The young man sitting next to me on the train was from Shanghai.

When the train rolled into the train station, I had unlocked the travel bag and lifted it onto my seat. The young man said to me, "Aunt, you have a pretty heavy bag. You go down to the platform and come around to the window. I will pass the bag to you through the window. That way, you do not have to carry the heavy bag through the crowded coach and down the steps." I thought that was a very nice offer. I thanked him. When the train stopped at the platform, I went down without the bag. But the minute I left my bag, I started to worry. What if he was a bad man? He could have arranged with somebody outside the window to get my travel bag before I got there. I said to myself, "I have been so careful throughout this trip. Why did I trust a stranger at the last minute?"

It did not take me very long to get to the window. As he had promised, the young man was holding my bag and waiting for me to get it from the platform. I thanked him profusely. I told myself that, after all, there were more good people than bad people in the world. After I thanked the young man, I turned around. There was my husband, who had come to meet me.

After the trip to Beijing, I became acutely aware that Shezhen worked and lived very far away from me. When Shebao graduated from college in January 1983, I told him not to get a job outside Shanghai. He listened and became a research professor of electrical engineering at his alma mater, Shanghai University of Science and Technology.

THE ANCESTRAL COMPOUND IS GONE

Up until 1983, Meifang's elder son and his wife had occupied the southeastern quarter of our old compound. Meifang, her husband, and her second son had moved out and built a house where Ah Bing's new house was. In 1983, the elder son applied for and was granted a new homesite near his brother's house. He tore down the old quarter and built a two-story house on the new homesite.

In 1984, Zhongming and Ah Juan decided to tear down their quarter and build a two-story house right next to our house on the west side. Their new house was to be a meter higher than ours. Traditionally, it was believed that the height of a house determined the prosperity of the family. This belief caused a lot of problems among neighbors in Wangjialong during the house-building frenzy of the 1970s and 1980s. My husband and I were aware of this belief, but decided to accept Zhongming's design. Shebao was working as a professor at the Shanghai University of Science and Technology. We knew that

9.4   The family home, when it was occupied by renters, 1990s

most probably he would establish a home in the urban area, so our village house would be kept as our ancestral home. I also believed that prosperity depended on the intelligence and diligence of the people in a family.

Taoming, Ah Bing's younger brother, owned the west side room. Because of the landlord label attached to the family, it was not easy for Taoming to find a wife, so he finally married matrilocally and moved to live with his wife's family. But he still inherited the side room. When Zhongming took down the southwest quarter, to which Taoming's side room was attached, Taoming tore down the room and took the reusable materials away.

Taoming did not do it without a complaint. He said that it was not right for everyone to move out and leave me, a woman, behind to stay on the home site of our common ancestors. I replied that this was not true, for Zhongming, a man, was also staying behind. But more importantly, I said that I did not drive them away and they could stay on or move back to our ancestral home site if they wished. Taoming's elder brother, Ah Bing, and his wife intervened and told Taoming to

9.5   A village similar to Wangjialong, late 1990s

shut up. They said that they moved out willingly and for the sake of
their growing family. With two sons getting married and establishing
families, their original home site was simply not big enough. Although
times had changed, the idea that only men were legitimate inheritors
was still strong in some people's minds.

Within ten or so years, the original compound we inherited from
our ancestors disappeared. In its place were two modern buildings,
one being our house (fig. 9.4) and the other Zhongming's house. The
descendants of our ancestors had built houses throughout the village
(fig. 9.5). Kaiyuan's new house was at the east end of the village, near
the Coal-cinder Road; Hanming's new house was in front of our
original compound; Ah Bing's new house was on the west side of our
village, and so were the houses Meifang's two sons had built.

NOTE

1   Xin Mama is a loosely-used term to call the wife of an uncle, who can be a parent's brother or cousin.

10

Farewell to Collective Life

I N the early 1980s, when Zhou Wei came to visit us during the Chinese New Year holiday, I was running my own warping shop inside our guest hall. I prepared lengthwise threads and reeled them onto a beam for home weaving. Zhou Wei had never seen a traditional warping shop, so he was very curious and took a picture of me while I was drawing lengthwise threads (fig. 10.1).

When I set up the warping shop, I ran into a problem. Our guest hall was two feet short of the required length of the warping frame. It was Ah Ming who helped me solve the problem. He made one end of the warping frame movable. During the day when I had business, I would move that end of the frame beyond the threshold of the guest hall so that I could have the perfect length. At night, I would move that end inside and close the door for safety.

Warping business had declined significantly. After Jinshan Petroleum Plant was established, synthetic clothing material was cheap to buy. Peasants were making more money by working in factories and engaging in sideline productions. The warping business was now reduced to making cloth for bedsheets and for simple work clothes.

10.1   Chen Huiqin in her warping shop, early 1980s

More and more young people could now afford not to wear home-made cloth, avoiding its association with earthiness and poverty. The warping business was becoming out-of-date.

My warping shop was just one of the many ways we used to increase family income. All of these were made possible by Deng Xiaoping's economic reform policies.[1]

PIECEWORK REWARD SYSTEM

Around 1980, the Dazhai system of recording work hours and appointing values to the work hours gave way to a piecework reward system, under which we earned work-points according to the pieces of work we completed. For instance, pulling up one bed of rice seedlings earned five work-points. Or cutting down a field of wheat earned ten work-points.[2] The calculation of work-points assigned to each task was based on the average number of hours taken to finish the job before the piecework reward system. Five work-points meant half a day's work. When the piecework reward system was implemented, it took less than half a day to complete either of those two jobs. People now had incentive to finish a job as soon as possible because the hours they spent on the job were no longer recorded or counted.

The piecework reward system turned out to be highly efficient. There was no more idling in the fields. People worked early mornings and late evenings. One day during the spring wheat-harvesting season of 1982, I delivered something to Shezhu's house early in the morning. I returned home, ate breakfast, and went into the fields right away. When I got there, some of the wheat had already been cut down. I went to the fields with wheat still standing. But at the beginning of every wheat field, a little bit of wheat had been cut down and a piece of clothing was put on the downed wheat. That meant that the field had been claimed by somebody. A total of sixty *mu* of wheat was cut down before noon that day. Before the piecework reward system, it would take a whole day and all the able-bodied workforce in the production team to finish the job. Some people earned twenty work-points that day.

I always wanted to earn more work-points whenever possible. One summer day, I was running a little fever, my whole body ached, and my legs were heavy. The production team leader was recruiting people to get manure from the brigade duck farm. The eleven production teams in the brigade took turns getting the manure as fertilizer. That afternoon, it was our turn. I said that I had a little fever and my legs were heavy. The team leader said that if I wanted to go, I could stay inside the duck farm and do the loading job. That way, I did not have to walk. I said I would go. I worked inside the duck farm, which was humid and hot, for the whole afternoon. I perspired so much that my clothes were dripping with sweat. My fever broke and disappeared while I earned work-points.

The piecework reward system also applied to sideline production, which was run collectively at first. Here is an example of how
it worked. The production team built thatched huts and grew mushrooms in them. Mushrooms needed to be covered by clay soil from
our farmland. Every one thousand *jin* of clay soil that had been dug
up, broken into two-centimeter diameter cubes, and brought to the
mushroom huts earned ten work points.

Mushrooms raised in Jiading County had a good reputation and
were sold to urban Shanghai and many other places.[3] Many production teams grew mushrooms to increase collective income. The more
collective income the production team earned, the bigger the unit
price for each work-point. With that understanding, most people supported collective sideline production and did not mind working hard.

Mushroom growth required warm temperatures. Since we did not
use heating or cooling mechanisms, we grew mushrooms only season-
ally. After the completion of the busy harvesting and planting season
in late August, we prepared the basic material for growing mushrooms, which consisted of pigsty manure and chopped dry rice straw.
The cement threshing ground was used to mix the chopped rice straw
with the manure. The mixture was covered by a big tarp and left
under the scorching summer sun for fermentation. Every other day or
two, we lifted the tarp and stirred up the mixture to give it air and to
facilitate the fermentation process.

When the basic material was fermented enough, we packed it
on bamboo shelves inside the huts, and then spread over the packed
mixture mushroom spores bought from Zhuqiao Mushroom Spore
Cultivation Farm. Onto the mushroom mixture we spread an inch-
thick layer of clay soil dug up from our farmland. The clay soil had to
be carefully broken into nuggets two centimeters in diameter.

One summer day in the early 1980s, I was digging clay soil when
Shebao came home from school and offered to help me since this was
a piecework job. I loaded the buckets with clay nuggets and he carried
them to the huts. The nuggets were weighed there and the amount
was recorded for reward under my name. Two full buckets of clay
nuggets weighed about one hundred *jin*. As I watched Shebao carry-

ing two buckets on a shoulder pole, I could tell that he was no longer a peasant boy. He walked with an effort. When I asked him if I should carry and he should help me break the soil into nuggets, he said no, adding that he was doing fine.

We worked until dark that day. The next morning, when Shebao got up, he said that he had sore shoulders. I took a look and saw two swollen shoulders, shiny and red. His skin was too tender for the shoulder pole. He did not complain about it, but my heart ached. I was glad that he did not have to do this for a living.

During the mushroom-growing season, we spread water every day and picked mushrooms whenever they were big enough. When it became too cold, we stopped spraying water and let the mixture dry up. When spring came and the temperature rose, we sprayed water over the dried-up mixture and mushrooms came up again. They grew until the temperature became too hot in the summer season. Then the mixture was thrown away. In the next season, new materials would be mixed and a new cycle begun.

At that time, Ah Bing's family had the most able-bodied farmworkers in our village. He and his wife were still in their prime, their three children were all adults, the elder son had taken in a wife, who was an additional work-point earner, and they were still living as one big family. Unlike some families, which had one person working in a local factory earning a separate income, everybody in Ah Bing's family earned work-points in the production team. Working in a factory was still considered a privilege. Although the landlord label had been officially eliminated, the lingering stigma was still there, keeping them away from such opportunities.

In 1982, Ah Bing's family received more than one thousand yuan as annual dividends, the most dividends earned by a family in Liming Brigade. This was such big news that people from other villages asked me how Ah Bing counted the more than one thousand yuan. At the time, there was no hundred-yuan bill. Although there was the ten-yuan bill, the commonly circulating bills were five-yuan and two-yuan. Ah Bing brought with him a flat bamboo basket to the village meeting place where dividends were handed out, and he counted the money in the flat basket right in front of the cashier.

One thousand yuan was a lot of money at the time and it was net income because it was in addition to the grain and fuel as well as the monthly cash credit the family had taken from the team throughout the year. To understand how great this annual net income was, here are some facts. It cost us 1,500 yuan to build the two-story house in 1975. There was very little change in the value of the yuan between 1975 and the early 1980s. One *jin* of brown sugar cost sixty-three cents and one *jin* of pork cost about seventy cents in the 1970s, and they were still the same prices in the early 1980s.

FAMILY RESPONSIBILITY SYSTEM

In 1983, the collective farmland in our production team was contracted out to individual families. Each person in the team was entitled to 0.65 *mu* of grain land (*kouliangtian*). Each adult was to contract about five *mu* of responsibility land (*zerentian*) to work on. Every family took its share of grain land, for that was the main source of staple food for us peasants, and most families contracted responsibility land.

For responsibility land, the state issued fixed quotas of harvested crops from each *mu* of land. These quotas were determined according to the average yields of the previous three years. They were rather generous and not hard to achieve. We now planted, cared for, and harvested crops in family units and then sold harvested and dried crops to the state to fulfill the quotas. Once the quotas were met, families could sell the surplus on the free market, or they could sell the surplus to the state. In the first few years of the contract system, families with able-bodied hands, such as Ah Bing's, wanted to contract more responsibility land because the state purchasing prices for agricultural products were high. Such families also chose to sell their harvests beyond the quotas to the state because they did not have to worry about marketing their crops on the free market.

I was among the very few adult persons who decided not to take any responsibility land. My husband said that I was fifty-three years

old in 1983 and no longer a young person. He also said that it would
be difficult for me to plant and harvest about six *mu* of land alone. For
instance, it would be a waste of electricity for a single person to thresh
rice or wheat on an electric-powered machine, which usually accom-
modated three or four working persons. If I contracted responsibility
land, I would inevitably incur "debt" when my cousins and neighbors
came to help. I agreed with my husband. In addition, he and I did not
want Shezhu and Ah Ming, who had a small baby and their own land
to take care of, and Shebao to feel the pressure of coming home to
help me at planting and harvesting times. When I told the production
team leader about my decision not to take any responsibility land,
he told me that several families had already expressed the desire to
contract more responsibility land than their share.

After the land was contracted out to families, the warehouse was
no longer needed, for it was the individual family's responsibility to
dry and take care of harvested crops until they sold to the state and
on the free market. Tools in the warehouse, such as brooms, shov-
els, rakes, willow vats, bamboo containers, and long bamboo sheets,
were all up for grabs. Since I was the warehouse keeper at the time, I
unlocked the doors to the warehouse. People rushed in to pick what
they wanted while I stood by and watched. When somebody asked
me why I did not take any, I replied that since everyone competed to
get a share, I preferred to avoid such a competition. If I took anything,
people would say that as the warehouse keeper, I had the privilege of
taking what was the most valuable. Therefore I decided not to take
anything.

The family contract system was quite popular. People now had the
incentive not only to work hard but also to find ways to increase the
yield from their contracted land. Dry land and rice land, good land and
bad land were divided equally. Each family therefore was cultivating
pieces of land at various places. No sign poles or paths were established between contracted pieces of lands. An outsider would not be
able to tell where one family's land ended and where another family's
land began, but we all knew exactly where our land was.

In planting and harvesting seasons, families volunteered to work together. For instance, Ah Juan, Hanming, and his wife would help Meifang thresh the rice Meifang and her sons had already brought onto the threshing ground. If this was done between one and four o'clock in the afternoon, then from four to eight o'clock, Meifang and her sons helped Ah Juan and Hanming thresh rice. Overall, people were reasonable and took turns using the only threshing ground to harvest their crops. The threshing ground was kept busy day and night during harvest seasons.

I grew rice, rapeseed to be squeezed into cooking oil, sweet corn, and vegetables on my grain land, which was 0.65 *mu*, and on our family plot, which was 0.3 *mu* at the time. Family plots were reassigned every several years as the number of people in families changed over time due to deaths, births, and marriages. The last time family plots were assigned was before Shezhu was married. Each person was entitled to 0.15 *mu* of land. We had 0.3 *mu*, which was Shezhu's share and mine.

After the Family Responsibility System was implemented, sideline production became privatized. In 1983 and 1984, I worked at the Zhuqiao Collection Station and personally witnessed the enthusiasm people had for growing and selling mushrooms and garlic, the two major products collected by the station. Garlic was harvested in May and by September it had been dried naturally for the market. After cutting off the dried stems and beard-like roots and peeling off soiled outer layers of the skin, families sold heads of garlic to the station.

From October to early December, the station collected mushrooms. Families utilized spare spaces in their houses or built makeshift sheds to grow this popular product. Some families had a small amount to sell, five or ten *jin* every few days. Others brought mushrooms to sell twice a day. A few families sold one hundred *jin* each day during the peak of the growing season. The station paid one yuan and five cents for each *jin* of mushroom. Those large mushroom-growing families made more than one hundred yuan each day during the busy season.

My husband's niece, Aidi, was one of the large mushroom growers in Zhuqiao Commune. She had received special training in mush-

room growing and worked on Zhuqiao Mushroom Spore Cultivation
Farm. Once families were allowed to engage in sideline production,
she and her husband made so much money that they were the first
ones to buy apartments in urban Jiading.

The buyer of the mushrooms we collected was Shanghai Yimin
Food Company. The company sent many plastic buckets to the collection station, each of which would hold fifty *jin* of mushrooms. After
mushrooms were collected, we put them into a big concrete sink and
washed them. After they were washed, we used strainers to get them
out of water and then put them into the plastic buckets. The filled
buckets were weighed on a scale. The company sent over its own
people to watch the scale, making sure that each bucket contained
fifty *jin* of cleaned mushrooms. The bucket was then filled with clean
tap water.

The filled buckets were loaded onto trucks. When a truck was full,
it was driven immediately and directly to Yimin's processing plant
in urban Shanghai, where fresh mushrooms were canned or bottled. During the peak season, no matter how late it was at night, the
washed mushrooms had to be delivered immediately to the processing
plant. We were told that the processing plant canned fresh mushrooms as soon as they arrived, no matter what hour of the day it was.

In addition to the white mushrooms, Aidi and other technicians
at Zhuqiao Mushroom Spore Cultivation Farm developed a variety
of other mushrooms, such as shiitake mushrooms, straw mushrooms,
and oyster mushrooms. Although growing shiitake mushrooms was
more complicated, they could be grown inside confined spaces, where
the temperature was more easily controlled. Besides, shiitake mushrooms were tastier and more popular; they could be sold for up to four
yuan per *jin* at a local farmer's market around the Chinese New Year
holidays.

Shiitake mushrooms grew on a mixture that was made of sawdust,
whole wheat grains ground to grits, and brown sugar. The mixture
was packed into plastic bags and had to be steamed for twelve hours
for total sterilization. After the steaming, we put mushroom spores
into the mixture in a sterile environment, wearing gloves and working

under a glass cover. When the spores spread throughout the bag, we cut open the bag, poured out the mixture, and pressed it firmly into wood frames.

The first batch of mushrooms emerged from the mixture sometime in October. Some families, such as Aidi's, would keep a coal stove in the room to keep the room temperature up so that they could still have fresh shiitake mushrooms around Chinese New Year's day, which is usually in the coldest month of January or February.

In the 1980s, most families in our area grew some shiitake mushrooms. But not every family went through the whole process I have just described. Some families pooled money together to run one furnace to steam the mixture. Or they paid somebody to steam the mixture. Some families, like mine, cut the process short by purchasing the steamed mixture from those families that ran a sterilizing furnace. Aidi's family was one of those that had such a furnace.

Mushroom growing generally involved the whole family. One autumn Saturday in 1984, Shebao, who lived in his university dorms in urban Jiading, came home in the afternoon. I had bought some shiitake mushroom mixture, and it was ready to be pressed into wood frames. Shebao helped me and we worked late into the night. I cooked a sweet soup with red beans as a nighttime snack. He ate some and went to bed.

The next morning, Shebao got up and complained about an acute stomachache. His father was also home for that weekend and so took Shebao to the medical center in Zhuqiao on his bicycle. When the doctor asked Shebao what he had eaten the night before, he replied that he had eaten a sweet soup of red beans. The doctor said that the stomachache was the result of eating "bad food." He prescribed two painkilling shots. One was administered immediately and the other was given to Shebao to take home. The doctor said that if the pain came back again by midafternoon, he should ask a local barefoot doctor to administer the injection.

The painkilling shot reduced the pain for Shebao, but he was not feeling well at all. By late afternoon, when the pain was back, I called Yan Meiying, the barefoot doctor, to administer the second shot.

When Meiying asked what had happened and examined Shebao, she immediately said that Shebao was suffering from acute appendicitis and needed to be rushed to the People's Hospital right away.

Shezhu and Ah Ming happened to be visiting us then. Ah Ming rushed Shebao to the hospital on the back seat of his bike while Shezhu went along on her own bike. I went to North Hamlet, where my husband was attending a dinner party, and told him the news. He rode his bike, with me sitting on the back seat, and rushed to the hospital. When we got there, Shebao had already been pushed into the operating room. The surgeon said that his appendicitis was "hot" and any further delay would have led to peritonitis. Clearly, Yan Meiying, the barefoot doctor, was far better than the so-called doctor at Zhuqiao Medical Center. I was and am still immensely grateful to her for saving my son's life.

Another major sideline was raising long-haired rabbits. In 1981, our neighboring Tanghang Commune developed a hybrid rabbit breed by combining a German rabbit with a local rabbit. The person who successfully developed this breed, Zhou Jinliang, was named a model worker in 1988 by the Shanghai municipal government. In the mid-1980s, the Tanghang rabbit became very popular and almost every family raised a few rabbits for commercial hair. A local ditty tells the high profit this rabbit brought to villagers in Jiading County: "Raise five rabbits, you can buy cooking oil, salt, fuel, rice, and vinegar; raise ten rabbits, the whole family will wear new clothes; raise fifty rabbits, you will become a ten-thousand-yuan family."[4]

These rabbits were fed with wild grass, which did not cost anything except labor. Families raised rabbits in spare spaces of their own houses, which required little investment capital, except for a little money to buy materials to build rabbit cages. Many people built two-story houses and now used their ground floor to grow shiitake mushrooms and to raise rabbits.

Shezhu and Ah Ming were very good at raising rabbits. Shezhu used her lunchtime at the factory to gather wild grass. She would do so again after she got off work. They grew vegetables on their plot as rabbit feed for rainy days. Ah Ming built cages for rabbits. He would shear rabbit hair once every two months. Rabbit hair sold for a very good price.

Ah Ming took the process one step further. He raised female rabbits and had them impregnated. He tagged rabbits with the date of impregnation. For one month, which was the standard duration for rabbit pregnancy, he watched the pregnant rabbits carefully day and night. One time, a rabbit had a difficult labor. After the labor, Ah Ming bottlefed the mother rabbit with milk to help nurse it back to health. When rabbits had diarrhea, he fed them anti-diarrhea pills. A pair of baby rabbits sold for fifty yuan in the 1980s. Ah Ming saved a lot of money by having his own rabbits multiply. By the mid-1980s, Ah Ming and Shezhu were raising over twenty rabbits.

Xianlin, one of my husband's distant nephews, made the most money in the region by breeding and selling baby rabbits. He and his wife made enough money from this sideline production to build the biggest house in Wangjialong. He became famous because of that.

My husband introduced another sideline production to our village. Chengdong Commune, where my husband worked, was now called Jianbang Town and had a chick-hatching farm. My husband talked to the people at the farm and arranged for us to sell them fertilized eggs. In order to have fertilized eggs, we had to feed a rooster. At first, I raised a rooster that traveled the whole village. Wherever it went, people would feed him so that he would remember to visit again. The rooster was big, beautiful, and fierce. I remember that one Chinese New Year holiday when Shezhen and Zhou Wei came to visit us, the rooster did not recognize them and attacked them. When we delivered chicken eggs to the farm, they were scrutinized under light to determine if they were fertilized. Each fertilized egg sold for fifty cents. The unfertilized eggs would be returned and eaten.

Another way of making extra income was to sell produce in the streets of urban Jiading. In 1984, the sweet corn I grew on our family plot produced an abundant harvest. The corn was very glutinous and sweet. I knew that urban people loved sweet corn. So, one afternoon, I filled two large bags with fresh sweet corn, boarded the public bus, and took them to Qinghe Road (Qinghe Lu) in downtown Jiading. I sold my corn easily and took the bus back home.

I tried everything to increase income. At that time, I did not have to do that. My children were all adults and no longer depended on my support. Yet it had become a habit for me not to lose an opportunity to earn money.

FACTORY WORK

After I completed work in the busy autumn of 1984 at Zhuqiao Collection Station, my husband said that he had found a factory for me to work in as a full-time worker. The factory was called Jianbang Chemical Machinery Plant and was one of the factories where my husband, as a leader in the commune, had implemented the piece-work reward system in the late 1970s, before the system was widely used. He ran a risk at the time, because giving material incentive to workers and peasants was still considered "taking the capitalist road." Under the piecework reward system, the factory became a very profitable business, and it was later recognized by the county authorities as a good example.

My husband had never used his official position to put family members or relatives into factories because working in factories was considered a privilege. When he contacted the office of Jianbang Chemical Machinery Plant in late 1984, he did not hold any official position in Jianbang Town, which had jurisdiction over the plant. Between 1983 and 1987, he worked in Jiading County's Office to Rectify the Communist Party (Zhengdang Bangongshi).[5] When he phoned the office of the plant and asked if they were recruiting more workers, the managers responded that they needed more workers in the packing workshop. He then said that his wife would like to work there.

So it was decided that I was to begin working in Jianbang Chemical Machinery Plant on January 1, 1985. Jianbang was on the east side of Jiading Town, while Wangjialong was on its north side. Since I did not ride a bike, it would take hours for me to commute to work by public transportation. So my husband rented a place in the urban section of Jiading Town called South Gate (Nanmen), which was right next to the plant.

We asked a carpenter from our neighboring Pandai Brigade to make a kitchen cabinet and some stools for our new home in South Gate. He came to our Wangjialong house and made the furniture for us. The cabinet was a big one, with two shelves in the upper part and a big space in the lower part. The upper part, with two screened doors, was to hold daily necessities such as cooking oil and soy sauce and to temporarily store leftover food between meals. The lower part, with two solid wooden doors, was for me to store dry food materials such as rice and flour. We did not have the time to have the new furniture painted in Wangjialong. After we moved to South Gate, we found a painter, who came and painted the cabinet and the stools for us.

In mid-December of 1984, my husband invited a few people from the plant to our house for lunch. This was intended to help them to get to know me and me to get to know them. I cooked several dishes for the lunch. While eating, they asked if we hired a professional chef to cook the dishes. When my husband told them that I cooked the dishes, they said that they liked them, and so they decided to have me work in the plant's dining room, instead of the packing workshop.

My husband had also invited a friend who drove a truck to join us at that same lunch. After lunch, this friend helped us move to our rented place in South Gate the modern bed, which was custom-made when Shezhen and Zhou Wei came to visit us right after they got married, a wardrobe, a square table, and a pair of cotton-padded quilts. A couple of weeks later, on New Year's Eve, I asked the tractor-trailer driver in our village to help move some other things to our South Gate residence. These things included a chamber pot, a couple of wash basins, kitchenware, and the newly-made furniture.

New Year's Eve was a cold day with snow flurries. I sat in the trailer, holding onto the kitchen cabinet, which was tall and wobbled in the trailer. Since the tractor-trailer had no covering, my clothes as well as my belongings were wet when we got to my new residence in

South Gate. After the driver helped me bring in the cabinet and the other things, I thanked him, and he left for home.

Our new residence had one room, in which we put the bed, the wardrobe, and the square table. Outside the room was a narrow passageway where I could hang washed laundry and my husband could park his bike. At the end of the narrow passageway was a small room. Inside that room there was a coal stove. My husband had bought some beehive coal, which was stacked in the room. Cooking was now dependent on that coal stove.

It was late in the afternoon now and I started to prepare for supper. My husband was working at Jiading County's Office to Rectify the Communist Party and was coming to the new place after work. Starting the coal stove turned out to be very difficult. The coal was damp and the stove was a simple one, without a chimney. I used old newspapers as kindling, but the damp beehive coal did not catch fire easily. After several trials and with no ventilation, the whole house was filled with smoke. I tried to fan the fire with whatever I could grab, but to no avail. I had not even thought of bringing a fan with me, for it was winter.

So when my husband came to the new residence after work, I had tears in my eyes. The tears were partially caused by the smoke. I also had cried because when I looked around, I saw this bleak and small place where I could not even start a fire to cook food. I thought to myself that I had a spacious and comfortable home in the village, where I had whatever I wanted. I asked myself, "What am I doing here?"

My husband comforted me. We got some food from a nearby small eatery. That evening, we went to the Chemical Machinery Plant, which was within walking distance of our house, filled two thermos bottles with hot water for drinking and washing purposes, and went to sleep. After the New Year's Day of 1985, I started to work in the kitchen of Jianbang Chemical Machinery Plant. I was fifty-five years old that year.

In time, I learned to maintain a coal stove day and night. We also bought a kerosene stove in case the coal stove died overnight. I used both the coal stove and kerosene stove when Shebao and Shezhu's family came on weekends. I learned to cook everything on the coal and kerosene stoves.

In springtime, our place in South Gate became very damp. After a few days of continuous rain, which happened very often during spring in Shanghai, we had water on the dirt floor inside our house. We had to put down bricks or wood planks to keep our feet dry. So one weekend, we bought cement and laid a thick layer of cement mixture in the house. It helped a great deal in reducing the dampness.

My work schedule was seven in the morning to two or three in the afternoon, six days a week. There were six of us working in the kitchen that served about two hundred people. We took turns serving a meal to those who worked the night shift. Only a small portion of the workforce in the factory worked the night shift. When it was my turn, I worked between three and six in the afternoon. When I did that, I would start the next day at ten in the morning, instead of seven.

Workers brought their own raw rice in a metal lunch box to the kitchen in the morning. They filled their own lunch box with water and we steam-cooked for them. Every day, the kitchen cooked five or six dishes at lunchtime. When workers broke for lunch, they came and picked up their own lunch box and bought one or two dishes of their choice.

The kitchen was about a five-minute walk from our South Gate house. Every morning when I got to work, I emptied the stove of coal cinders from the previous day, started the stove, boiled drinking water, and stored the boiled water in big thermal containers for workers to drink during the day.

We used about two hundred *jin* of coal for cooking each day. Coal was used for other purposes in the factory and so was not stored near the kitchen. In the morning, two of us had to fetch coal. We used a big willow vat to bring coal to the kitchen. One day right after I started working there, I took the shoulder pole and said, "Let's go and get some coal." Master Yuan, one of my coworkers, said, "Oh, no. It is too heavy for you. I will get a man to go with me to get the coal." I said, "How heavy is it?" He said, "It is about two hundred *jin*." I said,

"That would be one hundred *jin* to each of the two carrying the load. I can do that." My coworkers were all nice and considerate. I was in my fifties and was considered old, and I was also a woman. There was another woman about my age working in the kitchen. She had never volunteered to do that. So when I volunteered, they were surprised.

One of us did the shopping every day, early in the morning. When the shopper came back with meat, fish, and vegetables for lunch, we all worked together in picking, cleaning, and chopping. Master Zhao was the main cook. Lunch was served at eleven thirty. Only after all the workers had finished eating lunch would we kitchen workers eat our lunch, which was usually after twelve thirty. Some days, when the factory managers entertained visitors and/or business relations, we had to cook and serve a special lunch. If we served a table of visitors for lunch, then our lunchtime would be postponed to one or two o'clock.

I was overly conscientious about work. I did not think it was right for me to eat my lunch, even when I was really hungry, when it was service time. Nobody would have said anything if I stopped and ate something. In fact, some kitchen workers did that. But I just did not want to do so. I was foolish. Since I ate before seven in the morning, by noon I was really hungry. When it was my time to eat, particularly on those days we had to serve a guest lunch, I no longer had an appetite. Gradually, I developed stomach problems.

We peasants had always envied urban life. In the 1980s, urban housing continued to be very crowded, while many people in rural areas built spacious two-story houses. Yet this longing for urban life continued, and my family felt the same way. After I moved to South Gate, Shezhu's family came to our one-room house on Sundays, their day off from work. One Sunday, Shezhu had to go to work. So Ah Ming and Beibei came. After dinner, Beibei said that she did not want to go home and wanted to stay with me and her grandpa in South Gate. But Ah Ming said no and took her home.

The next Sunday, they came again. Ah Ming told me the following story. The week before he had taken Beibei home on his bike. Beibei tried to slide down several times from the moving bike because she did not want to go home. But Ah Ming was very persistent in taking her home. The struggle went on for quite a distance. Ah Ming said that he got so frustrated that he wished he had a big bag so that he could put Beibei in the bag and carry her home that way.

I told Ah Ming that he was too stubborn and should have returned and let Beibei stay with us that night. After that, Beibei stayed with us once in a while when Shezhu and Ah Ming returned home after a Sunday visit. Beibei was a very good girl. She never fretted and entertained herself during the day when my husband and I went to work. She watched TV, although there weren't a lot of TV programs during the day at that time. She cut and folded paper. We told her not to leave the house when we were not around and she listened. I would leave her in the morning when she was still asleep. After I had finished my morning round of work, I would sneak back a bit and get her breakfast. For lunch, I always had my rice steam-cooked in the kitchen, just like everyone else working in the factory. When Beibei stayed with us, I put a little more rice in the lunch box. When it was my lunchtime, I brought back the steamed rice and some vegetables and meat for her. Since lunch was often late, Beibei would be standing on a stool and looking out for me through the window. The window was high and she had to stand on a stool to see outside. Several times when I approached home, I saw her little face pressed against the window glass. From a very young age, Beibei said that she wanted to be a city person.

NOTES

1   Deng Xiaoping's economic reform policies mentioned here refer to a series of government policies issued between 1978 and 1983. These policies shifted away from the Cultural Revolution and stressed economic development by allowing sideline production and contracting land to rural families for farming. The policies which made the most impact are "Quanguo nongcun gongzuo huiyi jiyao" [Minutes of All-China Conference on Agricultural Work], Jan. 1, 1982, and "Dangqian nongcun jingji zhengce de ruogan wenti" [Problems of current rural economic policy], Jan. 2, 1983. In Zhonggong zhongyang shujichu nongcun zhengce yanjiushi ziliaoshi, ed., *Shiyijie sanzhong quanhui yilai nongcun zhengce*

wenxian xianbian [Selected documents on rural policies since the Third Plenary Session of the Eleventh Central Committee of the Chinese Communist Party] (Beijing, Zhonggong zhongyang dangxiao chubanshe, 1985), 24–58.

2   Rice seedlings are grown in beds. Each bed was about 1.5 meters wide and 15 meters long. A field of wheat was about 2.5 meters wide and 150 meters long.

3   According to *Jiading Xianzhi*, in the whole county, the amount of mushrooms sold to the state and collective markets grew from 1,295.8 tons in 1978 to 7,154.5 tons in 1984. *Jiading Xianzhi* [Annals of Jiading County] (Shanghai: Shanghai renmin chubanshe, 1992), 193. According to *Jiading Nongye Juzhi* [Annals of Jiading Agricultural Bureau], in the 1980s, Jiading County was the main producer of mushrooms in Shanghai. It was also one of the three main mushroom-growing counties in the country. These three counties were Jiading, Gutian in Fujian, and Liuba in Shaanxi. *Jiading Nongye Juzhi* (Shanghai: Jiading Nongyeju, 2002), 200.

4   *Jiading Xianzhi* [Annals of Jiading County], 202.

5   This was a comprehensive effort to clean and consolidate the Party after the Cultural Revolution. "Zhonggong zhongyang guanyu zhengdang de jueding" [Resolution of the Chinese Communist Party's Central Committee concerning consolidation of the Party], Oct. 11, 1983, accessed July 1, 2014, http://news.xinhuanet.com/ziliao/2005–02/07/content_2558439.htm.

11

Rural Customs and Urban Life

ONE day in the fall of 1985, Shebao came to our South Gate house from work at the Shanghai Science and Technology University and told me that he liked a girl at work. He said that the girl was from urban Shanghai. I immediately said that that was not good, for I was a country woman and would not know how to live with a girl from urban Shanghai. Shebao did not insist or protest.

The following spring, Shebao was organizing a youth trip to see the famous caves in Yixing of Jiangsu and wanted me to go with him. I did not want to go, but he insisted. So I agreed. Today, when we travel, we eat out. In those days, we prepared food and brought it with us. This was around the Dragon Boat Festival, so I made glutinous rice wrapped in bamboo leaves (*zongzi*) the evening before the trip.

Shebao had chartered a bus for the trip. That morning, when I got to the bus, it was already full, with no more empty seats. As the trip's organizer, Shebao had a reserved seat. He gave me the seat and stood all the way to Yixing. He told me to observe a girl who wore two braids and a checked jacket. He said that was the urban Shanghai girl he had mentioned to me earlier.

11.1   Shebao and Chen Huiqin outside the South Gate house, 1986

I paid attention to the girl, who was pretty and had a candid, straightforward personality. When we visited a cave, somebody said, "Now that we have visited the cave, we should live to be one hundred years old." The girl in the checked jacket responded, "Living to be one hundred years old would not be meaningful unless you were healthy." I agreed with her and liked her candor.

Sometime after the trip to Yixing, Shebao brought the girl to our place in South Gate after work, about suppertime. I was surprised and told Shebao that he should have given me some warning. He and the girl said that they deliberately came without warning to save me from preparing a fancy dinner for them. They stayed for supper with us. Since it was too late to shop, I did not have a lot to cook for them, so the supper was just everyday food. My husband and I formally met Xiao Xie, Little Xie, that day. My simple country cooking and our crowded one-room living conditions apparently did not bother Xiao Xie. After that visit, she came with Shebao to our South Gate house (fig. 11.1) quite often.

In rural areas, it had become customary for the family to invite relatives and friends to a banquet to announce an engagement. When I asked Shebao if we should do that, he said that it was not necessary and that people in urban Shanghai did not follow that custom. Also, the rural banquet to announce an engagement, called *zoutong*, or walk-through, was intended for the outsider to establish a connection with the family. Shebao said that Xiao Xie had already "walked through," for she had visited and eaten meals with us, thus had already established a connection with our family.

In 1986, Jiading County authorities decided to build an apartment building for former commune leaders who had been salaried government workers since the 1950s, who came from peasant backgrounds, and whose spouses were peasants working and living in the rural areas. Other commune leaders with urban backgrounds who had married non-peasant spouses were already living in government-built houses. Now it was time to account for those with peasant backgrounds and peasant spouses. My husband was among those entitled to a unit in the apartment building being constructed in downtown Jiading. This news came just as Shebao and Xiao Xie were talking about marriage. When my husband brought the news back home, we were all excited and went to see the building site immediately.

We had a big house in Wangjialong, but it was in the countryside. Those of us who had lived there all our lives were making every effort to leave it for the city. Shebao and Xiao Xie could make their bridal suite in Wangjialong and commute to work on their bikes every day. But they would have a hard time living there, for there were no flush toilets and cooking would have to be done on the brick stove. Xiao Xie had not grown up in a rural area, while Shebao had never cooked a meal on a brick stove himself.

We decided that my husband and I would continue to rent the house in South Gate, and Shebao and Xiao Xie would make their bridal suite in the new apartment. Before the building was completed, they visited it several times and walked through it. It was a five-story building with no elevator. When the building was completed, the county authorities conducted a blind drawing. My husband drew the lot and got an apartment on the fifth floor at the east end of the building. We liked it because it was bright and sunny. The sunshine turned the apartment into a hot place in summertime, but we appreciated it in winter. Shebao and Xiao Xie painted the inside walls of the apartment all by themselves. My husband helped them find a carpenter to make furniture for their bridal suite.

SHEBAO'S WEDDING

Shebao got married on the second day of the Chinese New Year in 1987. We consulted Xiao Xie's family to decide the day. At that time, factory and government workers had three days off for the Chinese New Year holiday. We decided that the wedding would take place during the holiday because many of our relatives and friends worked in factories or for the government. In the old days, most of our relatives and friends worked in the fields, so we did not have to consider whether it was a holiday. Instead, we usually held such an event in a slack farming season.

I went back to Wangjialong on New Year's Eve and started preparations for the wedding banquet. There was no longer a government policy against large banquets. We invited about twenty-five tables of guests, or about two hundred people.

My husband ordered pork, lamb, chicken, duck, fish, shrimp, delicacies such as winter bamboo shoots, and various vegetables. They were all delivered to our village house in the afternoon of New Year's Eve. We hired two professional chefs who also arrived that afternoon.

One of them was Master Yang, a very good chef and a good friend of my husband. The other was Master Yuan, who worked with me in the kitchen of the Chemical Machinery Plant. Meifang, Ah Juan, Shezhu, and I helped in cleaning meat and vegetables.

The two chefs had high standards. Winter bamboo shoots were very expensive. Meifang peeled off the tough sheaths and cut off the tough part of the bamboo shoots. When Master Yang saw the finished product, he said, "The winter bamboo shoots are not for pandas. You have to peel off and cut off much more." He added, "The tough part is bitter." Meifang told me later that she trimmed the bamboo shoots and showed them to Master Yang until he was satisfied. Shezhu was given the task of stirring the peeled and deveined shrimp after they were marinated. She stirred them until her arms were sore, but Master Yang said, "They have not been stirred enough. Stir some more."

The food they cooked earned many favorable comments from our guests. After the banquet, Meifang asked if she could hire the chefs the next time her family held a banquet. She said that at first she was rather reluctant to cut and peel so much of the winter bamboo shoots. After eating them, she said that the chef was right, because the dishes with the winter bamboo shoots were delicious.

New Year's Eve was a warm winter day. I was happy because we had to do the picking and cleaning in the open air and the warm temperature made our work easier. We used water from our own well, which had been dug several years earlier right outside our own kitchen. Well water is warmer than river water in winter. The warm temperature made me worry about the food, for we had no refrigeration for such large quantities of food and the banquet was two days away. Heaven helped. The next day when I got up, the temperature had dropped to below freezing.

In those days, we did not buy anything cooked or even semi-cooked. Everything was freshly cooked on the spot, including the seven chickens we raised ourselves and provided for the wedding. In the spring of 1986, I bought ten chicks, mostly for fun. When I bought them they had just come out of the hatchery and were cute furry yellow balls. I put them in a cardboard box and placed the box in the corridor of our South Gate house. I fed them rice and took care of them until they had grown their first feathers. Once they were strong and needed more space to play, I took them back to the village house, where Shezhu, Ah Ming, and Beibei were living, and Shezhu took care of them. All ten chicks survived and grew up. Three of them were roosters, so they were slaughtered for meat. The seven hens started to lay eggs by the fall. They grew wild and laid eggs everywhere. Some of them did not even come back to the coop at night. Shezhu had to look for them often and it was frustrating. So, as we were planning for the wedding banquet, Shezhu said that we should slaughter the hens for their meat.

These hens were small, about two *jin* each. Since we bought larger chickens for the whole-chicken dish on the banquet table, the seven hens were cooked and sliced to be an ingredient in the cold-cut platters. Everyone raved about how delicious the cold-cut chicken was. I was not surprised because we had raised the hens ourselves with organic feed.

For events like this, we always rented bowls, plates, spoons, and chopsticks. This time, when we asked the families from whom we usually rented, we learned that they had already rented out their ware, because the New Year holidays were a popular banquet time. As a result, Shezhu and Ah Ming decided that they would run their own rental business. They explained that we would have brand-new ware for Shebao's wedding banquet and after that, they would rent the ware out to make some money. So Ah Ming and Shezhu bought twenty tables' worth of dinnerware and had the Chinese character Ming carved on all the bowls and plates. The carved character made their ware distinct from ones owned by other rental businesses.

On the formal wedding day, we borrowed square tables from houses in our village. Most families owned such a table and it was customary for families to lend their tables out to the family which was holding a banquet. We had twenty tables placed in three rooms for the banquet. Zhongming's guest hall was spacious and we put eight tables in it. The two ground-floor rooms of our own house each had six tables.

We used Zhongming's kitchen for large-scale cooking such as steaming and deep-frying and Hanming's kitchen to cook rice. Our own kitchen was the headquarters, where all the banquet dishes were cooked or received final touches. Master Yang was the main cook. A group of relatives and neighbors helped to carry dishes to the banquet tables right after they were cooked and took away empty plates and bowls from the tables and brought them to the cleaning station. There, other helpers, who were also our relatives and neighbors, helped to clean them. Older relatives, such as Little Aunt and my maternal uncle, helped to maintain the fires in the brick stoves by feeding them with dried crop stalks.

In the morning on the wedding day, Shebao and two drivers, one driving a car and the other a minivan, went to urban Shanghai. There, Shebao took Xiao Xie's relatives and family out to a wedding lunch in a restaurant. After the lunch, Xiao Xie, her bridesmaids, and Shebao rode in the car while Xiao Xie's immediate family rode in the minivan to our village house.

When the bride arrived, we set off firecrackers and lit a bonfire of dry soybean and sesame stalks. Since the bridal suite was in urban Jiading, the bride and her party were entertained in our upstairs rooms until the banquet dinner began in late afternoon. The bride and bridesmaids were seated at the table of honor in our own guest hall. The table of honor was placed at the center and back of the room and the bride sat facing the south, toward the main door of the guest hall.

Very soon after the banquet began, my husband and I took Xiao Xie, accompanied by Shebao, to each table to pour wine or soft drinks for each banquet guest. When my husband and I introduced her to each of our relatives, she called these relatives by their appropriate titles, such as aunt or uncle. Senior relatives presented meeting-ritual money wrapped in red paper. We distributed wedding candies to the banquet guests as well as to every family in South Hamlet.

After the dinner banquet, the car and minivan took the newly-weds, the bridesmaids, the bride's family, and some other relatives to the bridal suite in urban Jiading. Shebao and Xiao Xie had prepared nuts, fruits, and candies for the party and decorated the apartment with beautiful paper hangings and colorful lights. Later in the evening, the van took Xiao Xie's immediate family back to urban Shanghai.

Xiao Xie's family were city people and had no idea about the practice of giving appreciation gifts. So I bought face towels and wrapped walnuts, dry longans, dry dates, and oranges in them and presented them as appreciation gifts to all the relatives who had given meeting-ritual money.

Since Xiao Xie and her family were urban people, we did not go through the steps of bringing wedding gifts over to Xiao Xie's parents and having her parents prepare bridal furniture. Instead, my husband helped to find a carpenter who custom-made a bed and other furniture for the bridal suite. Instead of us buying Xiao Xie jewelry such as a ring or a necklace, which was a common practice in our rural area at the time, her mother bought her a necklace. All the new quilts, new furniture, new clothes, and other miscellaneous wares Shebao and Xiao Xie bought together for the bridal suite stayed in the suite. So, on the wedding day, there was no moving or showing off of bridal furniture.

For our ancestors, we offered two tables of food in our village house right after the lunch on the wedding day. Offering food to ancestors was a traditional practice, so professional chefs knew about it. They calculated the food for this ritual in the overall plan and set aside two tables' worth of food when they cooked the banquet lunch. When the lunch was over, we pushed aside the other tables, moved two of them to the center of our own guest hall, and surrounded the tables with benches. We laid out all the dishes on the tables and lit candles and incense sticks for our ancestors. On the two tables we laid out many wine cups and many pairs of chopsticks. Just as we were joyfully celebrating the wedding of our son by inviting many guests, we imagined that our ancestors would also be happy, so they would invite their neighbors and friends to the feast. Those in Heaven and those on the Earth should share the happy event and celebrate it together.

11.2 Shebao and Xiao Xie on their honeymoon, 1987

In the spring following the wedding, Shebao and Xiao Xie took a honeymoon trip to Beijing (fig. 11.2). Shezhen was still in the United States at the time, so Zhou Wei took care of the newlyweds.

A FAMILY GATHERING

Shezhen's determination to study in the United States had finally had results—she was enrolled by the University of Utah in Salt Lake City. She left to pursue her big dream in the middle of 1984. Knowing that her American friends, Annina and Brown Beard, lived in that city made me feel a little better. After more than three years of studies in the United States, Shezhen received a master's degree in political science and was scheduled to return to China in the fall of 1987. She told us in a letter that she would go to Beijing first and then come to see us. On the day of her flight, we thought of her and hoped that her flight would be smooth. A week later, we thought she should be coming to see us soon. But there was no word from her, nor did she show up. We started to fear that she was not feeling well after the long flight. In my heart, I even wondered if she had arrived in Beijing safely. All kinds of worries occupied our minds.

For a few days, after my husband returned home from work, he would stand at the window of our South Gate house and look toward the bridge where Shezhen would cross if she were returning from Hongqiao Airport or from the Shanghai train station. Like many men, my husband did not express his emotions or his worries with many words. One afternoon around dusk, my husband called me over to the window. He pointed to a woman crossing the bridge and asked me, "Is that Shezhen?" I followed his fingers and said, "No, that is not our daughter." His concerns had led to a blurred or imagined vision.

Our worries were making us lose sleep. So my husband decided to go to Jianbang Town headquarters and use the telephone there to call Shezhen. Neither Shezhen nor we had a phone at home. When we had visited her in the early 1980s, we learned that there was a collective phone inside the apartment building in which Shezhen and Zhou Wei lived. The phone was in the stairway of the building. When the phone rang, whoever heard it would answer the phone and then knock on the door of the family the caller wanted. We got to the town headquarters and talked to Shezhen on the phone. Speaking with her was enough to lift the stone from our hearts.

Shezhen finally came to visit us, and Zhou Wei came with her. Our one-room South Gate house was now very crowded at mealtimes. We were a family of nine people. My husband had asked a local carpenter to make a movable round tabletop for us. So when it was time to eat, we would put the round top onto the square table. The table instantly became a round table that could seat ten people comfortably. When it was not mealtime, we would take off the round top and put it against a wall. That way, we would have some space to move around in the room.

Shezhen and Zhou Wei slept in Shebao's apartment. Shebao and Xiao Xie gave their bedroom to Shezhen and they slept on a makeshift bed in the kitchen-dining room. They arranged it this way because they had to go to work in the morning while Shezhen and Zhou Wei were on vacation and therefore could sleep in. From the kitchen-dining room, they could get their breakfast and leave for work without disturbing the two in the bedroom. They were considerate and that was a good arrangement. So while Shezhen was in Jiading, she and Zhou Wei shuttled between their sleeping place and their meal place on a bike. The distance between the two places was about a fifteen-minute bike ride.

While Shezhen was visiting us in Jiading, we took a family trip to Hangzhou. Shezhu and Ah Ming brought Beibei along. My children also persuaded me to go with them. When we got to Hangzhou by train, it was already late in the afternoon. In those days, there were not as many hotels as we have today and we had no travel experience. Everywhere we looked for a place to spend the night, we were told that they were all sold out. Finally, after it was already dark, we found a place. The hotel we stayed in for that night was inside a former bomb shelter. We slept in simple single-person beds.

That night, Shezhen suffered from stomach pains. She was sleeping in the bed right next to me. She turned and tossed the whole night. I saw her lying with her face down and putting the pillow under her stomach. I felt her pain. I realized that all the years of hard work had led to her stomach problem. Shezhen had mentioned to me that she sometimes had stomach pains, but to keep me from worrying too much, she said that it was a small problem. After watching her turning and tossing that night, I knew it was not a small problem. Some years after that, I learned that she had a stomach ulcer.

The next day, we visited the famous West Lake and walked the whole day. In the morning, Beibei walked very fast. By afternoon, her little legs were tired and Ah Ming carried her on his shoulders.

GRANDSON

The apartment building Shebao and Xiao Xie lived in was newly built and not yet connected to the natural gas pipeline. At the time, the pipeline was being extended to more and more residential areas in urban Jiading, but it had not yet reached that particular area. Some residents used compressed natural gas in tanks, but such tanked gas was a rarity. Each gas tank had a registered number. When the gas in the tank was used up, the owner had to bring the tank to the gas station to have it refilled. My husband managed to get a registered gas tank for Shebao and Xiao Xie so they did not have to maintain a coal stove for cooking.

In 1988, a new policy determined that my husband was entitled to an apartment with two bedrooms. We decided that Shebao and Xiao Xie should move to the new, larger apartment and we would move to the one-bedroom apartment. The new apartment was in a residential compound named Liyuan, Li Compound. New buildings in those days came with bare cement floors and roughly finished walls. Shebao and Xiao Xie put down hardwood floors and panels in the bedrooms and linoleum flooring in the kitchen, bathroom, and entryway. The entryway was made into a small eating area. They worked hard and used evenings and weekends to do all of those things themselves.

After Shebao moved to the new apartment inside Li Compound in April 1988, we left the one-room house in South Gate and moved to the one-bedroom apartment in downtown Jiading. By that time, our downtown apartment had been connected to the piped natural gas, but the one in Li Compound had not. So Shebao and Xiao Xie took the gas tank with them. They continued to come and eat with us on weekends. Sometimes, they also came after work and we would have supper together.

Li Compound was about a fifteen-minute bike ride from our downtown apartment, which was inside an old compound with a deep well that produced clean and sweet water. The tap water in urban Jiading at the time had a strong taste of chlorine and some other bad odors. So every time Shebao and Xiao Xie came to visit us, they brought with them two sturdy plastic bottles. Each could hold a gallon of water, so we referred to them as "gallon buckets." After their visit, they would return to their home with the gallon buckets filled with water from the well.

One weekend, Shebao and Xiao Xie arrived while I was in the kitchen-dining room preparing lunch. They put a slip of paper on the kitchen table and went to the bedroom. I took a look at the slip. Since

11.3   Chen Xianxi and
        baby Chen Li, 1989

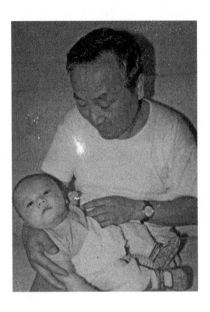

I could not read much, I was not able to tell what the slip said, but I could tell that it was a lab test slip. I took the slip to the bedroom and asked, "You have been to the hospital. Is everything alright?" Xiao Xie said, "Mom, I am pregnant."

Xiao Xie checked into Jiading Maternity Hospital in the morning on June 5, 1989. Shebao rode his bike to my place and told me. I went to the hospital right after I finished the day's work in early afternoon. The baby, a boy, was born around six o'clock in the evening. After the baby was born, the doctor said that we would be allowed to see the baby in two hours. Shebao and I decided to go back and eat our supper at my place. He rode his bike while I sat on the back seat. After supper, we went back to the hospital.

On the way to the hospital we passed through the center of urban Jiading. This was June 5, the day after the Tiananmen Square incident. There were thousands of demonstrators in the streets. The streets were so full that it was impossible to ride the bike through. We walked, with Shebao now pushing the bike. We finally got to the hospital and saw the baby for the first time. The baby was asleep. I noticed a cute and distinctive feature in the new baby, which was that his lower lip was so sucked in that I could only see his upper lip.

In those days, new babies were under the care of the hospital staff. Every day, there were fixed times that the staff would take the babies to their mothers for breast-feeding. The day after our grandson was born, my husband went to the hospital to see Xiao Xie and the baby. When all the new babies were pushed out in their little beds, I told my husband to look for the one whose upper lip entirely covered the lower lip. While other families asked the staff to identify their babies, we found ours easily (fig. 11.3).

The year our grandson was born, my husband was sixty years old. We Chinese consider sixty years as one complete sexagenary cycle (*jiazi*) and a full lifespan. My husband jokingly said that he would now start a new cycle of life and so he and his grandson were the same age.

Friends suggested that Shebao choose a name for the baby that was related to the Tiananmen incident. Shebao did not; instead, he named the baby boy Chen Li, *Chen* being our surname and *li* meaning "standing up." The character *li* is a very simple character. Beibei, who had learned some Chinese characters by that time, said, "Uncle is not fair. He named my little brother with a very simple Chinese character, but gave me the name *xi*, which is a very complicated Chinese character."[1]

At the time Chen Li was born, Shezhu and her family had moved to urban Jiading, where she worked for a housing development company. The family rented a room right above the company offices. The company had a big kitchen, where lunches were cooked for its workers. We used the company's kitchen to boil hundreds of eggs. After the eggs were boiled, we dyed them red. Beibei, who was eight years old at the time, enthusiastically participated in the dying of the eggs. Shebao bought cupcakes from his university's dining room. We delivered the red eggs and cupcakes to our relatives, friends, and neighbors, as appreciation for the maternity gifts they presented to Xiao Xie as well as an announcement of the birth of the new baby.

Within two months, Chen Li had his first haircut. I contacted an old barber who was a man from Yangzhou of Jiangsu. Barbers from Yangzhou were considered the best in their profession in our area. I arranged for him to come to our apartment to give Chen Li his first haircut. He told me to make a lot of tea ahead of his arrival. He would use tea water to wash Chen Li's head. He said that tea water would help keep the baby's hair clean and clear and prevent problems such as a crusty scalp or head blisters. After the hair was cut, the barber rolled the baby hair into a ball. Shebao and Xiao Xie took the baby-hair ball.

After Chen Li was born, I continued to work in the factory dining room. I told Xiao Xie that I would rather help to pay for a nanny than quit the job in order to help her with the baby. That was because I did not think that it was right to ask the factory to keep the job for me. Neither was I ready for retirement.

My husband's sister was working as a maid at the time, so she helped us to find a nanny, a middle-aged woman from a village in Zhuqiao Town. The nanny helped Xiao Xie take care of the new baby, but not for very long. Xiao Xie discovered that the nanny was a sound sleeper. When Xiao Xie needed help at night, the nanny was usually fast asleep. Therefore, she was not very helpful, so we decided to save the money we paid to the nanny. That was how we stopped using a nanny.

Xiao Xie returned to work after fifty-six days of paid maternity leave. She and Shebao put Chen Li in the nursery of the university for the day while they were at work. This family of three went to work on one bicycle. Xiao Xie held Chen Li in her arms and sat on the back seat of Shebao's bike. They ate lunch in the university canteen. Xiao Xie told me that one of them bought and fetched the lunch while the other held Chen Li. Chen Li was a good-natured baby. He did not cling to his parents. When colleagues offered to hold Chen Li and play with him during their lunch break, he responded happily.

The distance between the university and their home was about a ten-minute bike ride. On the way, they had to pass a stretch of rough, busy road near a farmer's market. In the morning when they went to work, this road was always crowded with people shopping for the day's vegetables and meat. On cold winter mornings after a rain, that part of the road would be slippery with frozen puddles, making the bike ride challenging. At that time, a new street, Bole Road (Bole Lu), which was to provide a more direct route to the university, was under construction. Shebao said several times that he was eagerly looking forward to the completion of Bole Road, for it would make his commute easier.

The bike was a very useful transportation tool. Shezhu and Ah Ming did the same thing when Beibei was little. Ah Ming rode the bike and Shezhu held Beibei and sat on the back seat. Shebao and Ah Ming both pedaled the bikes this way until the children were older. Then each adult would ride a bike and the child would sit in a little chair that was attached to the front bar of the bike, supported by the two arms of the adult riding the bike. As the child grew, she or he would then sit on the back seat of the bike.

We held the first-birthday party for Chen Li on the second day of the Chinese New Year in 1990 in our village house. My husband said that was the last major event he would sponsor in his lifetime,[2] so we invited all of our friends and relatives, just as we had when we held the wedding banquet for Shebao. Master Yang and Master Yuan were again the chefs for the banquet.

We put up a portrait of the Longevity Star in our guest hall and set up a table with traditional foods that conveyed all the good wishes. Shebao and Xiao Xie arrived from their urban Jiading home with Chen Li around lunchtime. Firecrackers and a bonfire welcomed Chen Li. Shebao helped Chen Li kowtow to the Longevity Star while all the guests watched. The table remained there for the rest of the day, while incense and candles continued to be lit. That afternoon, we delivered bowls of cooked noodles with glutinous rice balls and a big piece of meat in each bowl to every household in South Hamlet as "helping-child noodles."

When Chen Li was five years old, he went to the kindergarten run by the university, where his parents worked. We had heard stories of children being taken away from kindergartens by strangers, so we cautioned Chen Li not to go with anybody he did not know. Furthermore, staff members in nurseries and kindergartens did not allow anybody to take children unless they knew the person was a family member.

Usually, Shebao and Xiao Xie went to get Chen Li after they left work. Sometimes, when they had something special to attend to after work, they would let me know, and I would pick up Chen Li when I finished work. One day, when I got to the kindergarten, Chen Li was playing with other kids under the guidance of a staff member. When Chen Li saw me, he immediately got up from his little stool, took the stool and put it against a wall, came and took my hand, and then went to the staff member and said in a very serious manner, "This is my grandma. She has come to take me home."

From a very young age, Chen Li loved cars and learned the brand names of cars. One day, he came with his parents to our apartment on the fifth floor. While still huffing and puffing from having run up the stairs, he took my hand and asked me to go downstairs with him to the parking lot. He wanted to show me a car he had seen when he arrived with his parents. He pulled me by the hand to a car whose logo was four circles. He announced that was an Audi and a very good car.

When Chen Li came with his parents to have dinner at our apartment, he often insisted that I carry him down the stairs to see him off. Shebao and Xiao Xie would tell me not to pay attention to Chen Li's demand. They said that he was being too playful, but I admit that I loved doing what he asked.

Once, however, when I carried Chen Li downstairs, I sprained one of my ankles. Shebao and Xiao Xie asked if I had hurt myself. I replied, "No." Then, I went back up the stairs, washed, and went to bed. The next morning, my ankle was swollen tight.

URBANIZATION FOR BETTER EDUCATION

Shezhu and Ah Ming were determined that their only child, Beibei, would get the best opportunities possible for education. While Shezhen and Shebao had received college educations, Shezhu and Ah Ming had not had that opportunity. They were determined to do everything necessary to turn Beibei into a college student.

In September of 1988, Beibei came to live with me and my husband because she was enrolled at Putong Elementary School, which was in the vicinity of our downtown apartment. One morning, after breakfast, Beibei went to school and I went to work. As I did most mornings, I went with another person to get coal for the kitchen. While shoveling coal into the basket, I suddenly saw a little girl walking on the road toward the factory kitchen. I said, "That is my Beibei." I put down the shovel and ran to the road to meet her. Beibei said, "Grandma, I forgot to wear the red scarf and the school gatekeeper would not allow me to enter."

I told my coworkers what had happened and then left with Beibei to get the scarf from home. After we got the scarf, I accompanied her to the classroom. The teacher said, "Yang Xi is too shy." The teacher added, "If Yang Xi had explained, the gatekeeper would have excused her and allowed her to enter." The teacher apologized to me for the inconvenience.

That Beibei was attending school in urban Jiading prompted Shezhu and Ah Ming to think about resigning their current jobs and seeking work in Jiading Town. This was not an easy decision. At the time, Pengsha Factory, where they both worked, was doing very profitable business and workers' incomes were among the highest in the area. But their priority, which was to guarantee Beibei a good educational environment, was very clear. Ah Ming gave up his job at Pengsha Factory and was employed as a lathe worker in a village-run factory located right next to urban Jiading.

In the latter part of 1988, Jianbang Town established a division that was specifically devoted to the development of residential houses. This division became a company soon after its establishment, so we always refer to it as a company. There were already residential houses built around the borders of Jiading Town. Li Compound was one such residential community. The newly established company needed an accountant and a cashier. The company was building apartments on the outskirts of Jiading Town and therefore its company office was right next to where Ah Ming was working. My husband, who had returned to Chengdong Commune—now called Jianbang Town— after he finished the work at the Office to Rectify the Communist Party, was working as an advisor to the town leadership. He recommended Shezhu to the new company, which interviewed her and hired her as the cashier.

But Shezhu and Ah Ming did not have a place to live in the urban area, so they had to spend more than two hours riding bikes back and forth between their work and our Wangjialong house every day. Luckily, Shezhu's company offered her temporary housing. The company utilized a building on a former pig farm. The building had two stories: on the ground floor were the company's offices and a kitchen for its employees; on the second floor there were several empty rooms. Shezhu rented one of the rooms and took Beibei back to live with them. They had to make many sacrifices. They bought lunch from the company kitchen downstairs. They used an electrical stove and a kerosene stove to cook breakfast and supper. There were no flush toilets on the floor where they lived, so they had to use a chamber pot.

Because the building was part of an old pig farm, there were clouds of mosquitoes after it got dark in summer time. There were no screens on the windows of their room. They used a mosquito net over their bed. Shezhu said that when they slept at night, so many mosquitoes perched on the net that they turned the white net to black. They put Beibei in the middle when they slept and had to be very careful to stay away from the net. Whenever they accidentally pressed their arms or legs against it while asleep, they woke up with arms or legs swollen with mosquito bites.

After working as a lathe worker for some time, Ah Ming quit and started a repair shop. He repaired electrical appliances such as radios, TVs, fridges, and washing machines. He relied on the skills and knowledge he had gained when he maintained and fixed compressors in Pengsha Factory. He bought various technical books and studied them to gain more knowledge about electrical appliances.

On Sundays, still the only day off in a worker's week, Ah Ming and Shebao rode their bikes to the countryside and peddled their repair service to rural people. This was the time many people with special skills tried to earn extra income by offering services in their spare time. For example, teachers used weekends to tutor high school students for college entrance exams and received payment from the families using the service. Ah Ming and Shebao, whose college training equipped him with the skills to fix electrical appliances, were just riding the wave.

Xiao Xie and Shezhu, with Chen Li and Beibei, would come to our apartment for the day. By evening, they would be looking out from our fifth-floor apartment window for Ah Ming and Shebao. When the two peddlers rode their bikes into the compound and appeared below our window, Xiao Xie or Shezhu would eagerly ask if they had made any money. The two men would make some finger gesture to indicate how much they had made as they dismounted from and parked their bikes. They made between twenty and fifty yuan a day. Ah Ming and Shebao split the money. We referred to this as their sideline production income.

When the large refrigerator in the kitchen where I worked was out of order, I told the main cook that my son-in-law repaired electrical appliances. They contacted Ah Ming. Although it took several days for him to find and fix the problem, he succeeded. That was one of the first major business repairs for Ah Ming.

Shezhu and Ah Ming bought their first commercial apartment in urban Jiading in the latter part of 1989. The apartment cost 33,000 yuan and they paid about two-thirds of the total. They used all the savings they had accumulated from their years of hard work and frugal living. Before they paid it, I remember we helped Shezhu sort out all of the bank deposit certificates to add them up. The certificates of deposits ranged from fifty yuan to several hundred yuan.

Like Shebao's apartment in Liyuan, the apartment Shezhu bought had two bedrooms, a small dining room, a kitchen, and a bathroom. It was on the fifth floor of a building that had six floors. The new apartment had bare floors and walls. Shezhu and Ah Ming used their spare time to put up wallpaper and to lay down hardwood floors. The new apartment was not yet connected to the piped natural gas. Fortunately, Shebao's apartment in Li Compound was now connected, so Shezhu took over the gas tank that Shebao had used.

The gas tank had to be refilled about every three months. Since the gas tank had its own registered number, it could be refilled only at the particular station where it was registered. The filling station for our gas tank was located west of Little Aunt's village. When Shebao used the tank, every time he carried it on his bike to be refilled, he stopped and visited his grand aunt. When Shezhu took over the gas tank, Ah Ming took it to be refilled. He also made a stop at Little Aunt's home and visited her.

By the late 1980s, Little Aunt had suffered a stroke. She recovered from the stroke somewhat, yet she had difficulty walking and speaking. Although she could still take care of herself, she was no longer able to do housework, let alone work in the fields. Since she stayed home all the time, any relative who visited her would provide excitement. Little Aunt told me that about every three months, she would sit at the main doorway of her house and expect Shebao, or later Ah Ming, to visit her.

NOTES

1   People usually ask their children to address cousins as brother or sister. Beibei is referring to the fact that the Chinese character *li* 立 has five strokes while *xi* 曦 has twenty strokes.

2   The major events in a man's life are wedding banquets for his children, funerals for his parents, and finally first birthdays for his grandsons.

12

A House-Purchasing Frenzy

I N 1997, Shezhen called from the United States to tell us that she
had gotten a job as a history professor in an American university.
We were very happy for her. Shezhen had grown up a peasant,
and now she would be a college professor in the United States. My
husband said that our ancestors must have accumulated good deeds
for us to enjoy the benefits.

Shezhen had gone back to the United States in 1992 to pursue a
PhD degree in history. What she wanted to do now was way beyond
my imagination, but I was proud of her. Zhou Wei also went to the
United States for graduate studies, but did not stay there very long.
He went to work in Hong Kong, where he sold electronic equipment
to mainland buyers.

In the early 1990s we had our first telephone installed in our
apartment. One weekend not long afterward, Shebao, Shezhu, and
their families were visiting us just as they did on most weekends. My
husband must have been thinking about our elder daughter, for he
suggested that we make a phone call to Shezhen in the United States.
We knew it would be an expensive call, but all supported the idea

and so he dialed. Everyone spoke to Shezhen. Although we received letters quite regularly from Shezhen and my husband wrote back every time, it was thrilling to hear Shezhen's voice and communicate directly. When the monthly phone bill came, my husband read that the phone call to Shezhen had cost 384 yuan. We could not believe it was so expensive. My husband went to the telephone office and asked if there was a mistake. He was told that our phone call had lasted about fifteen minutes and that the charge was accurate. At the time, my husband's monthly salary was about six hundred yuan. The phone call was more than half of his monthly salary.

After Shezhen got the university teaching job, Zhou Wei quit his job in Hong Kong and joined her in the United States. That summer, Zhou Wei videotaped Shezhen's graduation ceremony as well as a party that her American friends held for her and sent the tape to us. We watched the tape many times, because every time a relative came to visit us, we would play the tape for them and watch it together. I thought that Shezhen's grandfather—my father—must be very proud of her scholarly achievement.

Another piece of celebratory news was our granddaughter Bei-bei's enrollment at Jiading Number One High School in the summer of 1997. Although there were many other ways to escape from the peasant fate, the best and the most desirable was through education. Many families hired tutors for their children. Entrance examinations for high schools and colleges were the most important events for such families.

Shebao helped with Beibei's education. When Beibei was going to elementary school, he subscribed to a magazine for her. Although I was not able to read the magazine, I heard them talking about what they were reading in the magazine quite often. Shebao also bought books for Beibei, so she grew up in a large family that empha-sized education. Shezhu and Ah Ming always told Beibei that they expected her to go to college and would do everything within their power to support her and help her.

Beibei was a smart girl, but she was not always careful about little things and made careless mistakes in tests. She could score very high on one test; on another one, she would perform poorly. Throughout the three years of high school, Shezhu and Ah Ming worried about Beibei's irregular performances.

In 2000, Beibei graduated from Jiading Number One High School and took the college entrance exams in mid-July. The mid-July weather in Shanghai can be very hot and humid, yet the schools where the exams were to take place were not air-conditioned. As the exam days approached, we watched the weather forecast every day, hoping that it would not be too hot or humid for Beibei. Many parents tried various ways to improve conditions that could bother their exam takers. Some rented hotel rooms near exam sites so that their exam takers did not have to travel too far. Others hired taxis to take their children to the sites. Those with their own vehicles drove their children to the exams. Ah Ming, who had bought a pickup truck for business use, offered to drive Beibei to the exams, but Beibei did not think it was necessary. She rode her bike to the exam site, which was her own high school. Beibei was always a calm and reasonable girl, much calmer than her mother about the exams.

Beibei performed well at the exams and was enrolled at Donghua University in Shanghai to major in mechanical engineering. When school started, Ah Ming drove Beibei and her belongings to the university. Shezhu, my husband, and I went along with them. My husband said with pride that Beibei was the third college student in our family.

NEW HOMES IN XINCHENG

In 1996, my husband learned that he could turn in the one-bedroom apartment in downtown Jiading to the government for some money. We were getting old, and climbing to the fifth floor every day was becoming tiresome. Large-scale construction around the apartment building had also made our living environment dusty and noisy. We decided to turn in the apartment and buy another one somewhere else.

The housing development company where Shezhu worked was responsible for constructing several buildings inside a new residential neighborhood known as Xincheng. With more and more people leaving rural areas and moving to live in urban Jiading, rural towns shrank in population while new urban administrative units were created. The shrinking rural towns merged together. For example, Zhuqiao and its neighboring Loutang merged to become one town, called Loutang Town. Jianbang and Malu were merged and became known as Malu Town. Xincheng was a new administrative unit inside Jiading District. It is the equivalent of a town, but was called *jiedao*, an urban neighborhood.

We visited a building site in Xincheng and decided to buy a two-bedroom apartment on the first floor of one of the buildings. We turned in the one-bedroom apartment and received monetary compensation. Combining the compensation with our savings, we bought the apartment before it was completed.

In 1997, the construction of the building was completed and we got the key to the new apartment. The apartment had bare concrete floors and walls. We hired Sun Yongqiu, the man who had saved Shebao's life when they both were little boys and was now running a tile business, to put down tiles in the living room, the kitchen, and the bathroom. Ah Ming did the electrical wiring. My husband hired a carpenter and a brick mason, who put down hardwood floors in the bedrooms, built wall panels, plastered the ceilings, and made closets in the bedrooms and cabinets in the bathroom and kitchen. They also put in a flush toilet and a bathtub. Before we moved in, we hired a man to put screens over the windows and install theft-proof window bars and doors.

In March of 1998, we moved into the new apartment. On the day of our move, we held a banquet and invited our close relatives. We rented a dining room in the neighborhood for the banquet. At that time, it had become a common practice for places like schools and offices to rent their dining rooms on weekends to families who needed bigger spaces to celebrate occasions such as weddings and first birthday parties for babies. Many rural people like us had moved to urban apartments whose limited space could not accommodate banquets. Yet rural people still maintained the tradition of celebrating important occasions with banquets. On our moving day, we invited seven tables of guests to the banquet. The tables we used this time were round and each seated ten people.

Before the moving day, I packed up many things. On the actual day, I got up very early and packed the rest of our household things. Ah Ming used his business truck to move our things to the new apartment. It was a small truck and had to make five trips altogether to transport everything. A few of our relatives came early that day and helped.

Our relatives presented money gifts wrapped in red paper when they came to the banquet. Traditionally, when a family built a house, relatives brought gifts in the form of foods such as pork and soy sauce. Those were practical and appropriate gifts then because the family building a house cooked meals and snacks for those involved in the building work. Now when people moved into a new apartment, the gift-presenting practice continued but gifts of food were no longer appropriate.

When we took the red packets of money, my husband marked each with the name of the gift giver. We provided our guests with both lunch and dinner that day. After lunch, we invited them to visit our new apartment. The dining room where we had our banquet was within walking distance of our new apartment. After the dinner, when our guests were leaving for home, we returned the money gifts to each of them. They were very surprised. We said that we had invited them because we wanted to show them our new home, so that they could come and visit us anytime. We added that we also wanted to thank them for their visits and gifts when my husband had been hospitalized for forty-five days for treatment of his high blood pressure and coronary heart disease in the previous winter.

The building we moved into was on the east edge of this new residential community called Xincheng neighborhood. Immediately east of our building, there was a construction site of more residential buildings. Beyond the construction site was open land for further residential development. In such a wild environment there were clouds of mosquitoes outside our apartment when summer came. Fortunately, we had screens over our windows and doors. When we went out after dinner to catch the summer breeze, we had to use our fans to keep mosquitoes away.

After we moved in, we redid the patio behind the apartment. The patio was large, had walls on all three sides, and was paved with bricks. We wanted to create an area for flowers. We pulled up the bricks, created a strip for flowers along the walls, and repaved the rest of the patio with concrete. For the flower strip, we needed more dirt to raise it so that our flowers would not be submerged in water in the rainy season. I saw a woman who rode a tricycle-trailer in our community every day to pick up plastic bottles, cardboard boxes, and other recyclable material from the garbage cans to sell. I asked her if she would use her tricycle-trailer to get some dirt for me. I said I would pay her fifty yuan for the job. She looked at the site and agreed to do it.

So she came one morning to do the job. She loaded plastic bags with dirt from the open land right outside our community and moved the loaded bags to our apartment in her tricycle-trailer. She carried the dirt through our apartment to the backyard patio.

I planted flowers and trees in the strip. When we lived in downtown Jiading, there had been a huge ginkgo tree outside our apartment. Its big branches stretched toward us, and we could easily pick its seeds from our balcony. Ginkgo seeds had medicinal uses and the tree was believed to provide a healthy environment. So I decided to try to plant ginkgo trees in our new place. I talked to a botanist I got to know when we lived in the downtown apartment. He gave me eight ginkgo seeds he had collected from a healthy tree. I planted them in the strip, and six of them came up. Four of them grew successfully.

The botanist also started an osmanthus tree for us. He was an expert in trees and plants. At that time, he was still living in the old building in downtown Jiading. He chose a healthy osmanthus tree in the compound, made a cut in a low branch, pulled it down to the ground, and buried the cut branch in the dirt. The buried branch was still connected to the tree and got its nutrients from the tree. He did this in winter. When spring came, the branch grew its own roots at the cut while it was still getting nutrition from the mother tree. When the roots were strong enough, the botanist cut the branch completely from the mother and the branch became its own tree. In early summer, the botanist called to let us know that the tree was ready. It was only about one foot high when I took it back and planted it in the strip in our backyard.

The ginkgo trees and the osmanthus tree grew to be big. Two of the ginkgo trees and the osmanthus tree grew into the space that the family living directly above us used to dry their clothes. So we trimmed them every spring so that they did not bother our upstairs neighbors. The other two ginkgo trees grew into the skies without bothering anybody. They were straight and healthy trees, growing beyond the second floor and into the views of the third floor. The osmanthus tree displayed very fragrant flowers in fall. When the growing trees began to overshadow the strip, I stopped planting flowers there and used pots to grow them, placing the pots on the concrete floor of the patio.

Shezhu and Ah Ming also sold the first apartment they bought in urban Jiading and purchased two apartments in Xincheng. Shezhu had a good income, for she was working for a very profitable company. Ah Ming was running a successful business, which installed window air conditioners in businesses and homes. The 1990s witnessed a rapid rise in people's desire for air conditioners. We had one installed in our apartment in downtown Jiading in the mid-1990s.

One of the apartments Shezhu and Ah Ming bought was in the same complex in which we lived. It took me about three minutes to walk from where we lived to that apartment. The apartment was on the first floor and was used as a warehouse for Ah Ming's business. The other apartment was in a neighboring complex on the fifth floor. It was a more spacious apartment, with three bedrooms and two full bathrooms. They moved into it in 1999. Shezhu's new home was about an eight-minute walk from our place.

Although the complex where Shezhu now lived was just across the street from our complex, it was still beyond the coverage of Xincheng residential phone service when Shezhu moved in. Ah Ming was doing business and had to have a phone. So before the coverage was extended to their community, they extended our phone line to their house. The direct distance between our home and their home was about three hundred meters. We lived in two separate residential communities and each was a walled and gated community. When we walked to their apartment, we had to leave our community through the gate, go around the walls of their community, enter the gate of their community, and then get to their apartment. So the actual walking distance was much longer than the distance in the air.

After the extension line was established, whenever the phone rang, we usually did not answer the call. We did not expect many phone calls, because most of our relatives lived in rural villages and had not yet installed phones. Ah Ming was doing business, so he had more calls. If the call was for us, Ah Ming and Shezhu would ask the caller to hang up and call again. When we heard the phone ring more than five times, we knew it was for us and would pick up the phone. We did this for about a year until the phone service was finally extended to their complex.

Many rural people bought apartments in urban Jiading in the mid-to late 1990s. Many of them had sons or daughters who were going to school or working in urban Jiading. My cousin Hanming, whose only daughter was working for the postal service, bought an apartment in downtown Jiading. One of my husband's nieces had a daughter working for Volkswagen, which ran a joint venture plant in Anting, one of the towns in Jiading District. The family bought an apartment in Li Compound. Aidi, my husband's other niece, made a lot of money in mushroom production and bought two apartments in urban Jiading.

My cousin Zhongming's son worked in an opera troupe in urban Shanghai. With their only son working in urban Shanghai, Zhongming and Ah Juan had not considered buying an apartment in urban Jiading. The house-purchasing frenzy, however, was affecting them. One day before we moved to Xincheng, we were attending the celebration banquet given by Hanming and his wife for the birth of their grandson. The banquet was in a restaurant in downtown Jiading. At lunch, Shezhu asked Xin Mama, or Ah Juan, if she was interested in purchasing an apartment in Xincheng.

This was the time apartments in urban Jiading were selling like hotcakes. Shezhu said that her company was completing several buildings and all the apartments had already been sold except for one. This one, on the second floor, was considered ideal, for it was easy to climb to in a building without an elevator yet it was high enough to be safe from robbers and thieves as well as high enough to be free of the shadows of shrubs. Shezhu explained that there were two apartments on the same floor and the other one had been purchased by her sister-in-law, Ah Ming's sister. Shezhu said that Xin Mama would already know her neighbor if she bought the apartment.

Ah Juan expressed an interest, but said that she had never been to Xincheng, so she asked Shezhu to go with her to see the community and the particular building. They rode their bikes to Xincheng that same afternoon. After seeing the apartment, Ah Juan said she would talk to Zhongming about it. Very quickly, they decided to buy the apartment. They followed us and moved into their Xincheng apartment in the latter part of 1998. Their apartment was about a fifteen-minute walk from ours.

NEW HOME IN URBAN SHANGHAI

Before we bought the Xincheng apartment, I told Shebao that his father and I would not mind moving into the Liyuan apartment if he and Xiao Xie were thinking of buying a bigger place. Xiao Xie said they were not. They were living a comfortable life at the time, financially speaking. If they bought a larger apartment, they would be in debt and would have to live on a tighter budget.

Then, right after we moved to Xincheng, an opportunity arose for Shebao and Xiao Xie to buy an apartment in urban Shanghai. At the time, Shebao had resigned from his job at the Shanghai University of Science and Technology and started to develop his own business, but Xiao Xie was still working there. The university had merged with several other colleges and was now called Shanghai University. The expanded university signed a contract with a building company in urban Shanghai so that its faculty and staff could buy apartments at a discounted price. Xiao Xie and Shebao decided to seize the opportunity and buy an apartment.

Xiao Xie and Shebao took us to see the apartment they were considering in urban Shanghai. These were buildings of seven stories and they were equipped with elevators. Such buildings were known as "little high-rises," a popular style desired by many people. According to a law, a building with six floors did not require an elevator, but a building of seven floors must be equipped with an elevator. The apartment we saw was on the sixth floor of a seven-story building. It had three bedrooms, a bright living room with big windows, two bathrooms, and two balconies.

They bought the apartment and moved into it quickly. Chen Li was finishing the fifth grade in elementary school in Jiading. Xiao Xie wanted him to attend his sixth grade in a good middle school close to the apartment they bought. The new residential community was good for Chen Li's growth in another way. Since many apartments in the community were sold at a discounted price to the university faculty and staff, most residents would be university-affiliated people, better than an unknown group of mixed backgrounds. Just like Shezhu, Xiao Xie wanted Chen Li to get the best educational opportunities possible.

In the summer of 2000, Shebao and his family moved to urban Shanghai. Chen Li started his sixth grade in September. The move also made it easier for Xiao Xie to get to work every day. After her university became a part of Shanghai University, her Department of Film and Television Arts moved to the main campus of the university, which was in urban Shanghai. Before they moved to the new apartment, she had to take a university bus from the Jiading campus to the Shanghai campus in the morning and take the bus back to Jiading in the evening. She spent a lot of time every day commuting. Now she used public transportation and got to the university herself. It was much easier and consumed much less time every day.

After they moved, they decided to sell the apartment in Li Compound. We suggested that they rent out the apartment. One of Xiao Xie's friends asked her if she would rent out the apartment because this friend knew somebody who was looking for a place to rent. Xiao Xie said that she did not want to rent it. She explained that she had gotten along very well with her neighbors in Li Compound. If she rented the apartment and found out that the renter was a troublemaker, she would feel bad for her neighbors. Xiao Xie is a friendly, generous, and thoughtful person. In this instance, she demonstrated empathy.

Subsequently, Shebao and Xiao Xie sold the apartment in Li Compound. We told Shebao to use the money to pay toward the mortgage they took to buy the Shanghai apartment, but they brought the money to us in a bag. Shebao said that that apartment belonged to his father and the money was his father's money. We said that he was silly. It is a common practice in our area for a father to prepare a house when the son gets married. So that apartment was his and the money was for him to keep or use. But our silly son insisted, and so his father deposited the money in a bank. Three years later, when the certificate of deposit matured, my husband took out the money and gave it to Shebao. This time, Shebao deposited the money in a separate account. Up to this day, he still refers to the money as his father's money.

In TV programs, in movies, and in everyday life, we see families arguing about money or even engaging in physical fights about money. My husband and I always say that we are very lucky. We do not have to face such headaches.

RETIREMENT AND FUN

My husband reached his official age of sixty,[1] which was the government-designated retirement age for men, in 1990. Jianbang Town held a luncheon for him to celebrate his retirement in December of that year. After the lunch, the town leaders drove him home, beating drums and gongs when they approached our downtown apartment. They all came up to our house and we entertained them with candies, nuts, and fruits in our kitchen-dining room.

My husband was very happy that day. He apparently had consumed
a lot of alcohol at the luncheon. He had a large capacity for alcohol, so
I had never seen him drunk. That day, I thought he had drunk a bit too
much because he was very talkative. He held Chen Li, who was two
years old, and said many times, "Chen Li, Grandpa is not drunk."

His friends and colleagues presented him with congratulation
gifts, which included wine and liquor. As we adults were entertaining
the guests in our kitchen-dining room, Chen Li wandered into the
bedroom, where the wine and liquor were. We suddenly smelled a
strong fragrance of wine. We went into the bedroom and found that
Chen Li had accidently broken a large jar of rice wine. The bedroom
floor was covered with wine, producing a strong wine fragrance for
the entire apartment.

We declared that this was a happy accident, and we shall always
remember the occasion of Chen Li's breaking the wine jar. It has
proven true, for every time we mention my husband's retirement
party, we remember the accident. Earlier, when Shebao moved to Li
Compound, we accidentally broke a thermos bottle. The breaking of a
thermos bottle made a loud noise. Xiao Xie said that other families set
off loud firecrackers when they moved from one place to another, but
we broke a thermos bottle for the sound instead.

After my husband's official retirement, he worked as an advisor in
an economic development company and received additional income
beyond his retirement pension. He worked there until 2001.

In 1991, I reached the official age of sixty. Since my husband and
I had been thinking of visiting Shezhen and Zhou Wei together, we
decided to travel to Beijing as a way of celebrating my sixty years of
life. In May 1991, we took the train to the capital city.

When we went to Beijing, we bought the basic tickets and so sat
on the train all the way. Zhou Wei and Shezhen said that it was too
tiring for us to sit on the train for twenty-some hours. So for our return
trip, Zhou Wei bought us sleeper tickets, which were more expensive.
There were six beds in one train compartment. There were three
levels of sleepers. I slept on the low level and my husband took the
middle-level bed right above mine.

At bedtime, a man came and slept on the floor between the two low beds. With him taking up the floor, it was difficult for the six of us in the compartment to move around. The man apparently knew the attendants working on the train so nobody told him otherwise. We all coped with it.

In the middle of the night, my husband got up to go to the bathroom. He had a very expensive cigarette lighter in his pocket. The lighter was a gift from a very good friend and my husband treasured it. As he put on his pants, the lighter dropped to the floor. Since it was the middle of the night, he decided not to disturb anybody. When we all got up in the morning, my husband looked for the lighter, but failed to find it. He asked the man sleeping on the floor if he had seen it. The man claimed that he had not seen it. Although we both knew that he had picked it up, we did not want to fight. I told my husband to let it go.

NEW JOBS

As I got older, I found the distance between our downtown apartment and the Chemical Machinery Plant was too much for me every day. So I quit the kitchen job and got a temporary job in Huilong Middle School in Jiading Town. The school ran an affiliated factory and a station that sold drinking water. My job was to clean the factory's offices, the water station, and its toilets, and to boil water on an electric stove for thermos bottles in the offices and the station. This was a much easier job, and it took me only fifteen minutes to walk to work. I would do a morning round of work and go back to my apartment for lunch. After lunch, I could take a nap. In the afternoon, I worked only a couple of hours more.

During the two years I worked there, I also served as a matchmaker. My husband's elder sister told me that one of her relatives was looking for a daughter-in-law. She said that the young man had graduated from a technical school and was now working at the Gear Wheel Factory, which was an enterprise run by Shanghai Municipality. In those days, such a factory meant better wages and benefits. My husband's sister further said that because this young man was now working in Jiading Town, he did not want to marry a girl still living in the rural area. So she asked me to keep an eye open for the right girl. I did not know this young man personally, but I knew his parents. I met them when I attended events such as weddings sponsored by my husband's sister.

At Huilong Middle School, I got to know a woman who worked in the dining room that provided lunch for students and school employees as well as workers of its affiliated factory. The woman was from Jianbang Town. She and her family were of peasant stock, but their village was right on the edge of Jiading Town and thus had been relocated for urban development. As a result, she and her family had become urban people.

One day, when this woman's daughter came to visit, I met the daughter. Afterward, I said to the woman, "Your daughter is beautiful." The woman said, "Well, are you going to find her a boyfriend?"

I thought of the boy my sister-in-law had mentioned. But I knew that my coworker would not marry her daughter to a family who did not have a house in urban Jiading. She had told me that her daughter would not know how to live a life without a flushing toilet.

Through my sister-in-law I found that the young man's family lived in a rural village but was buying an apartment in urban Jiading. With this information, I told my coworker about the young man. She was very interested and asked me to arrange a meeting for them.

So I did. I told both parties that we would meet at Little-Child Bridge in downtown Jiading. I met the boy and his mother. We waited on the north side of the bridge. The agreed meeting time came and went, but we did not see my coworker and her daughter. The boy kept looking at his watch and finally said that he had to go to work. We did not wait any longer and left separately.

The next day, I asked my coworker why she had not shown up. She said that they had gone to the meeting on time, waited a long time, and wondered why the other party had not shown up. I realized that I had not made the meeting site precise enough. I should have said that they were to meet on the northern side or the southern side of the bridge. Now that they had missed each other in a pre-arranged meeting, I thought they probably were not meant to be together.

Surprisingly, both parties asked me to arrange another meeting. My husband was aware of all of this and said, "Why don't you ask both parties to come to our apartment?" I thought that was a good idea. So both mothers and the boy and girl came to our apartment. I bought some candies and fruits and made tea for the meeting.

After a brief meeting and formal introduction, I suggested that the two young people go for a walk. They did. Their mothers came riding their own bikes and so they went home separately. The next day, my coworker told me that the boy walked with the girl and finally escorted the girl to her home. The girl asked him into her home, so her father also saw the boy. My coworker said that she liked the boy and so did her husband. Now she was waiting to see if her daughter liked the boy.

Later on, I learned from my coworker that the day after their first meeting, the boy went to see the girl after work. The two young people met several times more. They seemed to like each other, my coworker said. Then one day, the boy went to the girl's home and had dinner there. It started to snow that evening. The girl's father asked the boy to stay for the night because he was worried about him riding his bike in the snow back to his rural home. My coworker told me that her husband liked the boy so much that he was treating the boy as if he were his own child.

The relationship developed. After the boy's family bought an apartment in the recently developed South Gate residential community, my coworker's daughter and the young man made decisions together in fixing up the apartment as their bridal suite.

When they got married, the boy's family invited me to the wedding banquet as the matchmaker. The family sent a car to my apartment to pick me up. They insisted that my husband also go, so we went together to the wedding banquet, held in the boy's village home.

On the third day after the wedding, both the boy's and girl's families brought many gifts to thank me for being the matchmaker. The gifts included cakes and fruits and foods such as meat and fish.

According to local tradition, the boy's family would bring foods such as meat and fish to the matchmaker. But the girl's family did not have to do this. My coworker brought me many gifts to show her appreciation.

I have run into the parents as well as the young people many times since the wedding. Every time, I hear that they have established a happy family. Recently, I saw my former coworker, who was excited to tell me that her granddaughter graduated from elementary school last summer.

When we moved to Xincheng in 1998, I had stopped working at Huilong Middle School and so volunteered to cook lunches for Ah Ming and his workers. It is a common practice that a small-business owner takes care of lunches for his/her employees. Ah Ming's business of installing air conditioners picked up, and he had a couple of men helping him. He had a little store where potential buyers could visit and see various models and brands of room air conditioners. When a customer decided on one, Ah Ming and his helpers would go out and install the air conditioner.

Ah Ming had been giving money to the two helpers and the woman attending the store to buy their own lunches. He also had been eating his lunches wherever he happened to be. I had heard him complaining about the kind of fast food he had to eat. So one weekend when Ah Ming and Shezhu were at my home, I said, "Your father goes to work during the day. I stay at home the whole day with nothing to do. I can cook lunches for Ah Ming and his helpers." I added, "I could do so in your first-floor apartment, which is only about a three-minute walk from my home. That way, you can come and eat a warm and home-cooked lunch every day." Ah Ming and Shezhu liked the idea, but they both said that it would be too much work for me and that they should not put me to the task. I said, "Let me try."

The apartment had been a storage place for air conditioners. We cleaned up the kitchen-dining room. There was already a kitchen cabinet for me to store cooking and eating utensils as well as for things such as cooking oil, salt, and soy sauce. This was the cabinet a carpenter from Pandai Brigade had made for us when we moved to South

Gate in 1985. We continued to use the cabinet in our downtown apartment. But when we moved to Xincheng, our new apartment already had a built-in cabinet in the kitchen and so we no longer needed the old cabinet. I insisted that we keep it because it was still in good shape and was a useful piece of furniture, so we placed it in Shezhu's first-floor apartment. Now the cabinet was put to good use again.

Every morning, I went to the local market and bought vegetables and meat. I picked them, cleaned them, and cooked the lunch in the first-floor apartment. When Ah Ming and his helpers came to eat, I would pack a lunch box for the woman attending the store so that Ah Ming could bring it to her after lunch. Shezhu, whose office was about a five-minute bike ride away, also came to have lunch with us.

Ah Ming's mother was still living in his home village and grew rice every year on her grain land. She supplied us with rice and I cooked the rice in an electric rice cooker. Every day, I cooked a meat or fish dish, a dish with vegetables and meat, a vegetable dish, and a soup. If Ah Ming had a friend joining us for lunch, he would let me know, and I would add another dish. If a visitor came without advance notice, Ah Ming would buy some cooked food and bring it to the lunch.

I had my own purse and a separate purse for the money from Ah Ming. When I bought something to cook for Ah Ming, I used the money from that particular purse. At the end of the month, I was able to tell him how much I had used. He would give me more money for the following month.

MORE TRAVEL

I was not always working—I also traveled with my husband to a number of places. In 1998, we traveled to Shandong with a group of my husband's friends and their wives. We visited Confucius's hometown and then went to climb Taishan. The day we climbed Taishan was a very cold and rainy day. When we arrived at the foot of the mountain, we were told that it was even colder higher up on the mountain. Since this was in the month of May, we had not brought heavy clothes. Fortunately, there were stores that rented out long cotton-padded coats. We each rented one and took the cable car up the mountain. When we got out of the car to climb to the top of Taishan, it was raining very heavily. We bought disposable raincoats and wore them over the cotton-padded coats. We climbed to the top of Taishan in the rain. The cold and the rain made this quite an unforgettable experience.

In the autumn of 1999, the same group went to Lushan. On our way to Lushan, we stopped at a place called Yingtan in Jiangxi. There, we rode on a water raft. There was a drizzle that day so it was wet and chilly. We tried to use grocery bags to protect our feet from the water that came up from below and from the sides as the raft went forward, but this did not work. Water leaked into our shoes and soaked our feet. The ride was about five hours long. At one point, we had to ask the driver of the raft to allow us onto one of the banks so that we could relieve ourselves. We walked into the lower bamboo groves. We learned from the raft driver that the lower bamboo groves produced the kind of tender bamboo shoots we buy in the market. It is a delicate vegetable called *bianjian*. That was the first time I saw it growing in its natural environment.

During the raft ride, we learned about a local custom of burying dead people high up in the rocks of the mountains. On one side of the river, there were mountains. In the rocks on the mountains we saw holes. Although we could not actually see inside the holes, we were told that coffins were hanging there.

We drove to Lushan the next day. A van took us up a mountain on a spiraling road. Unlike Taishan, Lushan is a sprawling national park with hotels, shops, lakes, and other sightseeing places. The first night in Lushan, we checked into a hotel in an old house. Inside our room, we were surprised to see a down comforter on the bed, for it was autumn and at home in Jiading we used down comforters only in the winter season. Then when night fell, it rained and turned cold. We were glad to have the comforter keeping us warm. We learned that because of the town's high altitude, it rained most of the nights throughout the year, and it could be cold even during the summer.

The one-story hotel had a metal roof. When it rained at night, the raindrops made a lot of noise, so we did not sleep very well. The next day, we complained to the travel agent, who moved us to another hotel. This one was in a building that had four stories and we stayed on the second floor.

We did a lot of sightseeing during the three days inside the national park. We visited the place where Chairmen Mao held an important meeting in the 1950s. We saw a lake with pavilions in it, surrounded by mountain peaks. One day, the van that was taking us sightseeing had a flat tire. We had to get out of the van while the driver fixed it. We were already high up on a mountain; yet we saw still higher mountain peaks surrounding us.

In 2000, we went to Hainan, a very southern place. There, I saw several things that I had never seen in their natural environment. One of them was coconut. Coconuts were growing everywhere we visited. We learned to eat the fruit while there. After we bought one, we had to crack it open and then use a straw to drink the liquid. Our tour guide told us that the thick layer of white flesh inside the coconut was also useful. The coco flakes we could buy in grocery stores came from that white flesh.

I saw a large field of pineapples. I had never seen pineapples growing in fields. When I first saw them in a field from a distance, I thought they were turnips, but the local tour guide assured us they were pineapples.

When we were visiting Hainan, one of the things that tourists were eager to buy was anything made of sea turtle shell (*daimao*). We were told that sea turtle shell has medicinal effects: it can lower blood pressure and clean the body of bad elements. My husband and I did not totally believe this, but we still bought a bracelet and two rings made of sea turtle shell. My husband wore one of the rings for some time, since it was supposed to help lower blood pressure. We gave the other ring to my husband's sister. We did not use the bracelet; it was just a souvenir.

Our trip to Hainan was in March, but it was already hot there. So when we packed to come home, we put away our heavy clothes and wore only shirts. When we arrived in Shanghai and got out at Hongqiao Airport, we felt really cold, for it was still spring in our hometown.

NOTES

1   The "official age" is used here to distinguish it from the local way of counting one's age.

13

Crossing Borders and
Leaving the Ancestral Village

I N the old days, when my grandmother walked to Shanghai, she was considered an exceptionally daring woman. Most people, particularly women, in Wangjialong never visited Jiading Town in their entire life. My mother was an example. Other than being accompanied to see a doctor in West Gate, Mother never went to urban Jiading in her entire life.

When I visited Shezhen, who worked and lived in the New England region of the United States, my children told me that I was going to the other side of the earth. In terms of distance, they told me, I was going the farthest anyone could go from China.

My husband had always wanted to visit Shezhen in the United States, but I was worried about his health. He was diagnosed with high blood pressure and coronary heart disease when he was in his fifties. In the winter of 1997, during his forty-five-day hospital stay, his doctors, having observed his extremely irregular heartbeat and high blood pressure, told me that his heart could stop any time and we the family should be prepared for the worst. After that hospital stay, doctors prescribed medication for him, but they were not able to figure out what caused his irregular heartbeat. I had observed that any lack of sleep or irregularity in his life had an effect on his blood pressure and irregular heartbeat. I knew traveling to the United States involved long plane rides and a huge time difference and would upset his life in a significant way.

But my husband was determined. After Shezhen got her green card, we obtained our passports and began to apply for visas to enter the United States. The application for visas was complicated. Shezhen sent us all kinds of materials, including bank statements, tax returns, and a letter from her university. Shezhen said the materials were to show to American consuls that the intention of the trip was to visit our daughter and that our daughter could support us while we were there. We also prepared our documents showing our ownership of a house, our bank account, and the fact that we had a son, another daughter, and grand-children in China. Our documents should demonstrate to American consuls that we had many reasons to return to China.

Shezhen knew from experience how difficult it was to get a visa to enter the United States. When Zhou Wei worked in Hong Kong, one year he decided to use his Chinese New Year holiday to visit She-zhen. When he applied for a visa, the American consulate in Hong Kong refused to give him one.

In addition to documents, Shezhen also suggested that we bring a family photo with us when we went to the consulate for the interview. She said that we wanted the American visa consul to see that we had a large family, and that many of them were living and working in China. We took Shezhen's advice.

In March of 2001, my husband and I went to the American Consulate in Shanghai. We were very confident that we would get the visas. I said that I only wanted to go and see the place Shezhen worked and the home she and Zhou Wei had established there. If I could do that within one day, then one day would be enough. We never thought of staying in the United States for an extended period, let alone becoming immigrants. Since neither my husband nor I knew any English, we decided to make the trip in the summer when She-zhen was not teaching and could spend time with us.

While waiting for our number to be called, we saw people being called to the windows to meet with American consuls and many were denied visas. Then we were called. We went up to the window and were greeted by an American consul who spoke very good Shanghai dialect. He asked us a few questions and we answered them. Then he said that he could not give us visas because he suspected that we intended to immigrate to the United States. We both were very surprised and wanted to say something, but he had called the next person to the window.

We were very disappointed. It had taken us several months to prepare all the materials. We had to get up very early that day and waited for several hours outside the consulate and then inside the waiting room. And we had worked up our emotions and expectations. I was most concerned about the impact the denial would have on my husband's health.

But my husband was pretty calm. He said that we had done our best and that the result was beyond our control. He said he had given up, and I was relieved. When we returned home, we called Shezhen to tell her that we had been denied the visas and that we had decided not to pursue the trip any further.

Shezhen refused to accept the result. She told us that she had gotten support and help from her American friends and that she and her friends and colleagues were writing letters to American congressmen. These letters said that Shezhen was using her job to vouch that her parents had no intention of immigrating to the United States. At the same time, she decided to come back and visit us that summer.

When her semester was over, Shezhen came back. Those days, we did not have an Internet connection in our house, so she went to check e-mail at her sister's house one morning. That morning my husband answered a phone call from the American Consulate in Shanghai. The caller said we could get our visas to enter the United States at our convenience.

We could not believe what had happened. We knew what Shezhen had done, but we did not expect any success. We did not know that Americans also depended on connections in order to do things.

My husband waited at the window to tell Shezhen the news. When she returned, her father told her the news through the window before she entered the building.

A few days later, Shezhen accompanied us to the American Consulate in Shanghai. We again stood in a long line outside the consulate, then waited inside, and finally were called to a window. Without asking us any questions, the consul granted us the visas. With the visas in hand, we immediately bought our plane tickets. On July 10, we flew to the United States with Shezhen.

When we landed in San Francisco, I said to my husband, "We should follow Shezhen very closely now." We did not know a word of English and were not able to communicate with anybody. We were really in a foreign land.

From San Francisco, Shezhen took us to Salt Lake City, where she had earned her master's and PhD degrees. At the airport, Keith, Brown Beard's father, came to pick us up. We had seen him in many photos Shezhen had sent us, but this was the first time we met him in person. He and his wife had treated Shezhen as if she were their daughter. After Shezhen introduced us, he gave each of us a big hug. We felt very warm in this foreign land.

Shezhen was very familiar with the city and asked Keith to take us to a hotel. After we settled into the hotel, Shezhen took us out to a Chinese restaurant for dinner. We walked to the restaurant. I remember we saw a lot of construction. Shezhen said that the city was constructing a light-rail. After dinner, Shezhen paid the bill and gave a tip. I said that the tip would have bought the dinner if we were in Jiading. We took a taxi back to the hotel because it was already dark. It was only a short distance, for we had walked there, but it cost us twenty-three dollars. Then Shezhen gave a tip of seven dollars, when she gave the driver thirty dollars and told him to keep the change. So the cost of that short taxi ride was thirty dollars. At that time, an American dollar was worth eight Chinese yuan. When I did the math, I realized how expensive the American life was. Shezhen had told us about her income, her expenses, and other aspects of life in the United States, but we were very unprepared. Shezhen said that eating in a restaurant and taking a taxi were not regular parts of her everyday life.

I was worried about the impact of the jet lag on my husband. Right after we returned to the hotel, he was the first one to take a shower and went to sleep immediately. He slept like a log until the next morning. He said he did not feel the time difference. That was quite a relief to me.

The hotel provided a free breakfast in its lobby. There were tea bags and we made our own tea. We liked the bread that had a hole in the middle. There were also sweet breads.

After breakfast, Keith came to our hotel and drove us to his house. There, we met Elizabeth, Brown Beard's mother. We talked with them through Shezhen. We said that our hearts ached when we heard that their son, Brown Beard, had passed away.[1] We said that we were very fortunate to have met him in our home in Jiading. We learned more about Shezhen's life in Salt Lake City. They told us how hard she worked as a student and how much they liked her. We were very glad to have the opportunity to thank them in person for the care they and their family had given to our daughter. We had lunch at their house. Elizabeth cooked a meat-and-vegetable soup for us. With the soup there was also warm bread. Shezhen said that Elizabeth made the bread in her own oven.

Then we met Annina, a meeting of old friends. She took us to her house and invited us to stay. Shezhen accepted her invitation and so we moved to her house from the hotel. She took us out to a Chinese restaurant in Salt Lake City the first night we stayed with her. The following day, Shezhen took us to a Chinese grocery store and we bought Chinese things such as rice and vegetables. We cooked our own food in Annina's house. That was much better because we were not very used to American food.

We stayed in Salt Lake City for four nights. Shezhen took us to visit the University of Utah by bus. She showed us the two apartments she lived in when she was a student. When she pointed to a small window in the attic of a big house and said that she used to live there, tears welled up in my eyes. I thought of the loneliness she must have felt living in such an alien place, far away from family. She showed us the beautiful campus and the buildings in which she had an office when she was a teaching assistant.

One day, a big party was arranged for us at Leslie's house. Leslie was the daughter of Keith and Elizabeth. Her house had a big backyard and the party was late in the afternoon. There were chairs arranged on the green lawn in the backyard. Another son of Keith and Elizabeth also lived in the city. He came to the party with his wife and children. Elizabeth's sister also came. There were a couple of Chinese people from Beijing. They were friends with Shezhen and Annina. Annina cooked a chicken dish in her house and brought it to the party. Shezhen explained that Elizabeth and several other people also cooked and brought food to the party.

I thought that was a good idea. In China, when a family invites people to a dinner, it involves a lot of work for the host. The American party I witnessed that day involved less work for the sponsoring family.

The way to eat the food at this party was also very different. We took a paper plate, got some food from each dish, brought the plate of food to a chair on the lawn, and then sat there to eat the food. It was very casual and the host/hostess did not pressure you to eat more.

Another day, two of Shezhen's friends came and took us to their houses. They and their husbands had held a huge party to celebrate Shezhen's graduation when she got her PhD degree. Both women lived in big houses and their houses were beautiful inside and outside. Inside, there were soft carpets and comfortable sofas. They were very clean and tidy houses. Outside, they had planted flowers everywhere. When we admired their flowers, they decided to take us to see another house in the neighborhood, because that house was famous in the neighborhood for its flowers.

Indeed, there were so many flowers. The woman who owned that house showed us the flowers around the house. When we came to admire a particular kind of flower, she said that those flowers were perennials and they had been growing there for at least fifty years. I thought to myself: fifty years ago, we did not have enough food to eat, let alone grow flowers.

We left Salt Lake City for Boston by plane and landed in Boston
in the afternoon. When the plane flew into Boston, I saw big areas
of dark green color on the ground. I asked Shezhen what they were.
Shezhen said that they were wooded areas. After we landed, we
took an airport shuttle to a place where Zhou Wei met us. He drove
us to their house. On the way, we passed many wooded areas. I was
impressed. At home in Jiading, there had been a strong effort to plant
trees and flowers. What we had in Jiading were human planted trees
and flowers along the highways, while in the area where Shezhen and
Zhou Wei lived, trees were naturally preserved woods.

Shezhen and Zhou Wei lived in a clean house and a quiet environment. They invited us to sleep in a big bedroom with its own
bathroom. They slept in the other bedroom, which was also Shezhen's
office. There were only two bedrooms in the house, but there were
three bathrooms in it. The whole house was carpeted except for the
bathrooms and the kitchen. The carpet was very thick and soft. My
husband said that walking on the carpet required more effort because
it was so soft.

Every day, my husband and I took a walk in the residential complex. There was a swimming pool in the complex. In the afternoon,
we saw a few older people swimming and resting in the sun by the
pool. When we met people, they were all very polite. They would say
"hello" and "good morning." My husband learned "good morning"
and used it a few times. I walked on a wooded path one morning and
was startled by a long-tailed squirrel which suddenly jumped right in
front of my eyes from one tree to the next. After that, I avoided that
path when I walked.

Zhou Wei worked every weekday but Shezhen was home most of
the time because it was her summer vacation. She was writing a book
at that time, so my husband and I tried not to talk to her during the
day. On weekends, they took us out to see places. We went to a local
folk festival in the city where Shezhen's university is located. That
was the only time we saw many people on the streets. There were all
kinds of shows, but we did not understand them. Shezhen ran into
people she knew, and she introduced us to some of them.

Another weekend, Zhou Wei and Shezhen took us to Boston. We ate at a dim sum restaurant in Boston's Chinatown. They showed us the famous places in Boston. We shopped in a big Chinese grocery store. Only there did we see many Chinese vegetables and live and fresh fish and poultry. But Shezhen's house was far from Boston's Chinatown, and it was impossible for them to shop there every day.

Speaking of food, I found the variety to be lacking in the supermarkets near Shezhen's house. There were no *jiangdou*, *jiaobai*, *penghao*, or other ordinary vegetables we ate every day in Jiading. There was tofu, but it was expensive and there was only one kind. There were no live fish or shrimp. Seafood, however, was very good and fresh. We ate live lobster, fresh cod, and other kinds of seafood.

Shezhen also gave us a tour of her campus. She showed us her office, the classrooms she taught her classes in, and the library. One day, Shezhen was to teach a special summer class for a day. We went with her and sat in the classroom to observe her teaching. I did not understand a word she said, but I felt so much pride. I thought, "We must have done something right to bring up a daughter who is a professor in an American university."

Many times when I sat on the soft sofa in Shezhen's spacious living room or in the clean kitchen with big windows, I thought back on the forty-some years since Shezhen was born. We were so poor then, our house was so dark and crowded, we had no books in our house, I was illiterate. . . . Now this little country girl has a PhD degree, teaches in the United States, and owns this comfortable house. All of this was beyond my dreams. The greatest regret in my life is that I did not get an education. What Shezhen has achieved has brought satisfaction to me. I also thought that my father must be very proud of what Shezhen has achieved. He regretted that I did not get an education. He started to teach Shezhen to read when she was very little and was always happy when Shezhen brought home good grades from school.

Shezhen and Zhou Wei also took us to see the mountains. That day, Zhou Wei was the only driver, for Shezhen forgot to bring her driver's license. We had lunch in the mountains. On our way back,

Zhou Wei felt sleepy and so we stopped and he took a nap in the car. Shezhen could drive, but she did not do so because she did not want to get into trouble. I liked their careful attitude in life.

We went to visit New York City one weekend. We got up very early, drove to Boston Chinatown, and took a bus. We arrived in New York City before noon and had lunch in a Chinese restaurant in New York City's Chinatown.

We visited many places and walked a lot. Shezhen and Zhou Wei pointed out the Statue of Liberty and the Twin Towers in New York City while we were on a ferryboat to an island. Unfortunately, it was raining at the time, so we only saw the statue and the towers very vaguely.

After we returned to Jiading, on September 11, I watched the terrorist attacks on TV. My husband told me that the two buildings attacked by the terrorist planes were the Twin Towers we had seen in New York City in the previous month. It was a frightening scene and I felt a big chill inside me.

Shezhen and Zhou Wei also took us to see the United Nations. I saw a small dark house built with many guns. The gun house looked so frightening that I did not dare to get close to it. Shezhen told me that the guns were collected from all over the world. Behind each gun, there was a story of violence. Outside the building there was a statue of a gun. The barrel of that gun was twisted into a knot. I understood that the house of guns and the gun statue were antiviolence and anti-war demonstrations.

The night we spent in New York City was unforgettable. My husband started to feel an irregular heartbeat around midnight. He took his medicine and walked inside the small hotel room. He said that walking helped decrease the discomfort the irregular heartbeat created. The medicine failed to calm down the arrhythmia this time. I pretended to be calm, for I did not want to scare Shezhen and Zhou Wei. Inside I was so worried. I had learned to feel my husband's pulse. That night, as I held his wrist, I was able to tell how weak his heartbeat was and how the heartbeats were in clusters of two with long pauses in between. I thought to myself: my husband is in his seventies, so he is no longer young and has suffered from high blood pressure and irregular heartbeat for a long time. But I could not fathom what would happen if his life came to an end in a hotel room in New York City. I understood his desire to visit Shezhen in the United States and so supported it. Now I said to myself perhaps that was a bad decision. Dawn came and my husband's cardiac arrhythmia finally calmed down. We took the bus back to Boston and drove home in our own car.

Before the trip to New York City, my husband had experienced cardiac arrhythmia while at Shezhen's house. After the trip, the problem occurred more often. Then one day, he realized that he had miscalculated one medicine and that this particular medicine was running out. Shezhen said that she could take her father to see her physician and get the medicine. Her father said that an American doctor who had no knowledge of his medical history would surely put him through all kinds of tests before he could get the medicine. He did not want to go through such a process. After some discussion, my husband and I decided to go back to Shanghai as soon as possible. We had planned to stay for three months, but ended up staying for only forty-seven days.

Shezhen called the airline and changed our return ticket to the earliest possible date. Since we were to travel home alone, Shezhen requested special help from the airline. The airline people promised that they would make sure that we got Chinese language service on the plane and that they would assist us to the connecting flight at the San Francisco Airport. Shezhen explained to us that at San Francisco Airport, we should get off the plane and wait right there for somebody to come and escort us to the connecting flight. We called Shebao to let him know the arrival flight and time at Shanghai Pudong Airport and asked him to meet us there.

Shezhen prepared a note in both Chinese and English in case we failed to get help when we landed at San Francisco Airport. The note contained our flight information from San Francisco to Shanghai. We could use the note to ask for help and directions. She made a copy so we carried two copies of the same note.

We left on August 27 and Shezhen and Zhou Wei saw us off at the Boston airport. In the airport waiting room, I experienced a roller coaster of emotions. I was so proud of what Shezhen had achieved and was very happy to see the comfortable home she and Zhou Wei had established. I also liked the summer weather and the general environment Shezhen now lived in. But I realized how far she lived and worked from us. She is a part of me, yet she is so far from me. I was also worried about my husband's health during the long flight to Shanghai. If something happened to him, what could we do? I felt I was totally lost. Mixed emotions swirled inside me. I tried to control them but failed. I burst into sobs and could not stop. I knew I was scaring Shezhen, but I just could not help myself.

When we began to board the plane, Shezhen went up to the counter and asked the staff there to see if arrangements had been made for Chinese language service and assistance to the connecting flight for us. The staff said that the arrangement had been made and it was in the system. They looked at us and assured us that we would get the special help.

On the plane from Boston to San Francisco, we managed to get the drinks offered on the plane with gestures. There was no Chinese language service for us. When we landed at San Francisco Airport, we stepped off the plane and waited at the exit for assistance to the connecting flight. After about ten minutes of waiting, we saw a staff member getting off the plane. We handed him one of the copies of the note Shezhen had prepared for us. He took it and made a gesture to us. We thought that he said we should wait right there.

We waited another twenty some minutes, but nobody showed up. We now were worried that if we waited any longer, we could miss the flight to Shanghai. We pulled our bags and walked away from the exit gate. We stopped a man who looked kind enough to us and showed him the other copy Shezhen had prepared for us. This time, we held onto the piece of paper without letting it go, for that was the only thing that would help us get to the connecting flight. The man wrote down on our slip of paper the Arabic number of the gate from which our connecting flight was to take off and pointed us in one direction.

We thanked him with a bow and then walked in the direction he showed us. We were able to recognize Arabic numbers written on the gates. The number for our flight to Shanghai was in the nineties. As we walked, we saw the numbers increase. So we knew we were walking in the right direction.

Then we walked into a waiting area where there were many Chinese people, many of whom even spoke the Shanghai dialect. We checked the number on the gate, and it was the gate from which our flight was to take off. I finally was able to put my heart back into my chest.

When we arrived in Shanghai, it was late in the afternoon. Shebao and Chen Li came to meet us at Pudong Airport. Chen Li shouted, "Grandpa and Grandma" from a distance as soon as we walked into view. I felt an indescribable feeling, a feeling of family and a feeling of relief. Shezhu was cooking dinner for us at our Xincheng home. There is a local saying, "Gold house or silver house, nothing is better than the doghouse which is home." That was my feeling when we got home.

When we were eating dinner, Shezhen called on the phone to check if we had arrived home. When we told her that the airline had failed to deliver on its promise, she was not happy. Later on, she told us that she wrote to the airline and complained about it. The airline replied with an apology. We are glad that that trip to the United States was our first and last.

The visit to Shezhen's home gave me a physical sense of her house, workplace, and the larger environment she lived in. Quite often I imagine that Shezhen is driving to work or is driving home from work. When she called and said that she did not go anywhere and worked in her home office the whole day, I could picture her working at the desk upstairs and eating meals downstairs in the bright kitchen. When she sent me a photo of the flowers she grew outside her house, I felt that I could physically see the flowers, because I had been there.

I am glad that we made the trip and that we returned home safe and sound.

CHAPTER 13

VILLAGE RELOCATION

Most rural people in our area hoped that their village or their house would be within the zone of urban expansion or development so that they would be relocated. Relocation meant getting a new apartment and becoming a salaried worker for the young and getting a retirement pension for the old. Many towns and villages closer to urban Jiading had already experienced relocation. By the early 2000s, rural families without an apartment in urban Jiading could not even find wives for their sons, for most young women wished to be urban dwellers.

At the end of the 1990s, Little Aunt's village was relocated when a highway was built through its land. After her house was torn down and before a new house was built, Little Aunt and her family stayed in her granddaughter's village house. One day, I phoned her granddaughter and told her that I was coming for a visit. I took a city bus from Xincheng, changed to the rural bus, and got to Zhuqiao Town. From there, I walked to the village.

When I approached the first house of the village, I saw Little Aunt walking out from the guest hall of that house toward me. In rural villages, unlike in cities, people all knew each other and casual visits to another's house without prior notice was a very common practice. Apparently Little Aunt was eager to see me, for she had walked with difficulty—due to a previous stroke—to that house so that she could meet me as early as possible.

When I got close to her, I saw tears in her eyes. After the stroke, Little Aunt had difficulty speaking. When she was excited and could not express herself, her eyes welled with tears. I walked with her to her granddaughter's house. She showed me the room she and her husband stayed in. It was tight, but they had all the necessities for a simple life.

After Little Aunt and her family moved into the new house built by the relocation authorities, I continued to visit her regularly. The new house was very spacious and had two stories; Aunt and Uncle lived on the first floor. Outside the front door was a paved patio. When I visited her on a sunny and warm day, I would see Little Aunt sitting out on the patio. The houses built for Little Aunt and her fellow villagers were the envy of many rural people. Several times, we people from Wangjialong heard rumors that our houses were also to be relocated.

In the summer of 2003, I met one of my fellow villagers while doing my daily shopping in Xincheng. He said, "Have you heard that our village will be relocated?" I replied, "I have heard this before, but not recently. Is this real?" Since there had been such rumors before, I did not think too much about it. Two days later, I answered a phone call from our village head. He informed me of a meeting in two days and he said the meeting was about relocation. My husband and I went to the meeting and received all the details about the relocation.

The relocation was sponsored by Jiading Industrial Sector, which is an administrative unit equivalent to a town. More than three thousand families were to be relocated and Wangjialong was within the relocation zone. Yang Family Village (Yangjiazhai), Ah Ming's native village, was also within the relocation zone.

The local authorities were given the task of measuring and appraising our village houses for compensation. We were also compensated for the crops on our family plot. It did not matter what one was growing on the plot or whether one was growing anything at all. We were also compensated for the well we had dug many years earlier, and the trees in front and behind our house. The stone steps to the water that my father had put in before Liberation were also counted for compensation. Altogether, we received 344,310 yuan as compensation.

The relocation authorities showed us blueprints of the various styles they would build for the relocating families. The largest townhouse had three stories; in the middle was the two-story kind; and then there were apartments in multilevel buildings. My husband and I decided to buy a two-story townhouse, which cost us 289,310 yuan. We had 55,000 yuan left, which was about enough money to have the new house furnished for occupation. This style had a one-car garage, a living room, a dining room, a kitchen, and a bathroom on the first level. On the second level were three bedrooms, another bathroom, and a laundry room.

Families with four generations were entitled to buy an apartment in the apartment buildings, in addition to a townhouse. I say "entitled" because the houses built particularly for the relocating population were sold at a lower-than-market price. Families with four generations could sell their entitlement for money.

Ah Ming and Shezhu bought the largest townhouse with the compensation they received from their village house. They had just sold the Xincheng apartment in which I cooked lunches in the 1990s. They used some of that money to buy an entitlement and then used the rest to buy an additional three-bedroom apartment in a multilevel building.

Before we handed in the keys, we were encouraged to remove anything movable that we wanted to keep. I wished to keep the two traditional beds. One of them was made when my father and mother got married. The other one was made when my husband and I got married. Unfortunately, there was no space in our Xincheng apartment for them, so I had to let them go.

Shebao went home with me and took pictures of the house before it was torn down (figs. 13.1 and 13.2). People from nearby villages which were not within the relocation zone came to us and asked to take the wood items for firewood. A woman came to me, and I allowed her and her family to take the beds. They dismantled the beds into a big pile of wood and took it away in a truck.

In Wangjialong, our South Hamlet was the first to hand in our house keys. People in North Hamlet, my husband's native village, handed in their keys about two weeks later. One day after we handed in our house keys, my husband's nephews called to invite us to a ceremony at which they were to inform their ancestors about the relocation. We did not perform such a ceremony because I had already transferred the ritual site from our Wangjialong home to our home in Xincheng. On the day we went to the ceremony in North hamlet, I saw the destruction of the houses in South Hamlet.

Huge bulldozers knocked down the houses built with bricks and mortar. It was very easy for the houses to come down. I saw a bulldozer approach a house, stretch its arm, and knock at the house. The

13.1   Wangjialong house, 2003

13.2   Wangjialong bedroom, 2003

house crumbled like a toy house put together by a child. A column of dust puffed into the air. The house was reduced instantly into a pile of rubble.

A fellow villager in her eighties stood on the front road of the village and watched the bulldozers knocking down the houses. I happened to be near her when she murmured that she had forgotten to take the bottle of pickles she used at breakfast a while before. Right before the bulldozer came to her house, she walked toward the house, saying that she needed to go inside to get the pickles. Someone stopped her and said that it was already too late.

The house my husband and I worked hard to build was now gone. The homesite where I was born, grew up, and raised my children became almost unrecognizable. Fortunately, since the relocation authorities kept the river behind our old house, the Zhangjing River (Zhangjing He), and kept the Coal-cinder Road, I can still approximately point to the location of my ancestral home.

Aside from sentiment, I should say that our village house was really old and no longer structurally sound and safe. Since we did receive compensation for our old house and were able to buy a new one which is less than five hundred meters south of our original house, I consider the new house our ancestral home.

Before Liberation, we were totally dependent on land for living. We worked hard and lived frugally to buy land. After collectivization, working on the land was the last thing people wanted to do. We tried hard to find a way to make a living away from working the land. When people said, "I am still embroidering the earth," it indicated frustration and a sense of failure in life.

In the several years before the relocation, I seldom went back to the village. Even when I went back, I did not go far into the fields. Then one day before the relocation, I went to visit a relative, walked past the cropland, and saw fruit trees growing there. I asked people still living in the village about it and learned that the fruit trees were planted by a man they did not know. This man, who signed a contract with local authorities to work on the land, was very smart. After he planted the trees, he sowed fast-growing vegetables between the trees as he waited for the trees to grow up and bear fruit. Older people in our village worked for this man when he needed additional hands to pick vegetables for the local market and earned hourly wages. This man was running a very profitable business on our land.

After the relocation, all Wangjialong villagers were covered by small-town social security (*zhenbao*), which provided retirement pensions for men over sixty and women over fifty-five. The relocation authorities also provided stipends to those people who were under those ages until they found employment. Those who had reached retirement age were very happy. Some people said that the retirement pension was like a dream. As peasants, we never thought that we would receive such a pension. One woman said, "In the past, I worked so hard and sweated so much. Yet I never had any cash in my pocket. Now I sit at home doing nothing, but I receive money at the end of every month. I am living in a paradise."

Villagers younger than sixty or fifty-five found employment as gate guards, street cleaners, river cleaners, and garbage-can cleaners in the newly established residential communities for the relocated population or in residential communities in urban Jiading. Such jobs required little skill or education and so most people could do them. After the relocation, I ran into several people working such jobs in Xincheng, and they were from the relocated villages.

Jiading Industrial Sector paid part of the fee we needed to relocate our ancestral graves. Each family received a five-hundred-yuan coupon that could be used only at Green Bamboo Cemetery (Qingzhuyuan) in Waigang. We paid a total of 5,500 yuan for a tomb site for my parents inside that cemetery.

After having kept my parents' ash boxes in our village house for several years, I buried them in our own family plot in the early 1980s. Little Aunt came for the burying ceremony and helped me in the burial process. In the late 1980s, a clothes factory was to be built on the land where my parents were buried. Little Aunt came again and helped me move my parents' remains to the new family plot we were assigned to. When I dug up the ash boxes, they had disintegrated. Since the two boxes had been buried next to each other, the disintegration made it impossible for me to distinguish my father's ashes from my mother's ashes. So I gathered them into one earthen jar for the reburial.

I reburied my parents' remains in the earthen jar deep in the ground. At that time, I lived in urban Jiading. I knew I would be coming to work on the family plot less and less. Without me to tend the burial site often, I wanted to make sure that my parents would not be bothered. So on this hot September day when Shebao used a shovel to unearth his grandparents' remains, it was not an easy job. After much digging, he did not see any sign of an earthen jar. He asked me if I was sure he was digging at the right place. I assured him that was the place, because I had marked the gravesite with an evergreen plant. I informed Meifang's sons, who had been growing crops on our family plot, that under the evergreen plant were my parents' remains. They knew, as I knew, that a gravesite should not be touched. So the evergreen plant should not have been replanted and the remains should still be under it.

This was early autumn and the land was overgrown with crops. Sweet corn and sugarcane plants were much taller than any of us. Shebao was digging inside the overgrown crops and doing the physical labor he was not used to. In addition, it was an unusually hot September day. Sweat soaked his clothes. Shezhu stood by the digging site and said, "Grandpa, Grandma, your love for and care of your grandson is now paying off. You called Brother 'Big Man.' It is now the Big Man who is put to use." Shebao finally got to the jar that contained his grandparents' remains.

The new tomb site we bought at Green Bamboo Cemetery had two burial holes, so I had sewed two red-cloth bags for the ashes. My husband's nephew, who was a carpenter, made two ash boxes for us. I stretched open the bags while Shebao used his hands to get out the ashes from the jar and put them into the bags. After all the ashes were put into the bags, I tied the bags and put them in the boxes. My husband and I then each carried a box and walked directly to the Coal-cinder Road. There, we waited for a taxi, which took us to the cemetery. Shebao and Shezhu went with us.

13.3   Chen Huiqin, Shezhu, and Chen Xianxi, 2003

The tomb site in Green Bamboo Cemetery had already been
prepared. A tombstone with my parents' names carved on it had
been erected. When we arrived with the ash boxes, a staff member
of the cemetery came to assist us. It is believed that a cold burial site
is not good for the descendants of the dead. So we took away the
two slabs that covered the burial holes and the staff member lit a fire
to warm the holes. After the fire was out, we laid the ash boxes into
the warm holes and replaced the covering slabs. The staff member
used cement to seal the slabs and said, "Now you can rest assured
that your ancestors are very comfortable here. Nothing can get in to
bother them."

I performed a simple ceremony at the new tomb site. I brought
with me a candle and incense sticks, some red paper, some fruits and
cookies, a little wine, two plastic cups, and paper money I made with
my own hands. I spread out the red paper on the raised space right
in front of the burial holes, put out the wine cups, poured wine into
the cups, placed the fruits and cookies on the red paper, and lit the

13.4   Helen Community, 2012

candle and incense sticks. After that, I burned the paper money to my
parents on the ground right in front of the offerings (fig. 13.3).

In December 2004, we got the key to our new house. The new
residential community was called Hailun[2] (fig. 13.4). We do not
know who came up with the name, which sounds very modern and
foreign to us. The newly constructed community is very pretty.
There are no spiderweb-like wires or cables because they are all laid
underground. In the community, there are tidy streets, clean rivers
with wood-railed bridges, flower beds, grassy areas, wooded areas,
walking paths, and pavilions. We chose the style of our new house,
but its location was determined by drawing lots. We like the location
of our house very much. Our new house is in a cluster of two townhouses and our next-door neighbors, a family from South Hamlet,
are wonderful people.

My husband and I continued to live in Xincheng, where we had
easy access to hospitals, stores, and other facilities. We also lived very
close to Shezhu and her family, who had no plans to move to Helen

Community, either. Our new house in Helen Community was temporarily vacant.

NOTES

1 Brown Beard was Jeffrey Montague. He died of cancer in 1990.
2 Hailun is the literal translation of the English word "Helen." For smoother reading, Helen is used in the narrative.

14

Between the Living
and the Dead

IN the spring of 2006, my husband was bothered by serious irregular heartbeats. For a couple of weeks, he received IV drips in a
local hospital. Except for the irregular heartbeat, my husband was
a healthy man and so walked to and from the hospital. I always went
with him and stayed while he received IV drips. One late afternoon,
we were walking from the hospital toward home when he suffered
a heart attack. I tried to support him but lost my balance. We both
fell straight backward, with our faces up to the skies. I cried, "Mom,
Mom!" as I hit the concrete pavement while my husband fell on top
of me, with the back of his head hitting my chest. I thought to myself,
"What a perfect marriage! We are leaving this world together."

But we both survived. The accident left a bruise the size of my
palm on the back of my head while my husband sustained a little
scratch on the back of his head as it hit on the slider of a zipper on the
vest I wore that day.

The witnesses of our accident were from the neighborhood. They
said to me later, "Your ancestors are powerful and caring. They must
have protected you. Otherwise, how could you survive such a hard fall

with no concussion or internal injury?"

I do not know what happens when people die. But I know that if it is possible, my parents and ancestors would do everything to protect me and my family. In return, I have continued to hold the traditional rituals to remember our ancestors and to pay respects to Heaven, Earth, and bodhisattvas since I moved to urban Jiading in the 1980s. I do not worry about the format of performing the rituals. I believe that so long as I am sincere, the rituals are meaningful.

A PACEMAKER

After my husband's heart attack and the resulting fall on the sidewalk in the spring of 2006, Shebao did not think that doctors in Jiading hospitals were capable of taking care of his father, so he arranged for his father to be examined in Ruijin Hospital, the best hospital in Shangai for treating heart problems. At Ruijin Hospital, my husband was hooked up to an observation monitor around the clock and I accompanied him day and night. While sleeping in his hospital bed one evening, he experienced another fainting spell. Doctors rushed to perform emergency measures on him, concluding that my husband's fainting was caused by a temporary heart stoppage and that he needed a pacemaker.

Shebao and Xiao Xie came immediately after they got the telephone call from the hospital. With Shebao's signature, his father was wheeled into the operating room to receive a temporary pacemaker. We asked why it was a temporary one and what that meant. The doctors explained that the hospital was only responsible for putting in a pacemaker. The patient's family had to choose and buy one from among several suppliers of pacemakers. Once a pacemaker was placed into a person, it would be the responsibility of the manufacturer to check it and maintain it. Since this was nighttime, the suppliers were closed. It would be the next day before we could choose and buy one. Yet my husband's condition did not allow the delay until tomorrow, the doctors added. So they had to put in a temporary one.

After my husband was pushed into the operating room, Shebao

called Shezhu, who was at home in Jiading. Shezhu and Ah Ming responded quickly. Ah Ming at the time drove a pickup truck. Pickup trucks were not allowed on the streets in downtown Shanghai. Ruijin Hospital was in downtown Shanghai, so Ah Ming went to a friend, borrowed a sedan car, and drove to the hospital. It was late at night and the roads were almost empty. Ah Ming drove so fast that he exceeded the speed limits. About ten days later, the sedan owner received an electronic speeding ticket. The fine was two hundred yuan. The ticket showed the time and location of the speeding. Shezhu and Ah Ming willingly gave the owner two hundred yuan to pay the fine.

We were waiting outside the operating room when Shezhu arrived. I saw her coming out of the elevator and approaching us. She looked pale and was shivering so hard that Ah Ming had to support her.

My husband's illness had alarmed Shebao and Shezhu several times before. Yet this alarm was extremely frightening. First, this was preceded by their father's fall on the street. They had their father checked into this first-rate hospital because they worried that he might not survive another such event. Second, a second-rate hospital might send a false alarm, but this news reached them from a reputable hospital. I could imagine what was going on in their minds as they rushed to the hospital. Shezhu is especially emotional. She does not react well when she is emotionally upset.

When my husband emerged from the operating room, we were all at the doorway waiting for him. The first thing he asked was, "Has Shezhu come?" Shezhu quickly approached her father and said, "Diedie, I am here." Both father and daughter had tears in their eyes. My husband told us that inside the operating room and right after the temporary pacemaker was hooked up, Dr. Gu, the operating surgeon, said to him, "Lao Xiansheng (Old Mister), your life is now saved."

The doctors ordered that my husband remain in the hallway for that night. The hospital ward he stayed in had six patient beds. His bed was at the very end of the room. After the pacemaker was hooked up, the doctors said that my husband was still in unstable critical condition. They worried that he might need emergency care throughout the night. If emergency care was needed, every second would be important. It would take more time to move him from the end of that hospital ward to the operating room. So, that night, he stayed in the hallway and rested on that bed with wheels.

In order to hook up the pacemaker, a deep cut was made at the upper end of his right thigh in order to use the big vein there. A bag filled with sand was pressed against the cut in order to stop the bleeding. Because a blood thinner had been used in preparation for the angiogram, the blood in my husband's body was particularly thin. So we had to take care of the sandbag very carefully. The doctors particularly said that my husband had to lie face up with no movement or tossing whatsoever.

My children competed to stay the night with their father. In the end, Shezhu and Ah Ming stayed. They insisted that I go with Shebao and Xiao Xie to their house and sleep the rest of the night. I did go, but I was not able to sleep.

Early the next morning, Shebao, Xiao Xie, and I returned to the hospital. Together with Shezhu and Ah Ming, we decided to purchase the most expensive pacemaker for my husband. The pacemaker was a Medtronic, an American product. The cost was about 38,000 yuan. There were cheaper choices, but my children chose the most expensive one. They said that this was a lifesaving instrument and they wanted the best for their father.

In his retirement, my husband receives a monthly pension and has very good and comprehensive health insurance coverage. Just like all government employees, his health insurance is paid entirely by the government. The coverage pays for most of his hospital stays and the various medicines he takes every day. After the pacemaker was put in, we found out that his health insurance covered up to 5,000 yuan for a pacemaker. Shezhu and Shebao both wanted to contribute to our portion of the payment for the pacemaker, but my husband insisted that he pay it all by himself.

That morning, my husband needed to take a bowel movement. Since he could not move his body without risking his life, Xiao Xie thought of an idea to help. She went to the hospital shop and bought a packet of toilet paper. We gently put the packet under my husband's body and told him to relieve himself. It worked very well. Xiao Xie helped to solve a life-threatening and awkward problem. We are really lucky to have such a thoughtful and kind daughter-in-law. The operation to insert the permanent pacemaker took place in the afternoon of the same day. The pacemaker has been keeping my husband relatively healthy since May 2006.

REMEMBERING ANCESTORS

Until the mid-1990s, I went to our village house every year to hold traditional rituals on the death anniversaries of my parents and my grandmother and on the ancestor-remembering festival (*qingming*). Because my father passed away on September 30, the day before the National Day holiday, I used the holiday to remember him. I usually went to the village house the day before the ritual, opened all the windows to let in fresh air, and cleaned the house. I bought meat and vegetables and brought them to our village house to cook dishes. I folded paper money ahead of time and burnt it at the ritual. The rest of my family came on the day.

The ritual was always at lunchtime. We moved our square table to the middle of the guest hall, placed the dishes in the middle, and lined wine cups and pairs of chopsticks along the three edges of the table. The adults in the family took turns pouring wine for our ancestors, a little at a time. Two candles and incense sticks were lit and put on the remaining edge of the table, which was the side closest to the entrance door of the guest hall. We also offered fruits and candies on the table. I assumed that my father, together with my mother and other ancestors of ours, would come to the lunch. When the incense sticks burned down to about their last third, I would burn the paper money. While the paper money was burning, each of us knelt down and kowtowed three times in front of the table.

When the incense sticks burned to the end, the ritual was over. We would take everything on the table back to the kitchen, clean the table, move it to one side of the guest hall, put back the dishes, and sit down to have our lunch.

My mother's death anniversary occurs seven days before the Chinese New Year's Day. I combine the ritual to remember my mother with the end-of-the-year family dinner (*nianyefan*), which is another occasion to make offerings to our ancestors. At the combined ceremony, I have one urn that burned paper money to my mother and another urn that burned paper money to all our ancestors. My grandmother's death anniversary is close to the ancestor-remembering festival in April (*qingming*), so I combine the two together. I again separate the paper money into two urns, one for my grandmother and the other for all our ancestors.

All of us, except for Shezhen and Zhou Wei, who lived and worked too far away, came to the three rituals every year. For my mother's death anniversary/*nianyefan* and my grandmother's death anniversary/*qingming*, we would choose a weekend that was the closest to the anniversary so that all of us could be present. I would always say at the rituals, "Father, Mother, or Grandmother, we are early or we are late for the anniversary because we work or go to school. We can only gather together on a weekend."

We never held a separate ritual for my grandfather. Grandmother did not perform any ritual for her husband. We asked her when my grandfather died. She said it was on the twelfth of the second month on the lunar calendar. When we asked why she did not make offerings to Grandfather on his death anniversary, she said it was because he gambled away the family fortune, so he did not deserve to be remembered. According to traditional beliefs, the practice of remembering a person's death anniversary should begin right after the death occurred and should continue regularly. If a family did not make offerings to a dead person after his or her death, then the family was not supposed to start doing so after many years had passed.

Around the mid-1990s, my husband suggested that we move to hold the rituals in our apartment in downtown Jiading. He said that I had to clean the house in Wangjialong every time we held a ritual. I agreed. Then came my father's death anniversary. On that day, only my husband and I went back to the village house and held the ritual there. During the ritual, I told my father and our ancestors that this would be the last time I made offerings to them in the village house, that I would hold future rituals for them in our urban Jiading home, and that I would show them the way.

After the ritual, we ate our lunch there. My husband called a friend, who was a driver, and asked him to drive us back to Jiading Town. I lit an incense stick as I left the village house and held the stick in my hand while riding in the car. I carried the incense stick all the way to our apartment in downtown Jiading. That way, I felt that I had shown my ancestors the way to get to where I now lived. After that, I conducted the rituals in our downtown apartment.

When we moved to the Xincheng apartment, I held a ritual in the downtown apartment, told our ancestors that we were moving again, lit an incense stick, and carried it to the new apartment while riding in Ah Ming's truck to show our ancestors the way. After that, I conducted rituals in our Xincheng apartment.

ZHAKU AND DAOCHANG

Both of my parents passed away during the Cultural Revolution, so we did not perform traditional rituals at their funerals. I felt really bad about that. My parents had me marry matrilocally partly because they wished to have a family take care of them in their old age and after they left this world.

Under the reform policies, many traditional practices were revived. Shamans, who are believed to have the ability to contact dead people and act as liaisons between this world and the world of the dead, became available again. No ordinary person would wish to be a shaman. It is usually a person who has suffered a severe illness and has to act as a shaman in order to live a healthy life.

In the early 1990s, I decided to find out how my parents were doing in the other world. One weekend, Shezhu and I went to see a shaman in a remote village near Jiangsu. We were inexperienced and got there too late. We waited the whole day but did not get the service. There were simply too many people ahead of us.

I went again, this time on a weekday. I took the day off work. Because it was a weekday and Shezhu was busy at work, I asked Meifang, wife of one of my cousins, to go with me. We went earlier that day, and it was less crowded. We still had to line up but got the service before lunch. I provided the shaman with the necessary information, which was my father's name, the date and year of his death, his age at the time of his death, and the location where he passed away. The shaman lit an incense stick and whispered certain chants. After a while, she said, "Here he comes, a tall man." My father was a tall man. In fact, his nickname was "Long-legged Ah Di." Then the shaman became the liaison between my father and me, that is, my father talked to me through her.

My father said, "Thank you, children, for coming to see me." I replied, "Speaking of children, how many do you have?" Father replied, "I only have one and it is you. I regard you as a son." Meifang quickly asked, "Why do you say that you only have one child? Then who am I?" Father smiled and said, "You are a relative of mine."

By that time, I had become emotional and started to sob. My father said, "Don't cry. I am fine here. This is a very rare opportunity and let's talk." I asked him where he lived. He replied that he lived in a temple and got his food there in exchange for his service. I asked why he lived in a temple and what kind of service he provided there. He replied, "Don't you remember that I am a Daoist priest?" I then offered to send him a house so that he did not have to live in a temple. He replied, "That would be a lot of trouble. I have lived in the temple for so many years that I am now used to living there." But I insisted. So he finally said, "You could do it, but don't do it in a loud and fancy way." He lowered his voice and added, "Be practical and include some money in the house."

The language used by the shaman was characteristic of my father. He was calm when he talked to me and courteous when he talked to Meifang. When he advised me not to do things in a loud and fancy way, that was typical of my father. Although Father was a master of rituals and ceremonies, he preferred substance over formality.

I contacted a married couple in Zhuqiao Town who specialized in
zhaku, making paper houses for the other world. Just like tailors and
carpenters who go to work in customers' homes, paper-house makers
also work in customers' houses. The couple came to our village house
and made a paper house with bamboo sticks, reeds, and paper. It was
a two-story house with a lot of details such as a guest hall, bedrooms,
a kitchen, and a bathroom. The couple also made furniture, which
included two beds, a desk, and a chest with drawers in the bedroom;
sofa chairs and a TV set in the guest hall; and a gas stove and a refrigerator in the kitchen. They also made a washing machine and a car
for my father. Basically, whatever we the living had or desired to have
was available in the paper house.

It took the couple three full days to make the house. Since I was
still working in the dining room of Jianbang Chemical Machinery
Plant, I contracted the work out to the couple. That way, I did not
have to entertain them with lunch or dinner. I asked Little Aunt to
come to our village house and fold paper money while accompanying
the couple who made the house and the furnishings. I bought tin-
plated paper and Little Aunt folded a lot of paper money.

Every day of the three days, I went to work during the morning.
When I got off work in early or mid-afternoon, I bought afternoon
snacks for the paper-house makers and my aunt and delivered them to
our village house by taking a bus. In late afternoon, I returned to our
urban apartment on the last bus of the day so that I could go to work
the next morning.

We chose a weekend to deliver the paper house to my father.
My husband and I, my children except for Shezhen and Zhou Wei,
and my grandchildren all went to the village house and attended the
ceremony. Little Aunt, her family, my cousins and their families all
attended the ceremony. I asked Bai Yingzhou, who had learned to be
a Daoist priest from the same master as my father had, to preside over
the ceremony at which the paper house, which contained the furnishings and the paper money, was delivered to my father. The ceremony
featured chanting by Bai Yingzhou. Candles and incense sticks were
lit. We offered a table of food, wine, and fruits. We walked around the

paper house and the car parked outside the house three times before setting them all on fire. Our grandson Chen Li was only about four or five years old, so we held him in our arms when we did the walking around. Our granddaughter Beibei was old enough to walk on her own.

After our village relocation in 2003 and the reburial of my parents' remains, I wanted to know how my parents were doing in the other world through a shaman. This time, I decided to call on my mother. When I mentioned my idea to Shezhu, she enthusiastically supported me. This time, we learned that there was a shaman in a village in Huating Town in the northernmost part of Jiading District. One morning in late fall of 2004, Ah Ming drove Shezhu and me to the village. When the car got to the village, we learned that the shaman's house was on the other side of a bridge. We drove to the bridge, but found that the bridge did not accommodate motor vehicles. Ah Ming dropped us there and went back to attend his business in urban Jiading. Shezhu and I walked across the bridge and to the shaman's house.

Just like my last visit to a shaman, many people had arrived earlier than we had. We decided to wait. I noticed that next to the room where the shaman worked was the family kitchen. A middle-aged woman was picking and cleaning vegetables for lunch. Shezhu and I went over and talked to her and offered her our help in the kitchen. We learned that the woman was hired to cook lunches for the shaman and her family. After some conversation, the woman offered to help us. She went to the shaman and asked her to see us next. The shaman agreed. Because there was a line of people waiting for the service, the kitchen helper explained to the waiting crowd that we had arrived very early in the morning and went out to get breakfast. With her help, we jumped the queue and received the service before lunch.

After I gave her the information about my mother, the shaman said that it had been a long time since my mother's passing and it might be difficult to find her. Quite often a shaman failed to find a dead relative for a family. When Shezhu and I went to call on my father but failed to get the service because we got there too late, we witnessed such a case. A family came to call on a son who had died hundreds of *li* away from home and the dead body was not shipped home for burial. The shaman tried hard to find him but failed.

The shaman lit an incense stick and whispered chants. We waited silently. After a long while, the shaman said, "Here she comes, wearing a long gown of blue-color fabric [*shilinbu*]." Through the shaman, my mother called me "Ah Lin." My nickname is Linshe. Shezhu asked, "Then who am I?" My mother replied, "You are Ah Ni, Number Two." Shezhu is my second child. I then asked, "Mom, where do you live?" She said, "I live in the house you gave to your father." She then added, "I do not leave the house often. These days, people wear modern clothes, yet I am still wearing the old *shilinbu* long gown. I feel embarrassed and so do not leave the house." After my mother died, she was cremated wearing an old *shilinbu* long gown. I promised my mother that I would send her some new clothes.

After I heard what my mother said, I felt really bad. She had lived her entire life frugally and refused to accept new clothes in life. When she passed away during the crazy years of the Cultural Revolution, I did not even have the opportunity to make her a set of new clothes. So she left this world with that old *shilinbu* long gown. After the visit with my mother ended and the shaman had come back to this world, I told her that I wanted to do something for my mother and asked her for advice. She said that I could perform a day of chanting (*daochang*) for my mother in a nearby temple.

I started to plan a ritual for my mother when we learned that Shezhen was coming home on a sabbatical leave in January of 2005. She was to stay with us in Jiading for almost half a year. She told us that she was doing research about our home village. I decided to perform the ritual for Mother in the spring of 2005 so that Shezhen could also participate in it.

In preparation for a day of chanting in a nearby temple for my mother, I bought a set of clothes, a pair of shoes, and a pair of socks; I knitted a hat with my own hands; and I bought tin-plated paper and folded a lot of paper money.

In early spring of 2005, I contacted the Wuxing Temple (Wuxing Si) in Waigang and scheduled the ritual day for my mother in May.

When I called the temple, all the weekends of the spring season had been booked, so our scheduled day was during the working week. When the day approached, Shebao said that he could not leave his factory on that day and asked me if he could be excused from the ritual. I replied that he did not have to attend and that his factory business was more important. On the chosen day, my husband and I, Shezhen, and Shezhu took a taxi and arrived at the temple before eight in the morning.

At exactly eight o'clock in the morning, six monks began to chant. We followed the instructions from the head monk in kneeling down and kowtowing to my mother. After a round of kowtows, we sat in the same room where the monks chanted. One session of chanting took forty-five minutes and ended with our participation, again kneeling down and kowtowing to my mother.

At the end of the first session, the lead monk read aloud a previously prepared document that contained my name and my husband's name, our residential address at the time, and the date, month, and year of the chanting ritual. After reading it, he lit the document and burnt it.

There were three sessions of chanting and kowtowing in the morning. We had lunch in the temple cafeteria, which offered all-vegetarian food. There were three more sessions in the afternoon. At the end of the all the chanting sessions, the clothes, the paper money I made, and three gift boxes from Shezhen, Shezhu, and Shebao were thrown into a huge urn on the temple grounds and burnt as a way to deliver them to my mother. The monks again chanted at the burning ceremony while we stood near the urn.

By the time we did the ritual for my mother, remembering ancestors with such a ceremony in Wuxing Temple had become a very popular practice. The temple had regular monks working there, sold gift boxes, and accepted reservations. The temple charged us 1,000 yuan for the day of service.

I do not know if the other world really exists, but I would like to believe that my mother and father know I miss them and remember the love they bestowed on me. They gave me my life. We were poor when I was little. Yet I never felt deprived of anything while growing up. They helped me raise my children. They saved in every way for me and for my family. I know I will never be able to pay back what they did for me, but I am doing my best to show them my appreciation.

AMITABHA

Since the revival of traditional practices in the 1980s, fortune-tellers, shamans, monks, and Daoist priests have all been very busy people. Temples are crowded places, particularly on the first and fifteenth day of the lunar month and on festivals such as the birthday of Guan Yin, the Bodhisattva of Mercy and Compassion, which is the nineteenth day of the second month on the lunar calendar. On the eighth day of the twelfth month on the lunar calendar, people donate rice and other foods such as red beans, lotus seeds, and dried dates to local temples, which in turn cook winter eight porridge (*labazhou*). Everybody can eat such porridge at a temple free of charge on that day. Or one person can go to a temple and take some home to share with the family. The porridge is believed to be blessed.

I do not like to do things in a fancy way or to follow fads. Besides, I do not ride a bike, so must take public transportation to get to a temple. I worked until I was sixty-six years old. While I was working, I did not have free time to go to a temple on the first and fifteenth day of the lunar month. I, however, do believe in the existence of the Buddha, who watches us and looks after people of good conscience. There was a story about a man surviving a shipwreck in a vast sea. The story said that when the ship was wrecked, he sank into the deep sea. Seashells wrapped around his body and floated him up. The seashells were sent by the Buddha. The Buddha saved him because this man's mother had been a sincere and kind person who said Amitabha at home every day. I do not know if such an event really took place, but I like the moral of the story.

In the early 1990s, I began a daily chant of Amitabha. My husband and I were living in the downtown apartment. At first, I filled a Sprite bottle, whose top part was cut off, with sand and used it as an incense burner. I put the Sprite bottle, or my incense burner, on the desk in our bedroom. One day, a relative came for a visit with his baby son. The little boy was not yet walking or talking, so he held him in his arms. I showed them the apartment, since they, like most of our relatives, still lived in the village. When we were in the bedroom, the little baby pointed in one direction and uttered some sound. I asked if the baby wanted something, and the baby's father said that he wanted the Sprite bottle. Recently, I learned that this baby is now an employee at the Volkswagen auto factory in Anting Town. He is twenty-one years old. I use that incident to calculate that I have been doing the daily chant of Amitabha for about twenty years.

Every morning, after I got up, brushed my teeth, and washed my face, I lit an incense stick, stood it in the incense burner made of a Sprite bottle, clasped my hands in front of me, and chanted Amitabha for about a minute. Soon after I started, my children saw me doing this and gave me support. Shezhu bought me a copper incense burner and Xiao Xie bought me a porcelain statue of the Guan Yin Bodhisattva. To protect the wooden desk from hot incense ashes, I used an enamel tray and put the incense burner and the statue of the Guan Yin Bodhisattva in the tray.

When my husband and I traveled, we saw zodiac birth animals made of all kinds of materials for sale at souvenir shops. We playfully bought a Horse, which is the birth animal for my husband, and a Sheep, which is my birth animal. The Horse and the Sheep are both porcelain. After we brought them home, I put them on the enamel tray, together with the incense burner and the Bodhisattva.

When Shezhen came back from the United States for a visit, she saw what I was doing and bought me a lacquer statue of the Guan Yin Bodhisattva. I put the two statues together and have been lighting two incense sticks each morning since then.

I have continued this daily chant of Amitabha ever since I started with the Sprite bottle. I have not missed a day unless I was not home or could not get out of bed due to illness. Besides the daily chant of Amitabha, I light a pair of candles and a bunch of incense and burn some paper money on important occasions such as Chinese New

Year's Day, the Lantern Festival, and the Mid-Autumn Festival. I
pray for the health and safety of my entire family and for bumper
harvests and peace in the world. I do not do it in an elaborate way, but
I do it with sincerity and devotion.

A MODERN FUNERAL

One of my husband's sisters died very suddenly in late 2005. She
suffered acute and sudden diarrhea accompanied by vomiting and
was rushed to Jiading Central Hospital. When doctors there did
not know what to do, she was transferred to a hospital in Shanghai.
There, she went into a coma. After several hours of investigating and
testing, while her belly swelled, the doctors said that it was intestinal
cancer at its last stage. Knowing that her illness was no longer curable,
her family decided to take her home. Local people prefer to go home
when they become aware of the status of their illness. If one dies
outside home, the dead body is not supposed to enter the house. My
husband's sister was thus taken home with life support and under
doctor's care in an ambulance. After she reached home, the doctors
pronounced her dead.

My husband's sister died at the age of eighty-one. She left this
world in such an unexpected way that everybody was extremely sad.
The two daughters wept profusely. It was heart-wrenching to see the
loud weeping of the son-in-law. The daughters and the sons-in-law
said that death came too suddenly. They wished that they had had
an opportunity to perform their filial duty by nursing her for a while.
The deceased's husband also wept. It was even sadder to watch an old
man weep.

The family planned an elaborate funeral service that ran for four
days. The first day was the planning and announcement day. They
contacted West Gate Cremation Station for services, eight Daoist
priests to perform chanting, a band to provide music during the rituals, and professional chefs to cook banquet-style meals. Close relatives
and neighbors were sent out to inform other relatives about the death
and the funeral arrangements. Many relatives and neighbors helped

in food preparation and in folding paper money.

The second day was the day for relatives to call and for the dead body to be cleaned and clothed. This used to be done by a few men in the village. Now professionally trained people from the cremation station did it.

The third day was the actual funeral day. Before lunch, eight Daoist priests chanted while family members kowtowed and paper money was burnt for the deceased. After lunch, a funeral service was performed; this included a band playing funeral music, the village head giving a eulogy, and a family representative and a relative representative remembering the deceased. Finally, there was the procession of sending the coffin to the West Gate Cremation Station. The procession was led by the band and then neighbors holding funeral wreaths. Wailing family members walked next in the procession, followed by close relatives. Two of the priests walked at the end of the procession, one beating a pair of cymbals and the other a gong.

The procession stopped at the village entrance, where a truck and a bus, chartered by the family, waited. The truck took the coffin—attended by the daughters and their husbands, sitting on temporary benches—to the cremation station. My husband, the only living sibling of the deceased, did not go to the cremation station due to his poor health. I went on the chartered bus. At the cremation station, I represented my husband and myself in paying last respects to his sister. After the cremation, the daughter who had been married matrilocally carried the ash box home.

The fourth day was a day of chanting sponsored by the daughter who was married out. Again, eight Daoist priests performed the ritual service. Neighbors and relatives helped to fold more paper money. Professionals had been hired to make a paper house and all the furnishings. The Daoist priests chanted while the sponsoring daughter and her husband knelt down and kowtowed. In the middle of the afternoon, the paper house, with its furnishings and lots of paper money inside, was burned for the deceased.

The four-day affair demonstrated the filial piety of the two daughters and their husbands. Relatives and neighbors sang praises, commenting that my husband's sister had raised filial children and left this world in splendor and elegance.

About two months after my sister-in-law's death, in January 2006, Little Aunt passed away at the age of eight-six. She had been bedridden for some time. When I visited her a couple of weeks earlier, she was mentally alert but physically weak. Her son-in-law is a medical doctor. Because he took good care of Little Aunt while she was bedridden, she did not suffer from any bedsores. She and the bed she slept in were always immaculate.

Little Aunt did not give birth to any children. She and her husband raised the daughter they adopted from Big Aunt, her own elder sister. This daughter married matrilocally and had a son and a daughter, both of whom carried her father's surname.

After Little Aunt died, her daughter and son-in-law held a grand funeral service. It was also a four-day affair, including everything that was done at the funeral service for my husband's sister. I had always been very close to Little Aunt and regarded her as one of my dearest elders. I attended the four-day funeral service and paid my last respects to her at the West Gate Cremation Station.

Little Aunt lived a long and good life and left this world with splendor and elegance. Relatives and neighbors all said that although she did not have any biological children, her funeral service showed that she had filial descendants.

15

All Our Children
Are "Plump Seeds"

W HAT my children and grandchildren do in their professions is
beyond my imagination, but I am proud of them. My husband
compared our children and grandchildren to crops we grew in
the fields. He said that in every batch of harvested grain, there is chaff.
But he said with pride that every one of our children and grandchildren is "a plump seed" (fig. 15.1).

BEIBEI'S WEDDING

Beibei, Shezhu's daughter and our granddaughter, graduated from
college in 2004. She got a job working for a Japanese company in
urban Shanghai. Her job was related to mechanical designing, which
was what she was trained for in college. Commuting between her
Jiading home and her workplace in urban Shanghai took a few hours
every day. Beibei thought of renting an apartment near her workplace,
but we worried about her safety. After all, she was an innocent young
girl, although we all believed that Beibei was mature enough to take

15.1   Standing: Shebao, Chen Xianxi, Chen Li, Chen Huiqin, Ah Ming; squatting
and sitting: Beibei, Shezhu, Shezhen, Xiao Xie. Photo by Zhou Wei, 2002.

care of herself. Then Xiao Xie and Shebao said that Beibei could live
with them if she wanted.

That was a good arrangement. Beibei lived with her uncle's family
during the working week. She returned to her parents' Jiading home
over weekends. She did this for about a year. Within that year, Beibei
got accustomed to a regular professional schedule, made friends in

urban Shanghai, and became a regular member of Shebao's family. Furthermore, Beibei and Chen Li got along well. Beibei is an avid reader and loves cartoons. Chen Li has the same interests. Every time they came to visit us, I heard them talking about books and cartoons. They often turned on the TV in our Xincheng home and watched cartoon programs together.

On New Year's Day of 2005, Shezhu was shopping in a local market when she ran into a woman she had gotten to know when she was in accounting school in the early 1990s. They had not seen each other for more than ten years. This woman said that her husband usually did the daily shopping, but that day, she had decided to do it. They chatted for a while. Shezhu remembered that this woman had a son who was a very good student and was about the same age as Beibei, so she asked the woman about the boy. The woman said that her son had graduated from Jiaotong University and was working in urban Shanghai while doing graduate work for a master's degree. Shezhu told her about Beibei. They also learned that neither of their children was engaged or married at the time.

Shezhu liked this smart and capable woman. After Shezhu got the basic facts about her son, she thought he must be very smart. Jiaotong University is one of the best schools in Shanghai and one has to score very high in order to enroll there. So Shezhu called the other woman and proposed that the two young people meet and get to know each other. The woman liked the idea very much. When the mothers told their respective children about the proposal, the young people agreed and obtained each other's cell phone numbers.

The young people talked on the phone first and decided to meet in person. They had no idea what the other looked like. Since the two families both lived in Xincheng and the two young people knew where Xincheng neighborhood's administrative building was, they decided to meet in front of that building. After they met, they went to a Kentucky Fried Chicken restaurant in downtown Jiading and had coffee. Beibei came back and told us that the young man's name is Minjie.

After that meeting, Beibei and Minjie talked on the phone often. They worked during the day and called each other in the evening, which was the time Chen Li and Beibei used to talk or watch cartoon programs on TV. So Chen Li was very unhappy about the long phone conversations between Minjie and Beibei. Chen Li was still young and did not understand courtship.

Shezhu did not intervene and trusted Beibei's ability to decide for herself. One weekend, when Beibei came for a visit, I said to her that there was no such thing as a perfect match. Every person had his or her own personality. If she was 70 percent happy about who Minjie was, that should be enough. I said further, "If you do not think there is potential in developing a meaningful relationship, then let Minjie know. Do not mislead him. Once he gets deeply involved in what he thinks is a serious relationship, it will hurt to learn otherwise." When I talked, Beibei nodded. Then she said, "Grandma, I know that."

At the same time, Beibei found a girlfriend on the web. How she did it is beyond me, but I know that this friend was from Sichuan and was also a college graduate. When the girl told Beibei that she was coming to Shanghai to prepare for a graduate exam for the famous Fudan University, Beibei decided to move out of her uncle's house and rent an apartment to share with her friend in urban Shanghai. Before this friend arrived in the city, Beibei found an apartment near her workplace and near Fudan University. When this girl arrived in Shanghai by train, Beibei and her parents went to the train station to pick her up. Since this friend was coming to Shanghai for the first time, she had a lot of luggage. Ah Ming used his car to help her move the luggage to the apartment Beibei had rented.

During one long holiday, Beibei invited her friend to spend the holiday in her Jiading home. Shezhu also invited us to her house. That is how I met Beibei's friend, a very nice girl. I told Shezhu that she did the right thing to invite the girl to her house during the long holiday. The girl reminded me of Shezhen, who lived and worked far away from home. Shezhen told me that when she was a student, she was invited by her friends to their homes over holidays. What Shezhu did was our family's way of paying back the society that had been good to us.

When we met Minjie in person, we liked him. He was very modest, intellectual, and gentle. I found him a very sincere young man, became very fond of him, and treated him as one of my own children. I am aware that I am an old woman and an earthy person. But anytime Minjie came to visit us, he liked what I cooked. That made me very happy.

Beibei and Minjie became engaged in the spring of 2006. Minjie's parents held an engagement banquet in a restaurant in urban Jiading. My entire family was invited to the banquet.

Shezhu and Ah Ming are very open-minded people. Some people of their generation with only one child, a daughter, insisted on keeping the daughter at home, that is, to have the daughter marry matrilocally. Shezhu and Ah Ming did not believe that raising a child was for the purpose of carrying on the family name. Instead, they wanted Beibei to find a husband she loved and live a life she wanted. Ah Ming's mother, however, thought that Beibei should marry matrilocally. Ah Ming told his mother, "You are being closed-minded. So long as the two young people are happy, we are happy. Beibei is our daughter and she will forever be our daughter. Any children she will bear will be our grandchildren. It does not make a difference what surname the children will take."

At that time, Minjie was working at General Electric Company (GE) in Shanghai. He became aware of a job opportunity at GE that fit Beibei. He told Beibei, who applied for the job. She was interviewed and got the job.

It is still our local practice that the young man's family prepares a house for the engaged couple, so Minjie's parents looked for an apartment to buy in urban Shanghai. After much searching, they were unable to find an appropriate and affordable one. Then one weekend, Shezhu and Ah Ming were in Pudong on an errand. Ah Ming had done a project in that part of Pudong. He drove to show Shezhu a very nice residential complex. There, they saw an apartment for sale. They asked a real estate agent to show them the apartment. They instantly liked it and believed that Beibei would also appreciate it. GE Shanghai was located in Pudong. They called Beibei, and she came immediately and fell in love with the apartment.

With Minjie's parents' agreement and support, Beibei and Minjie decided to buy the apartment. Shezhu and Ah Ming contributed a large sum of money toward the purchase. They said that they did not think that preparing a house for Beibei and Minjie was entirely the responsibility of Minjie's parents. They would do what they could to help the two young people establish a home. I believe Shezhu and Ah Ming were doing the right thing as parents, and I admire the open-mindedness and generosity they showed in this matter.

Beibei and Minjie got married in March 2008. Although the two families consulted each other in choosing the wedding day, Minjie's parents still delivered a formal proposal to Shezhu and Ah Ming. In the envelope that contained the formal proposal, Minjie's parents included two sums of money. The larger sum, known as a wedding gift (*caili*), was to help Beibei prepare her dowry, such as jewelry and clothes. The smaller sum was appreciation money to thank Shezhu and Ah Ming for having raised Beibei. Shezhu and Ah Ming accepted the formal proposal and the appreciation money but returned the larger sum of money to Minjie's parents. Shezhu and Ah Ming said that they wanted to prepare a dowry for Beibei.

The wedding banquet was held in a hotel in Jiading. In the old days, we had to hold wedding banquets in cold weather to keep food fresh since we had no refrigeration. Nowadays people choose to get married in warm weather because the bride wears a wedding gown made of very thin material and the groom wears a suit and tie.

Beibei and Minjie hired a company to run the wedding ceremony. This company provided a makeup service for Beibei on the wedding day, took photos of the wedding day events as well as videotape them, decorated the wedding hall inside the hotel, and provided a professionally trained ceremonial master for the marriage ceremony. Holding the banquet in a hotel and hiring a company to run the wedding ceremony were new to us.

Shezhu helped Beibei shop for wedding clothes. Ah Ming drove them all the way to Suzhou, where there were many famous wedding-clothes stores. There, they chose the styles and had wedding clothes custom-made. Beibei chose an all-white wedding gown, an evening gown that glittered in candlelight, and a traditional-style dress of red satin with woven flowers. Shezhu also helped Beibei prepare quilts for the bed in the Pudong apartment. In addition, Shezhu bought many sets of bedsheets with pillowcases as appreciation gifts (*huantun*) for those who would give meeting-ritual money (*jianlitian*) to Minjie at the wedding. The appreciation gift has evolved greatly. In the old days, it was a homemade apron; then it became a face towel; now it was a complete set of bed sheets.

Shezhu also prepared a suitcase, known as the golden chest. Into the golden chest she put underwear for Beibei, socks and shoes for both Beibei and Minjie, and a lot of goodies for a bridal suite party such as walnuts, dried longans, peanuts, and sugarcane. This is also part of traditional practice, representing the parents' wishes for a happy marriage and many children. Sugarcane was significant in the golden chest because it rises joint by joint and therefore symbolizes good wishes for success in life. Shezhu also put some money in the suitcase to help the newlyweds start a life together.

In addition, Shezhu made a descendants' bundle (*zisunbao*), which contained the traditional contents of shoes and hats for potential babies, and two bowls of raw rice, dry dates, and peanuts. They all represented best wishes from the parents. The day before the wedding, Shezhu wrapped the selected items in a piece of homemade cloth. Sticking out in the middle of the bundle were fresh leaves from an evergreen plant. The evergreen leaves again symbolized good wishes.

On the wedding day, the makeup artist came to Shezhu's house early in the morning to prepare Beibei. Beibei had two bridesmaids— one of them was her cousin from her father's side and the other was her friend from Sichuan. They came early that morning and helped in Beibei's preparation.

I regarded Beibei's wedding as a grand event and even had my hair permed. On the wedding day, my husband and I went to Shezhu's house at about nine thirty in the morning. At about ten o'clock that morning, Minjie, handsomely dressed in a suit and necktie, came to Shezhu's house to take the bride. He poured tea for Beibei's elders, including me. According to the instructions of the ceremonial master, Beibei, now dressed in her red-satin clothes, closed her bedroom door. Minjie knocked on the door, asking to marry Beibei. He was allowed into the bedroom by the two bridesmaids only after he gave them each a red packet of money.

After Minjie obtained Beibei's positive response, we all went together to the big hotel for the lunch banquet. The banquet was grand and huge in scale. Shezhu and Minjie's parents held the banquet together. They invited a total of fifty tables of guests and each round table seated ten people. The banquet hall was divided into two sections, one for guests from the bride's side and the other for those from the groom's side. Dividing the two sections was a long corridor. In the front of the huge banquet hall was the main table for the bride and groom, Shebao, who was a representative of the bride's family, Chen Li, who carried the descendants' bundle, Beibei's paternal uncle, who carried the golden chest, the bridesmaids, and the groom's best men.

At the lunch banquet, Shezhu took Minjie, accompanied by Beibei, to pour wine and soft drinks for all the guests on Beibei's side. As Shezhu introduced Minjie to Beibei's relatives, Minjie addressed them each accordingly. Relatives such as Beibei's uncles and aunts handed Minjie meeting-ritual money wrapped in red paper. Shezhu, in turn, immediately delivered a set of bedsheets to each of the gift-giving relatives. Xiao Xie and others helped by handing pretty packages of bedsheets to Shezhu as she went around the tables with Minjie.

After lunch, we went to Shezhu's Helen house, which was the ancestral home for Beibei. In that house, Shezhu and Ah Ming had prepared a bedroom for Beibei. They had also prepared tea, coffee, nuts, and candies in the living room to entertain everyone. While we sat down to rest and chat in the living room, the makeup artist helped Beibei change her hairstyle and clothes in the bedroom.

In the middle of the afternoon, Beibei emerged in her pure white wedding gown and was a beautiful and elegant bride. Beibei and Minjie, while holding each other's arms, walked outside and down the steps of the Helen house toward a car that was decorated with fresh flowers and the Chinese character of double happiness. Walking in front of them were a little boy and a little girl, who scattered flower petals. Relatives and neighbors said that the scene reminded them of wedding ceremonies held by rich families they had seen on TV. At the side of the decorated car, Shezhu helped Beibei change into a pair of red leather shoes. Then the bride and groom entered the decorated car. The red color represented good luck. Putting the red shoes on in front of the public conveys the mother's best wishes to her daughter.

At this point, a bonfire of dry soybean and sesame stalks was lit right outside the house and firecrackers were set off. The car with Beibei and Minjie led a fleet of eight shining cars. Sitting in the other cars were bridesmaids and best men; Shebao; Beibei's paternal uncle, who carried the golden chest; Chen Li, who carried the descendants' bundle; and the flower boy and the flower girl.

The fleet drove straight to Minjie's parents' house, which was in Xincheng. I did not go with them, but I know what happened there. Minjie's parents burned a bonfire and set off firecrackers when the bride and groom arrived. They prepared tea, coffee, and other treats for the bride and her guests. Chen Li would deliver the descendants' bundle and Beibei's uncle would deliver the golden chest.

By dinnertime, the eight cars had taken the bride and the groom and their entourage to the hotel. All the guests by now had been seated at the tables. In the middle of the wedding hall, along the long corridor, a red carpet had been laid down. Halfway down the red carpet was an arch decorated with fresh flowers.

With the ceremonial master announcing the start of the ceremony, music began to play. Minjie walked from the raised platform in the front of the hall toward the arch while Beibei walked from the other end of the corridor toward the arch, holding her father's right arm. At the arch, Ah Ming formally gave Beibei to Minjie. When Minjie and Beibei walked arm-in-arm toward the raised platform, Ah Ming stood at the arch with his eyes full of tears. Ah Ming loves Beibei and would do anything for her. I am sure he was happy for Beibei, but he must have been emotional when he so formally and publicly gave Beibei away.

In the old days, it was the mother who gave the final touches to the daughter when she left her home on the wedding day, so people usually commented on the display of emotions between the daughter and mother at that critical moment. Now it was the father who was the center of the entire banquet audience's attention as he experienced the complexity of such a moment.

The wedding ceremony was formal and beautiful. Shebao represented Beibei's family and spoke at the ceremony. On behalf of all of us, he thanked Minjie's parents for having raised such an excellent young man. He hoped that Beibei and Minjie would be filial and responsible to both sets of parents. He said that he was sure that the two young people would live successful lives, making both sets of parents happy and proud. Both Minjie's father and Beibei's father also spoke at the ceremony. They were filled with delight and wished the bride and groom happiness together.

While on the raised platform, Minjie put the wedding ring on Beibei's finger and Beibei put the wedding ring on Minjie's. The ceremonial master then declared Beibei and Minjie a married couple. Loud applause came from all the guests. The newlyweds then cut the wedding cake that had six tiers and was stacked in the shape of a pagoda (fig. 15.2).

The newlyweds disappeared from the raised platform for some time. When they appeared again, all lights in the banquet hall were turned off, leaving only candles on the banquet tables. Beibei had now changed into her evening gown that glittered in candlelight. Minjie and Beibei walked together again on the red carpet, holding a light on a stick. They went onto the stage and lit the huge candle there. It was then that smokeless fireworks exploded along the red-carpet corridor and in front of the raised platform. I heard people sitting around me singing praises. They said, "We have never seen such a grand wedding ceremony."

The dinner banquet had been going on for some time now. With electric lights turned back on again, Beibei went to each table to pour wine and soft drinks for Minjie's relatives. Minjie's mother went with Beibei, introducing her to all the guests. As Beibei addressed Minjie's

15.2 Beibei and Minjie cutting
wedding cake, 2008

relatives and received meeting-ritual money wrapped in red paper,
Minjie's mother delivered appreciation gifts that contained the same
four-piece bedsheets.

The newlyweds spent their wedding night in the bridal bedroom
Minjie's parents had prepared in their Xincheng apartment. The next
day, Beibei's male cousin from her father's side went to invite her and
Minjie to visit Beibei's ancestral home in Helen Community. The
bride and groom brought with them gifts that included traditional
foods such as glutinous rice wrapped in bamboo leaves (*zongzi*),
which expressed the best wishes from Minjie's parents, and modern
gifts such as a cream cake. My husband and I attended the lunch and
dinner sponsored by Shezhu and Ah Ming for Beibei's post-wedding
visit. On this day, Shezhu held a ritual to inform Ah Ming's ancestors of the marriage between Beibei and Minjie. A table of food was
offered to the ancestors. Beibei and Minjie kowtowed together as
a married couple in front of the table. Only then was the wedding
ceremony complete.

Minjie is a wonderful addition to our family. His parents raised
him well and we are very lucky to have him as the loving husband

of our granddaughter. Shezhu and Ah Ming are very happy about Beibei's marriage. The two young people are successful professionals and they love and care for each other dearly.

SHEBAO'S PROFESSIONAL DEVELOPMENT

When Shebao worked as a research professor at Shanghai University of Science and Technology, which merged with other colleges to become Shanghai University in the mid-1990s, he successfully designed a sensor and the factory affiliated with the university manufactured it. We were happy for him and proud of him. But he was not happy there. He said that there were too many bureaucratic limitations and too much red tape for his career development, so he resigned from the job in 1997.

My husband and I did not like Shebao's decision. We thought he had an iron-rice-bowl job, was an engineer, and worked in a university. To people with peasant backgrounds, he had everything any person could desire. But I knew that once Shebao decided to do something, nobody could stop him.

After he resigned, he devoted his time and energy to developing a machine that welded eyeglass frames. In the development of the machine, he had to go to a factory outside urban Shanghai to test it. This factory was in Shanghai County, on the southwestern side of urban Shanghai, whereas Jiading is on its northern side. He could get there by taking the rural long-distance bus system. But rural buses ran very infrequently and it took him hours to get there. So most of the time he rode a bike for about two hours to get there. The rural roads he had to ride on had no clearly defined bicycle lane, and it was not safe. His father was not happy and said to Shebao, "You are a college graduate and an engineer. Yet you are riding an old bike to your work. Peasants with no education and working temporary jobs are not doing that these days. Why can't you find a job?"

Then one day, Shebao came and announced that he had found a job working for an American company in urban Shanghai. He had seen a job ad in a newspaper, sent in his application, and been interviewed and hired. His job was related to designing televisions. After several months, his salary was increased. But Shebao was not happy, so he resigned from the job. The American company wanted to keep him and so raised his salary again in response to his resignation, but he quit the job anyway.

By that time, I had stopped cooking lunches for Ah Ming, so Shebao used the spare space in Shezhu's first-floor apartment to work on the welding machine. When he finally found buyers for his machine, he hired a helper to work with him. In addition to the welding machine, he designed other electronic parts. In 2003, he rented some space in a manufacturing center near his home in urban Shanghai and moved his small manufacturing business there. About a year later, he hired six people to work on his products.

In the latter part of 2005, Shebao was looking for housing for his little company. The lease for the building in which he had run his company was coming to an end. He could have renewed the lease, but this was an opportunity for him to find another place. Ah Ming suggested that Shebao use our Helen house to run his business. That was a great idea. First, Shebao's company made small electronics. It involved a lot of technology, but it did not require a lot of space. It was environmentally clean and quiet. So running it in a residential community should not create any problems. Second, the townhouse was empty and my husband and I had no plans to move into our Helen house.

Besides space to run his business, Shebao also needed to take care of his workers' housing needs, as it is common for local small businesses to do. While Ah Ming's workers were local married people who returned home after work, most of Shebao's workers were unmarried young people and from places outside Shanghai. Ah Ming generously offered to help Shebao. He said that Shebao's female workers could live in the townhouse he and Shezhu owned. He said that his mother would not mind having a few female workers share the three-story house with her. In addition, Ah Ming said that the three-bedroom apartment they bought in Helen Community was vacant, so Shebao could turn it into a dormitory for his male workers.

Shebao accepted Ah Ming's suggestion and help. When his lease in urban Shanghai ended in November, he moved his factory to our Helen house. The house had a spacious kitchen. He hired a local middle-aged woman to cook lunch for the workers.

When Shebao first moved there, Helen Community was not yet connected to the natural gas pipeline. The gas tank, which had traveled all over among my family and relatives, became useful again. It provided fuel for the middle-aged woman to cook lunches for the workers. We also moved the kitchen cabinet, which had been cus-tom-made for us when I moved to South Gate in 1985, to the Helen kitchen as a storage place for utensils.

After Shebao moved his company to Helen Community, com-muting back to his home in urban Shanghai demanded better trans-portation. He registered for a driving course, which was required of everyone who wanted to get a driver's license, and passed the road test in the spring of 2006. He bought an old Volkswagen Santana and used it as his transportation.

After moving to our Helen house, Shebao developed and made joysticks for large machines such as bulldozers and cranes. He worked day and night and over weekends, and he traveled a lot. He was the designer, the salesman, the owner of a business, and the customer-re-lations person. His hard work paid off and the business began to grow.

In a casual conversation, I heard Shebao say that he had some money and would like to buy an apartment in one of those apartment buildings inside Helen Community if someone was willing to sell one. One day, when I was visiting an acquaintance in Helen, I heard an old woman say that her family was selling their apartment for cash. I said that my son was looking to buy such an apartment. When the woman learned that my son was running a business, she latched onto me. Her grandson had lost a great deal of money in gambling. The family needed cash and needed it as soon as possible, because the debt collector was pressing them for the money and the debt was accumu-lating interest every day. I told Shebao about the situation. After we looked at the apartment, Shebao decided to buy it. After the purchase, the female workers who had lived with Ah Ming's mother moved to this apartment. This was much better, for Shebao did not want to impose on Ah Ming's mother for too long.

As his business picked up, he hired more people. As the clean and quiet work environment without night shifts appealed to local people, the new workers were mostly from the area. One of the new workers had actually been in school with Shebao. Local workers made things easier for Shebao, for they returned home after work so he did not have to provide housing for them.

For years Shezhu had been the accountant for Shebao's business. Now he wanted her to help manage the day-to-day business for his growing company. Shezhu wanted to help her brother, but she had a very comfortable job at the time. The company she worked for was within walking distance of her home in Xincheng. She was able to do the daily shopping and cooking and make sure that she and Ah Ming had dinner at a regular time every day. Working for Shebao meant traveling to Helen Community. If she took public transportation, it would mean two or three hours on the road every day. In winter, it would be completely dark when she got home after work. She would still have to shop and cook for dinner. Dinner would be late due to the time she spent on the road.

Shebao asked me about getting Shezhu to work for him. I said that if Shezhu agreed to do so, she would have to sacrifice a lot and that she would also need Ah Ming's support. Shebao understood. When Shezhu asked me about working for Shebao, I reminded her of all the inconveniences that she would encounter and the sacrifices that she would have to make. When they both were present, I said, "Both of you are my children. Both of you are married and have families. It is entirely up to you to decide what to do. Whatever decision you make, I will see it as the reasonable and right choice."

Shezhu finally resigned from her job and went to work in Shebao's company. Most days, Shebao would stop outside Shezhu's residential complex and give her a ride to work in the morning and back to the complex after work. Helen Community is about twelve *li* north of Xincheng, where Shezhu and we lived. Since Shebao lives in urban Shanghai, which is south of Xincheng, giving Shezhu a ride involved no detours. Shezhu had to use public transportation whenever Shebao traveled on business trips or attended to business needs in urban Shanghai.

Ah Ming supported Shezhu's decision to work for her brother. Shezhu said that no matter how late she got home from work, Ah Ming never complained. In fact, sometimes when Shezhu got home late, Ah Ming would say, "Let us go out to eat so that you do not have to cook." I was aware of the sacrifices Shezhu was making. Sometimes, I would cook a fish or some meat and tell Shezhu to stop at my place on her way home and take the dish. That way, she would only have to cook a vegetable dish for a complete dinner.

Shebao is generous and kind to his workers. He has organized company vacation trips. One time, he took his workers to Huangshan, the Yellow Mountains. Another time, he took his workers to a famous hot-spring resort in Ningbo. He not only paid for everything on the trip, he reserved three-star or four-star hotels for his workers. On various festivals, he prepares gifts for his workers. On each Dragon Boat Festival, which is in the spring, he prepares glutinous rice wrapped in bamboo leaves (*zongzi*) for his workers and their families. One year, I volunteered to make the gifts. The woman who cooked lunches in the company and I made about 250 *zongzi*, which took thirty *jin* of sweet rice and eight *jin* of pork. He gives out gifts again for Mid-Autumn Festival every year. The biggest gifts of the year are the ones given at Chinese New Year (*nianhuo*). My husband and I have shared in the gifts so I know how much and what he gives to his workers. This past year, he bought cookies, nuts, chocolates, and other treats and put them together in large bags. Each worker received one bag. Shezhu bought the items for the Chinese New Year gifts and said it cost a hundred yuan for each bag. Every time Shebao gives gifts, he prepares one set for each of the neighbors.

Shebao's kindness toward his workers goes beyond what I have mentioned. He has a lot of compassion. For example, a woman worker in the company had a sick mother who lived in Sichuan. He told the worker that whenever she needed to go to her mother's side, she could do so. The worker appreciated the offer, but said that she was aware of how busy the company was and she should stay to help. Shebao replied, "Family always comes first. Work can wait."

When the woman's mother became seriously ill, she decided to fly back to Sichuan to be with her. Shebao gave her money and told her to spend as much time with her mother as she needed. That worker was able to be with her mother when her mother died. She stayed in Sichuan and took care of her mother's funeral service. Only after that did she came back to work. Shebao gave the worker full pay for all the days she was away from work.

"Family is more important than work" is what Shebao tells us all the time. When my husband and I need a ride to see a doctor, we always hesitate because we realize how busy he is. When he learns of our need, he comes to us immediately. He says, "I am busy. But to me, your health is more important than anything else."

One day, one of his workers got into a small traffic accident on her way home. When Shebao heard the news, he had not yet left the office. He got into his car and drove straight to the accident site. He took the worker to Jiading Central Hospital in his car. He stayed with her through the whole process of getting an emergency check-up and X-ray exam, dressing the external wound, and getting the medication. He then drove the worker home.

The next day, the worker and her husband went to the company to see Shebao. The worker said that her husband was at work the night before and so missed seeing Shebao when he brought her home. So he came to thank Shebao in person. Shebao said he had only done what he should. He told the worker to go home and rest until the wound healed. He added that her wages would continue as usual during her sick leave. The worker was extremely grateful. She went home with her husband that day, but returned to work the following day. She said that the injury on her face was superficial and it was no longer painful. She further said that she used her hands and eyes to work and so the injury on her face did not interfere with her ability to work.

Since Shebao moved his company to our Helen house in 2005, I have heard from a number of people who were neighbors or whose family members worked in Shebao's company. They all told me that

I have raised a generous and kind son. Shebao is very much like my father, who was generous and kind to his extended family as well as to his neighbors and fellow villagers.

Nonetheless, Shebao's generosity sometimes goes beyond my comprehension. One woman worker resigned from Shebao's company after having been trained to do the work. This was a loss for Shebao because it took time and money to train a worker. Yet Shebao wished her well. About two years later, she came back and asked to be employed again. I said to Shebao, "If I were you, I would not want to accept her." But Shebao allowed her to come back. Then, some time later, she left again. She said that one of her relatives had found her a better job. Shebao again wished her well. Not too long after that, another worker told Shebao that that woman was not happy with her new job and wanted to return. I did not think Shebao would take her back this time, but he did. When I asked Shebao why he had done that, he replied, "Young people should be allowed to explore for themselves. They will decide what is really good for them. Now that she wants to come back, she will stay and devote herself to her work in my company." Shebao was right. This woman is now a devoted worker. She tells other workers in the company that she now knows the outside world and knows that Chen Gong (Engineer Chen) is the best man to work for.

By the way, Chen Gong, or Engineer Chen, is how everyone in his company addresses him. Shebao started his own company from scratch and has been running it since the early 2000s. At the end of 2011, he employed more than twenty people. But he never regarded himself as "boss." Many people prefer to be called boss (*laoban*) when they run a small business. The title *laoban* connotes somebody who is rich and powerful. Shebao prefers to live a low-key life.

I do not want to see Shebao's business grow too big. I believe that so long as he is able to make enough money to meet his family's needs, it is good. I know that running a big business involves too much and is too tiring.

A couple of years after the company moved to our Helen house, Shebao's business had outgrown our townhouse. One of the neighboring townhouses, which was owned by another Wangjialong family, was vacant at the time. When we asked if the owners were willing to rent it, they gladly said yes. Shebao's growing company now occupied two townhouses. Through its website, the company was selling products all over the country.

In 2010, Shebao moved his company to a newly-built manufacturing center about six *li* north of Helen Community. He said that his goal was to create a brand name in the industrial joystick business. The manufacturing center has its own huge dining room so the company employees now eat in the dining room and Shebao pays for their lunches.

After the move, my husband and I went to see the new factory. It was huge. Besides workshop spaces, there was a sales office, a warehouse, a conference room, an accounting room, a room devoted to developing new products, and Shebao's office. All the rooms were equipped with air conditioners and/or electrical fans.

In addition there was a special area reserved for badminton and a set of ping-pong tables. After lunch, workers played ping-pong and badminton. To celebrate the Chinese New Year in early 2011, the company organized a ping-pong contest. All the workers were invited to participate. Shebao asked Shezhu to buy many toiletry sets with items such as shampoo and hair conditioner on the web. The winners of the contest were awarded the toiletry sets as prizes.

In 2011, Shebao found a partner to run the expanded business with him. The company now has an office in urban Shanghai while its factory is still in the manufacturing center in northern Jiading. The company expenses are now high. I sometimes express my worries. Shebao and Shezhu tell me not to worry. When I ask Shebao if he is making any money, he tells me that he does not run the company to make money, but to do something worth doing. I have lived all my life thinking about doing things to earn money so that my family can live a better life. I guess Shebao is beyond that. According to my way of thinking, I say I have raised a "silly" son, a son who is not interested in making money. Yet I am proud of him.

CHEN LI GOES TO JAPAN

When Chen Li was in high school, Shebao and Xiao Xie wanted their son to see the world. They sent Chen Li to Canada on an exchange program during one of his summer vacations. In 2007, Chen Li took the college entrance exams and scored high enough to be admitted to Shanghai University, where he chose communication engineering as his major.

Many Chinese people, old and young, believe that the United States is the best place on earth. Shebao and Xiao Xie hoped that Chen Li would do graduate work in the United States but Chen Li apparently did not want to. The summer before he became a senior in college, he asked his parents for some money to pay for a Japanese language course. He studied the Japanese language very seriously. Before this, his foreign language was English. When Shezhen brought some American friends home, Chen Li had no problem communicating with them. Nonetheless, he wanted to learn Japanese and planned to do graduate work in Japan. Shebao and Xiao Xie said that they would financially support Chen Li's pursuit of further education and it did not matter where he chose to do it.

In the spring of 2011, Japan experienced a tremendous earthquake, which was followed by a disastrous tsunami and frightening news about the nuclear plant. We saw the news coverage on TV. My husband told me that this disaster was happening not very far from Tokyo, Japan, where Chen Li was planning to go. I learned that earthquakes happen rather frequently in Japan. I also learned that nuclear radiation could last a long time. So I called Chen Li and asked him to reconsider his decision. Chen Li told me that there were still many months before his planned trip and that he would wait to decide.

In the summer of 2011, after Chen Li graduated from Shanghai University, he took the Japanese language test and scored very high. Within one year, he had mastered this second foreign language. The news from Japan was now calm and Chen Li stuck to his decision to go there. My husband and I wanted to buy Chen Li a gift. We knew that he loved Apple products because when Shezhen visited us with her Apple laptop, Chen Li played with his aunt's computer and praised it for its beautiful and smart design. At the same time, he had his own laptop, which was not an Apple. He kept up with news about Apple products all the time. When a new iPhone was to be released, he said to his father, "Dad, your cell phone is too old and should be updated." Shebao replied, "What you really want is to buy a new iPhone and give me your old one. Is that right?" Chen Li admitted, "That is right." Since Shebao also loves electronic things, he told Chen Li to go ahead and buy what he wanted. On the first day the new iPhone was available in the store, Chen Li got up early and stood in line for hours to get one. When he got the iPhone, he came to Jiading and showed it to me and my husband. He said, "Grandma, this phone is more important than my life." I replied, "Don't be silly. Nothing is more important than your life."

My children talked about Apple products when they gathered at my house. I recognized the Apple logo, which was an apple missing one bite. So when the owner of the Apple company died, I saw the news on TV. When Shebao came to have dinner with us that same day, I said, "I heard the owner of the Apple company has died." Shebao was surprised and said, "Mom, you also know that!"

Therefore, my husband and I decided to buy Chen Li an Apple laptop, the kind Shezhen used. We gave Chen Li the money and he bought the computer himself. Shebao told us that after Chen Li bought the Apple laptop, he carried it home but did not open the box that contained the computer. When he sat down to dinner with his parents, he took out some wine and asked his father to drink with him. He said that he wanted to celebrate the opening of the Apple computer box with wine. So he and his father poured wine, clicked their wine glasses, and sipped some wine; then he opened the box.

After Chen Li obtained a visa to enter Japan, his parents bought him a plane ticket. Then he called us to say that he was coming to see us and to show us the new laptop. He came and spent the whole day with us. He told us that the computer would allow him to do many things, including have video chats with us while he was in Japan. He logged on to the web and showed us the school he was to attend, the

apartment he had rented for himself, the light-rail he would take to
go to school every day, and the prices of various food in Tokyo, Japan.
We were amazed by how much information he obtained from the
web. He even showed us a drawing of the apartment he had rented. It
indicated where the bed was, where the bathroom was, and where he
would be cooking his meals. We knew that Tokyo was a very crowded
city and every inch of space was as valuable as gold. Therefore, housing was very expensive. The apartment Chen Li had rented was very
small. Yet, just like the little sparrow which has every organ to live its
life, the apartment had everything Chen Li needed to live his daily
life.

As he showed us the prices of food, he explained to us the
exchange rate between Chinese money and Japanese money. We realized that food in Japan was very expensive. Since we knew that Chen
Li did not have a habit of spending money in a wasteful way, my
husband told Chen Li, "Don't worry about money. Buy and eat what
you want. I will be glad to help out financially if such a need arises."
Chen Li responded, "Grandpa, I know what you are saying. But my
father has promised to support me financially."

Before Chen Li was scheduled to leave for Japan, Shebao and
Xiao Xie sponsored a send-off dinner and invited the entire family to
it. When we went to the restaurant for the send-off dinner, I was in
the same car with Chen Li. I said to Chen Li that I wanted to share
with him two things, although they might not be the right things to
say. Chen Li said, "Grandma, go ahead. I will listen." I said, "First, I
do not want you to marry a Japanese girl." I explained, "I have visited
your aunt in the United States and know how big cultural gaps can
be." Chen Li said he would consider my advice. A few days later, he
told me that he had decided to accept my suggestion and would not
marry a Japanese girl. The second thing I said to Chen Li was that he
could spend as many years abroad as he wanted and needed for education, but he should come back and pursue his career and establish
a family in China. Chen Li replied, "I will see what happens. It is too
early to make such a decision now."

Because National Day celebration, a week-long holiday, was

approaching, I asked Chen Li to leave for Japan after the holiday, but he was very eager to go, so he left right before the holiday. As soon as Chen Li arrived in Tokyo, Shebao brought his laptop to our house. He got on to the web, and we chatted with Chen Li, who used his Apple computer and showed us his apartment. We saw the sleeping area, the kitchen area, and the bathroom area inside his one-room apartment via the Internet.

The web is just wonderful. Shebao and Xiao Xie are in touch with Chen Li every day. I remember when Shezhen went to the United States at first—it took more than ten days to receive a letter from her and it cost a lot of money to make a phone call. Now we can see Chen Li and talk to him almost anytime we want and it is free.

During the National Day holiday, the entire family came to my house, just as they usually did. While eating dinner, we talked to Chen Li via the computer. We showed him a table of dishes, many of which he loved. He showed us the food he had prepared for himself. When I asked him if he envied the food on our table, he said he did not. I understood that he had decided to go study in Japan, so a few homemade dishes did not make him regret his decision.

16

Return to Ancestral Land

AFTER Shebao moved his company to the new manufacturing center in 2010, our ancestral house inside Helen Community became vacant. I decided to move to the Helen house for several reasons.

First, the fixtures, walls, and floors in our Xincheng apartment were getting old. We had moved there in 1998. I cooked in the kitchen for every meal and many family gatherings, so the kitchen was greasy. The bathroom was also getting old. The inside of the apartment needed a lot of work.

Second, we were never happy about the fact that we did not get much sunshine any time of the year. The buildings in front of us and behind us were too close and blocked the sun as well as the wind from our apartment. Besides, more and more people who owned the apartments above or beside us had moved to larger apartments or to newer residential communities with better ambience. They either rented out or sold their apartments to people who were often from other provinces. These people were less responsible about their living environment. They threw trash from their windows. If I did not clean our patio for a week, it would be covered in cigarette butts, candy wrappers, tissues, and other dirty things. They would also hang laundry that had not been spun dry and was dripping water, and I had to be very careful when I put out my laundry. Many times, I had to move my clothes several times during the day to avoid their dripping laundry. Since they did not speak the local dialect and we did not speak their dialects, it was difficult to communicate with them about such problems.

Because of these conditions, my children claimed that our residential community had become a slum. I did not think that it was that bad, but it was true that our living conditions had deteriorated.

Third, Shezhen told us that she had been granted another semester-long sabbatical leave and planned to come back and spend half a year with us. Although we had two bedrooms in the Xincheng apartment, they were small. Every time Shezhen came back to visit us during her summer vacation, she had to work in a corner of her small bedroom. I had visited her house in the United States and knew how spacious and comfortable her house was. Shebao and Shezhu also told me that although their elder sister never complained about it, it must be difficult for her to adapt to the crowded living space in a slum-like environment.

Fourth, Shezhu and Ah Ming bought a new apartment in a new residential complex. They were scheduled to move into the new house in the spring of 2012. The new complex is located in the northern part of urban Jiading. Since Xincheng is in the southeastern part of urban Jiading, we would have to cross the entire urban area in order to get to Shezhu's new house once she moved into it. And her new house is only about a fifteen-minute bus ride or a seven-minute car ride from our Helen house, which is on the northwestern outskirts of Jiading Town. Plus, Shezhu worked in Shebao's factory, which is north of Helen Community. After Shezhu moved to her new house, every day that she went to work at Shebao's company, our Helen house would be on her route while our Xincheng apartment would be totally out of her way.

Fifth, my husband and I were getting old, and I started to think about a time when we would need assistance in our daily life. There were several ways to get assistance. One of them was to move to a retirement home. We had heard terrible stories of life in a retirement home. So that was not an ideal option for us. Another way was to continue to live at home with the help of a maid. I thought that the latter option would be much better. It would be best to hire a middle-aged woman who was not a complete stranger to us. It would be easier for us to find such a person in our native home, where we have extended family as well as many acquaintances.

In the summer of 2011, I asked Ah Ming to find a remodeling company to prepare our Helen house as our home. I asked him for the help because he was in the air-conditioning business and knew many people in the remodeling business. I told Ah Ming to make all the decisions for us. We did not want anything fancy, but we did want to have the house ready for easy and comfortable living. Ah Ming contracted the work out to a company and made all the decisions for us. The remodeling project was completed in November 2011, and we gave the money to Ah Ming to pay for the work.

My husband, however, was worried that life in Helen Community would be inconvenient. He was concerned about getting his medicine, since his health depended on the medicine he took every day. But we found out that a new hospital, within walking distance of our Helen house, had just opened. It was the same kind of hospital as the one near our Xincheng apartment where my husband had been getting his medicine. We could also easily take a bus outside Helen Community and get to the hospital that way. He was also worried about not having easy access to various stores since Helen Community was in a rural area. I understood his concerns and said that we would not move any essentials from our Xincheng apartment so that we could return if we did not like living in Helen.

Since we were not moving most of our furniture from our Xincheng apartment, we had to buy new pieces for our Helen house. Xiao Xie helped us with this. She shopped around and found a furniture company in urban Shanghai, where she and Shebao selected two sets of bedroom furniture and one set of living-room furniture for us.

We then gave Shebao and Xiao Xie the money to pay for the furniture they bought for us. We decided to move our dining-room furniture from our Xincheng apartment to our Helen house because it was hardwood furniture and a set that we treasured. We said to ourselves that if we needed to move back to Xincheng, we would buy a cheaper set for the dining room there. Our children bought housewarming presents for us. Shebao and Xiao Xie bought a reclining sofa for our bedroom. Shezhu and Ah Ming bought us a big-screen TV set.

My husband and I bought curtains in a Xincheng store for our Helen house. The store provided very good service. They drove to the house and measured all the windows. We then chose the materials and the styles, and they made the curtains. They again drove to the house and put up the curtains for us. The new living-room and bedroom furniture was delivered directly to our Helen house around the same time the curtains were put up.

We decided to move to our Helen house before Chinese New Year's Day and before Shezhen's scheduled arrival. Ah Ming was very busy those days, coordinating several projects outside Shanghai. I saw a neighbor who was moving some furniture and asked the neighbor about the moving company and obtained the company's business card. I told Shezhu that I could contact that company and move our stuff that way. But Shezhu insisted that Ah Ming do the moving for us.

So on the Sunday before Shezhen's arrival, Ah Ming squeezed time out and used his pickup truck to move our dining-room table and chairs, a nightstand, some clothes, and the bedding. My whole family came to help, with the men helping with the moving and setting up of the furniture and the women helping with setting up the beds.

My family asked me what I was going to do with my bodhisattva. I said that I would take it to the Helen house personally. I packed everything carefully and carried the package in my arms to our new house. I put the nightstand in the smaller bedroom and placed my precious statues of the bodhisattva, the incense burner, and the birth animals on the nightstand. Since then, I have been chanting Amitabha and lighting two incense sticks every morning in front of the bodhisattva at our Helen house.

Shezhu prepared traditional housewarming things for us and brought them over on our moving day. She bought a bag of rice, a bottle of cooking oil, a family-size bottle of spring water, two sticks of sugarcane, a rice cake, and several glutinous rice dumplings wrapped in bamboo leaves (*zongzi*). The rice, the cooking oil, and the spring water are basic materials for life and represented Shezhu's wishes for our family never to suffer shortages of basic materials. The sugarcane, the rice cake, and *zongzi* were symbols of best wishes for success and fortune.

At last we moved to our Helen house, which is built on our ancestral land. Our house has two stories. On the first floor we have a living room, a dining room, a kitchen, a bathroom, and a one-car garage. On the second floor, we have two large bedrooms and a small bedroom, a laundry room, and another bathroom. The kitchen is equipped with built-in cabinets above and below and has extensive counter space. The two bathrooms have tiled walls and floors for easy cleaning. The house has a roofed balcony for hanging washed laundry. All the rooms are equipped with air conditioners.

We consider the new house our ancestral home and the land it stands on as our basic homesite. According to local traditions, after a house is built and a family has moved into it, the family should hire a Daoist priest to perform a ritual to calm the homesite (*zhenzhai*). I contacted a Daoist priest on the phone and made an arrangement for him to perform the ritual for us. The day before the scheduled ritual, I called to ask him how to prepare for the ritual. He told me to buy a bottle of Chinese liquor, a bottle of Chinese wine, and a live chicken and to prepare three vegetable dishes and three meat/fish dishes. He also told me to prepare eighty paper ingots, which I made myself with tin-plated paper.

Shezhu is always thoughtful and caring. The day before the ritual, she called to ask if she should come and help us at the ritual. I told her that it was not necessary and that her father and I could manage. But she was still worried, so she got up before dawn on the ritual day, took public transportation from her Xincheng home, and arrived at our Helen house to assist us.

The Daoist priest came to our house at 7:30 in the morning. He brought six pieces of paper on which six different gods were drawn and put them on our dining-room wall. He placed our dining table against the wall under the six gods. On the table, Shezhu and I laid out the six dishes we had prepared, the rice cake, the *zongzi*, and six wine cups in which we poured Chinese wine. Two candles and a bunch of incense were lit on the table. In the same dining room were the bottle of spring water, the bag of rice, the bottle of cooking oil, and the two sticks of sugarcane. The sugarcane sticks were tied together with a piece of red thread and stood against a wall.

The Daoist priest chanted in front of the table and before the six gods. After the chanting, he asked my husband, who was the head of the household, to go through the entire house with him. The priest had a sword in one hand and a chain in the other. He brandished the sword in all the rooms, making sure that he approached all the corners of each room. At the same time, my husband used his mouth to spray the Chinese liquor in every room and into every corner of each room. Shezhu accompanied her father in this task, holding the liquor bottle and pouring liquor out into a bowl for her father. Afterward, my husband said that he felt his mouth was burning from so much high-proof liquor. The priest told us that all this was to drive away any bad spirits in the house.

The Daoist priest then took the six pieces of paper, which represented six gods, down from the dining-room wall and burned them with the eighty tin-plated paper ingots I had prepared. Next he killed the live chicken and, with my husband following him, dripped the chicken blood around the outside of our house. This, the priest said, was to protect the house from bad spirits. The ritual thus cleaned the house and placed it under the protection of the six gods.

It turned out that Shezhu's help was very much needed. She held on to her father's arm when he went throughout the house and outside the house. Right after the ritual was over, she went to work at Shebao's company. After we moved into the new house, she talked to us several times a day to check on us. She worried about her father not being used to the new environment. She worried about my being exhausted from the packing and moving.

Right after we moved in, Shezhen arrived and kept us company in the new house and new environment. Our other children and grandchildren came many times before and during the Chinese New Year holiday. They were able to come because their work schedules became relaxed before the major holiday and they had seven days off for the holiday. They came also because they wanted to chat with Shezhen, who was not always with us at this time of the year.

We held a traditional ritual to remember my mother on the twenty-third of the twelfth month according to the lunar calendar. Just as I had been doing in the past years, this ritual was also our family's end-of-year dinner (*nianyefan*). When I held the ritual to remember my father on his death anniversary in the previous October, I made the announcement that we would be moving back to our ancestral home inside the Helen Community before the coming Chinese Year. So I assumed that my mother knew where to go for the anniversary and that our ancestors knew where to go for the end-of-year dinner.

On the twenty-third, Shezhen and Xiao Xie, who was on her school's winter break, helped me prepare the food and for the ritual. Shebao, Shezhu, and Ah Ming came at lunchtime and joined us in kowtowing to my mother and the rest of our ancestors. We laid out the ritual table in our dining room but burned the paper money outside the house to avoid polluting the inside with smoke. I was able to burn paper money outside because the ground right outside our townhouse was part of our homesite. When I lived in our urban apartments, we had to burn paper money inside because we lived in an apartment building that housed many other families and burning paper money outside would be confusing to our ancestors.

Our children brought not only joy to me and my husband but also the hustle and bustle we needed to warm the new house. With the hustle and bustle and with Shezhen living with us, my husband and I settled smoothly into our new environment. My husband has found new walking routes and takes several walks every day. My daily routine includes doing the shopping, cooking the meals, and cleaning the house, the same daily routine I had when we lived in Xincheng.

Since we moved back, I have run into many people that I knew but had not seen for many years. I see them mostly when I am shopping for our daily vegetables and meat/fish in the market across the street from our residential complex. I also see them when I walk in the community. Some of these people are from Wangjialong and use my nickname and say, "Linshe, you are shopping here. Have you moved back here?" If they are not from Wangjialong but are of my generation, they say, "You are that warping lady, aren't you? I came to your warping shop for service many times." If they are a generation younger, they say, "You are that warping aunt, aren't you? When I was a little girl, I came with my mother to your warping shop."

Several of my cousins and two of my husband's nephews have also moved back to their ancestral houses in Helen Community. They come often to visit us and have given us help. When we first moved to the new house, we had access to Internet service since Shebao did not stop it when he moved his factory away. But our Helen house did not have cable TV service, so we had to open an account, and it had to be done in the communication service office in Loutang Town. It happened that Shebao was on a business trip at the time. My cousin Zhongming heard about our need and offered to help. He rode his battery-powered bike to the service office and opened the account on our behalf. One of my husband's nephews fixed the lock on our garage door and lubricated the moving parts of the door. I feel really at home living in Helen Community.

On the east side of our house is a strip of land on which we can grow trees and flowers. When Shebao ran the factory here, he planted a couple of orange trees. There were also some non-fruit trees planted by the community management. But there was still open space for more trees. One morning when I was shopping in the market, I saw a man selling young fruit trees from his truck. I found out that he sold all kinds of trees and that he was coming the next day. So the next day, my husband and I went to the market together and we bought three little fruit trees. They were a calamondin tree, a pear tree, and a peach tree. Shezhen helped me plant them in the open space in that strip of land.

My husband is now used to living in our new ancestral home. We have a supermarket here that supplies most of what we want and

CHAPTER 16

16.1   Bus stop near the family home in Helen Community, 2013

need. The nearby vegetable/meat/fish market is a little smaller, but as sufficient for us as the one in Xincheng. The hospital in Zhuqiao provides the same service as the one in Xincheng. There are three bus lines we can take to get into urban Jiading. They all stop outside our residential complex to pick up or to discharge passengers (fig. 16.1).

Spring in Shanghai is wonderful, with comfortable weather. Around our house, the trees and grounds are turning green. Our neighbors have a peach tree whose branches are now full of peach blossom buds. In a couple of weeks, we shall have peach blossoms in our living environment.

Recently, Shebao came to visit us. He asked for a shovel, saying that he wanted to show me where he had planted the peonies I gave him. I obtained these peony plants from one of our Xincheng neighbors. This neighbor raised peonies that won a prize in a gardening contest in her hometown. I asked her for some roots and she graciously honored my request. So that fall, she gave me two peony roots. I asked Shebao to plant them in the strip of land on the east side of our Helen house. Soon after he planted them, he moved his factory to the manufacturing center. One day after he moved, I visited our Helen house. Our next door neighbor told me that somebody had stolen our peony plants. I was sad, but I did not think I could do anything.

When Shebao said that he wanted to show me the location of the peony plants, I told him that they had been stolen. But he took the shovel and went to the location where he had put down the roots. I went with him and watched as he gently scratched off the dried weed over a patch. There, we saw many deep red sprouts just emerging from the soil. It turned out that only one of the plants had been stolen. I put some fertilizer around the sprouts and am now watching them grow every day.

I take a walk almost every day so long as it is not raining. The planners of Helen Community kept all the rivers in my hometown as well as the Coal-cinder Road. So I can still identify many meaningful places although my village itself has disappeared. During the New Year's holidays, my children walked with me to our old homesite. Zhangjing River (Zhangjing He), the river that flowed behind our old house, had a slight bend about ten meters west of our stone steps to the water (shuiqiao). The slight bend is still there, so I could almost precisely point to the place where our old house had stood. On that particular site now stands a cluster of two townhouses. I did not know the people who owned these two houses. East of this cluster, however, were two townhouses occupied by people I knew from Wangjialong. They were home for the New Year's holiday, so we chatted with them a little that day.

I walk on the central walkway inside our complex very often. The walkway is brick-paved, wide, and flanked by trees, green bushes, and flower beds. Although this is still early spring and there are no flowers, I can imagine flowers in these places when the weather becomes warm. Along the walkway are several areas with pavilions, built-in benches, playgrounds, and basketball courts, as well as exercise equipment such as leg-stretching and arm-stretching machines and sit-up benches. I use some of this equipment often, stretching my arms and legs.

Where this walkway spans the Zhangjing River, there is a fancy wooden bridge. Besides allowing people to cross the river, the bridge is a wide wooden platform on which there are built-in benches under a glass-covered corridor and a glass-covered pavilion. The river is widened at this place so that part of the wooden platform is above the water. The people who have experienced the summer season here have told me that in summertime, it is particularly cool on the wide platform because you are basically above the water, which helps to cool the air. On the west side of the wooden bridge is where our family plot used to be. That is where my parents' ashes were buried for a number of years.

On the southeast corner of our complex is a community park. This park is right beside the old Coal-cinder Road, which has been widened and paved with asphalt. The park is also equipped with benches for people to rest on. The north end of the park is right at the entrance gate of our complex and the south end is at the Big Stone Bridge. The bridge, just like the road, was there when I was little and has been widened and rebuilt several times.

When I walk inside this roadside park, I can pinpoint the spot where we owned one *mu* of land before Liberation. This was one of the first pieces of land my family bought. It was not irrigable land, so we usually grew cotton there. With the land itself devoted to the cash crop of cotton, my mother grew sesame on the edge of our land along the Big Official Road as well as on the little path that separated our land from the land that belonged to another family. We cut down the sesame plants in August, brought them home to dry in the sun, and then harvested the seeds. We kept the seeds until around Chinese New Year's Day. Then we made sesame-and-peanut candies. Since we were small eaters, the candies, as our sweet snacks, usually lasted until April or May of the following year.

We are back to our native place. But it is no longer the place of rustic living conditions that we all tried to escape. I have seen many earth-shattering changes in the last eighty years and have endured a lot. Ever since I became aware of things, I have worked hard. Sometimes I wonder if I have been a fool who does not know how to enjoy life.

Overall, I think I am a pretty lucky person. I grew up in a harmonious environment under the influence of people with many good qualities. My grandmother was capable, bold, and far-sighted; Grandpa Bai

16.2 Chen Huiqin and Chen Xianxi on their fiftieth wedding anniversary, 2001

was kind and loving; my mother was kind, wise, and selfless; my father was reasonable, principled, open-minded, and generous.

I married a good man. My husband has a kind and loving temperament. He trusts me and respects me. We have never quarreled with each other, not even once, in the more than sixty years of our married life (fig. 16.2).

My children are just wonderful. They did not give me much trouble while growing up. They have established themselves in life and have achieved things far beyond my expectations in their professional lives. At the same time, they are thoughtful and filial children, ready to attend to my needs and those of my husband.

My husband and I are getting old. We take care of ourselves and try our best not to be a burden to our children. Our current life is good, and we are grateful for the family and health we enjoy every day.

GLOSSARY

FAMILIAL TERMS OF ADDRESS

ah po　阿婆　granny

bobo　伯伯　uncle, father's brother

diedie　爹爹　dad

gufu　姑父　uncle, husband of father's sister

Hedong Niangyi　河东娘姨　East River Aunt, mother's sister living on the east side of the river

Hexi Niangyi　河西娘姨　West River Aunt, mother's sister living on the west side of the river

m'ma　姆妈　mom

meimei　妹妹　younger sister, or a local way to address a younger woman

momo　嬷嬷　Big Aunt, father's elder sister

niangjiu　娘舅　uncle, mother's brother

niangniang　娘娘　Little Aunt, father's younger sister

taitai　太太　great-grandmother

waigong　外公　maternal grandfather

waipo　外婆　maternal grandmother

yifu　姨夫　uncle, husband of mother's sister

MEASUREMENTS

jin 斤 half a kilogram, or about one pound
li 里 half a kilometer
mu 亩 about one-sixth of an acre
shi 石 156 *jin*, or 78 kilograms
yuan 元 Chinese dollar

PLACE NAMES

Anting 安亭 town in Jiading County/District
Baziqiao 八字桥 Eight-Letter Bridge, hamlet in Jiading County/District
Baijiazhai 柏家宅 Bai Family Hamlet of Wang Family Village
Baihe Jiang 白河江 river in Qingpu County/District
Baiqiang 白墙 brigade/village in Jiading County/District
Beicun 北村 North Hamlet of Wang Family Village
Bole Lu 博乐路 Bole Road in Jiading Town
Chengdong 城东 commune in Jiading County/District
Dazhai 大寨 brigade promoted as a national model during the Cultural
   Revolution
Dengta 灯塔 brigade/village in Jiading County/District
Dianpu He 淀浦河 canal in the suburbs of Shanghai
Dianshan Hu 淀山湖 lake in Qingpu County/District
Dongfeng 东风 brigade in Jiading County/District
Hailun 海伦 Helen, residential community in Jiading District
Hangjiacun 杭家村 Hang Family Village in Jiading County/District
Huating 华亭 town in Jiading County/District
Huizhou 徽州 region in Anhui
Jiading 嘉定 county/district in Shanghai
Jiafeng Fangzhi Chang 嘉丰纺织厂 Jiafeng Textile Mill in Jiading County
Jianbang 戬浜 town in Jiading County/District
Jinshan 金山 county/district in Shanghai
Lijiang 沥江 brigade/village in Jiading County/District
Limin (or Liming) 利民 Benefit the People or 黎明 Dawn High-
   Stage Cooperative and brigade/village in Jiading County/District

Lixin　立新　brigade/village in Jiading County/District

Liyuan　李园　Li Compound in Jiading Town

Loutang　娄塘　town in Jiading County/District

Malu　马陆　town in Jiading County/District

Meilong　梅龙　town in Minhang District of Shanghai

Nancun　南村　South Hamlet of Wang Family Village

Nanmen　南门　South Gate of Jiading Town

Pandai　潘戴　brigade/village in Jiading County/District

Penglangzhen　蓬朗镇　town in Qingpu County/District

Qinghe Lu　清和路　Qinghe Road in Jiading Town

Qingpu　青浦　county/district in Shanghai

Qingzhuyuan　清竹园　Green Bamboo Cemetery in Jiading District

Ruijin Hospital　瑞金医院　hospital in urban Shanghai

Songjiacun　宋家村　Song Family Village in Jiading County/District

Tangjiazhai　汤家宅　Tang Family Village in Jiading County/District

Waigang　外冈　town in Jiading County/District

Wangjialong　汪家弄　Wang Family Village of Jiading County/District

Wuxing Si　吴兴寺　Buddhist temple in Jiading County/District

Xijing He　锡泾河　river on the west side of Wang Family Village

Ximen　西门　West Gate of Jiading Town

Xincheng　新成　residential neighborhood in urban Jiading

Xuhang　徐行　town in Jiading County/District

Yangjiazhai　杨家宅　Yang Family Village in Jiading County/District

Yunzaobang　蕴藻浜　river in the suburbs of Shanghai

Zhangjing He　张泾河　river behind Wang Family Village

Zonghe Factory　综合厂　commune-run factory in Jiading County

Zhoujiazhai　周家宅　Zhou Family Village in Jiading County/District

Zhuqiao　朱桥　town in Jiading County/District

GENERAL TERMS

baileitai　摆擂台　welcoming challenge

bantuochan ganbu　半脱产干部　one who worked half-time as a cadre and half-time as a peasant

bao　保　administrative unit containing ten villages; used before Liberation

baozhang　保长　head of a *bao*

biandou　扁豆　flat bean

bianjian　扁尖　tender bamboo shoot

caili　彩礼　wedding gift

changgong　长工　year-long hired hand

changshan　长衫　long gown

chi　池　pool

chujishe　初级社　initial-stage cooperative

citang　祠堂　family memorial hall

cunzhang　村长　village head

Daguanlu　大官路　Big Official Road

daimao　玳瑁　sea turtle shell

dajiao　打醮　chanting ritual after a harvest

Dalu　大路　Big Road

daochang　道场　chanting ritual

Daoshi　道士　Daoist priest

ding　疔　a boil or furuncle

dingshenggao　定升糕　sure-to-rise cake

Dun Hou Tang　敦厚堂　Hall of Honesty and Sincerity

fangweixing　放卫星　launching satellite

fengshui　风水　geomancy

gaojishe　高级社　high-stage cooperative

gongliang　公粮　public grain

Guan Yin　观音　Bodhisattva of Mercy and Compassion

huangjiu　黄酒　yellow wine

huanglian　黄连　bitter herb

huangmei　黄梅　rainy and damp season

huantun　还囤　appreciation gift

huimenri　回门日　after-the-wedding visit

huqin　胡琴　Chinese violin

jia　甲　administrative unit containing ten families or one natural village; used before Liberation

jiazhang　甲长　head of a *jia*

jiangdou　江豆　long bean

jianggua　酱瓜　pickle

jianlitian　见礼钿　meeting-ritual money

jiaobai　茭白　vegetable grown in water

jiazi　甲子　sexagenary cycle

jiedao　街道　urban neighborhood

Jifei　季匪　Ji bandit

jihualiang　计划粮　planned grain

jisuhun　鸡宿昏　chicken night blindness

ketang　客堂　guest hall

kouliang　口粮　grain for the mouth

kouliangtian　口粮田　grain land

labazhou　腊八粥　winter eight porridge

lao xiansheng　老先生　old mister

laoban　老板　boss

litong　立桶　standing bucket for children before they learn to walk

mantou　馒头　steamed bun

meigancai　梅干菜　preserved vegetable

mianzi　面子　face

minban laoshi　民办老师　peasant teacher

nianhuo　年货　New Year's gift

nianyefan　年夜饭　end-of-the-year family dinner

penghao　蓬蒿　green vegetable belonging to the chrysanthemum family

pipa　枇杷　Chinese plum

putonghua bisai　普通话比赛　Mandarin-speaking contest

qingming　清明　ancestor-remembering festival

Qingxiang Yundong　清乡运动　Clearing the Villages Movement

qipao　旗袍　traditional Chinese dress

she'm'geng　舍呒更　maternity gift

shengganjiu　生甘酒　raw sweet wine

shilinbu　士林布　blue cotton fabric

shiyuezhao　十月朝　day to remember the dead in the tenth lunar month

shuiqiao　水桥　stone steps to the water

sijiaoling　四角菱　four-horned water caltrop

sileifenzi　四类分子　four categories (of class enemies)

Siqing　四清　Four Clean-ups

tian　田　land

tianjing　天井　sky well

tonggou tongxiao　统购统销　unified purchasing and marketing

wobuyaochi　我不要吃　I do not want to eat

wubaohu　五保户　family of five protections

xiafang ganbu　下放干部　sent-down cadre

xiang　乡　township

xiangmenjian　祥门间　fortune gate room

xiangzhang　乡长　head of a *xiang*

xiansheng　先生　mister

xingzao　行灶　movable stove

xingzhengcun　行政村　administrative village

xuexiban　学习班　study course

yuantuan　圆团　glutinous rice balls with sweet or meat fillings

zerentian　责任田　responsibility land

zhaku　轧库　making paper houses for the other world

Zhangjia Daoshi　张家道士　Zhang Family Daoist priests

zhenbao　镇保　small-town social security

Zhengdang Bangongshi　政党办公室　Office to Rectify the Communist Party

zhenzhai　镇宅　ritual to calm the homesite

Zhongshan chuang　中山床　Zhongshan bed

Zhongshan zhuang　中山装　Zhongshan jacket

ziliudi　自留地　plot of land allotted to each rural family during the collective period

zisunbao　子孙包　descendants' bundle

zisuntong　子孙桶　descendants' pot

zongzi　粽子　glutinous rice wrapped in bamboo leaves

zoutong　走通　walk through or engagement (for marriage purpose)

zuoqun　作裙　work skirt

zuzhang　组长　head of a group

INDEX

Note: page numbers in *italics* refer to illustrations.

A

adoption, 16, 45, 65
Ah Bing, 49, 50, 170–71, 195–97, 202–3
Ah Du, 180–81
Ah Juan, 169, 176, 192, 195, 205, 221, 245–46
Ah Lin, 290. *See also* Chen Huiqin; Chen Tian'e; Linshe
Ah Ming, *298*; air conditioning business, 244–46, 253–54, 309; and Beibei, 190–92, 214–15, 227, 232, 234–35, 239–40, 300–302, 304–5, 307–8; engagement, 178; and Helen Community, 271–72; repair shop, 235–36; and Shebao, 208, 235–36, 309–12; sideline production, 208–9, 222; urban apartments, 236, 244; 282–83, 286, 289, 307–12, 321–23, 326; wedding, 184–86, *185*

Ah Xing, 117
Aibao, 83
Aidi, 205, 206, 207, 245
American company, 308–9
American Congressmen, 260
American Consulate, 259, 260
Amitabha, ix, 292–93, 323
ancestor, 13, 19, 20, 21, 38, 49, 68, 196–97, 277; and marriage ceremony, 62, 224, 307; power of, 36, 145, 238, 280–81; and relocation, 272; remembered, 284, 285, 286, 326
ancestor-remembering festival, 284, 285
ancestral compound, 19, 195
ancestral home, 12, *196*, 273, 274, 324, 326, 327; for Beibei, 304, 307
ancestral tablets, 20, 125
Anhui, 29, 30
Annina, 188, 225, 262–63
apartment, 9; in Beijing, 193–94; as condition for marriage, 251, 252; in Japan, 318–19; and relocation, 270–

North Hamlet, 19, 28, 36, 41, 46, 48, 50, 55, 62, 65, 70, 81, 84, 86, 90, 93, 97, 104, 111, 117, 126, 140, 183, 208, 272, 334

O

Office to Rectify the Communist Party, 210, 212, 246, 338
104 Document, 166, 167, 172n1

P

Pan Guanghua, 47–48
Pan Shouwen, 47–48
Pandai Brigade, 211, 253, 335
Panjia Mama, 70, 87n5, 111
paper house, 9, 288–89, 295
paper money, 85, 134, 175, 178, 278, 284, 285, 290, 295, 326
peasant, 9, 64, 72, 75, 90, 100, 104, 106, 121, 127, 131, 137–38, 155, 163, 168, 176, 198, 202, 203, 210, 214, 238; association, 42, 47, 73; backgrounds, 219, 308; cadres, 93; calendar, 178; experience, x; family, 3, 4, 6, 165; fate, 168, 239; house, 114; life, 151, 162; middle, 48; and pension, 275; poor, 7–8, 47, 48, 49, 50; rich, 7–8, 48, 77; -run furnaces, 92; spouses, 219; stock, 251; teachers, 126, 349
Penglang Town, 39, 43, 335
Pengsha Factory, 234–35
pension, 9, 249, 270, 275, 283
People's Liberation Army, 40
piecework reward system, 199–201, 210
policy, 107n1, 109, 127, 185, 220, 228; Cultural Revolution admission, 9; economic reform, 199, 215n1, 286; land reform, 47; local government; one-child-one-family, 86, 191; "Three Fixes," 75; unified purchasing and

marketing, 72–73
production team, 99, 102, 103, 114, 125–26, 142, 151, 159, 162, 170, 190, 201–3; leader, 101, 116, 128, 152, 156, 168, 200, 204
Pruitt, Ida, 5–6
public project, 84, 153, 161, 163
Pudong, 301, 303; Airport, 267, 269
Putong Elementary School, 233

Q

Qian Caiqing, 44
Qingpu, 35, 36, 335
Qilong, 188
Qinghe Road, 210, 335

R

Red Guards, 8, 125, 126, 154
relocation, ix, 270–72, 274–75, 289
responsibility land, 203–4, 338
Resting Horse Bridge, 36–37
ritual, 8, 10, 13, 33, 131, 150, 272, 281, 284, 285, 286, 287, 326; to calm the homesite, 324–25, 338; chanting, 23, 290–91, 294–95, 336
Ruijin Hospital, 281–82, 335

S

Salt Lake City, 225, 261–62, 264
San Francisco, 261, 268; airport, 267, 268
"sent-down" cadres, 105, 338
sexagenary cycle, 149, 150n2, 230, 337
Shaanxi, 5
shaman, 9, 286–87, 289–90, 292
Shandong, 4, 5, 44, 254
Shanghai, ix, 2, 3, 9, 15, 33, 35, 41, 42, 51nn1,2, 76, 83, 89, 90, 100, 105, 111, 121, 134, 135, 162, 171, 173, 184, 192, 194, 201, 219, 223, 240, 245, 248,

X

Xianlin, 209

Xiaomei, 83

Xiao Xie, 298; and Beibei, 298; care for and support of parents-in-law, 281–83, 322–23, 326; and Chen Li, 229–33, 247, 316–19; engagement and wedding, 219–225, 225; urban apartments, 219–20, 226, 228, 246–48, 249

Xijing River, 17, 145, 335

Xincheng, 27, 240–42, 244–46, 253–54, 269–72, 275, 278, 286, 299, 305, 307, 311, 320–24, 326, 328, 335

Xingying, 97

Xiuqin, 84

Y

Yan Family Temple, 44, 63, 82, 125

Yan Shoufu, 32–33, 63, 142–43

Yang Family Temple, 42, 125

Yang Ji'an, 73, 113

Yang, Martin, 4

Yang Xi, 191, 234, 237n1. *See also* Beibei

Yangzhou, 230

Yangzi valley, 4

Yingtai, 255

Yixing, 217–18

Yunnan, 4

Yunqing, 44

Yunzaobang River, 167, 335

Z

Zhang Family Daoist Priests, 13, 23, 338

Zhangjing River, 19–20, 22, 40, 97, 106, 274, 329, 335

Zhang Zhigao, 114, 119

Zhongming, 81–83, 168–69, 174, 176, 180, 195–97, 222–23, 245–46, 327

Zhou Family Village, 16–17, 335

Zhou Jinliang, 208

Zhouqiao Comprehensive Store, 155

Zhou Wei: care of parents-in-law in Beijing, 194, 225, 249; engagement and wedding, 177, 179, 182, 183–84; job in Hong Kong, 238, 259; in the United States, 238, 239, 264–68; visits in Jiading, 198–99, 209, 211, 226–27

Zhuqiao, 2, 25, 38–40, 44, 67, 69, 82, 96, 102, 104, 106, 112, 114, 145, 148, 154, 187, 190, 207, 231, 241, 270, 288, 328, 335. *See also under* commune

Zhuqiao Central Elementary School, 103, 116

Zhuqiao Collection Station, 205, 210

Zhuqiao Farm Machine Plant, 163, 190

Zhuqiao Medical Center, 208

Zhuqiao Middle School, 144, 146, 155

Zhuqiao Mushroom Spore Cultivation Farm, 201, 206

Zonghe Factory, 148, 335